EXTRASENSORY
PERCEPTION

EXTRASENSORY PERCEPTION

A CIBA FOUNDATION SYMPOSIUM

★

Editors for the Ciba Foundation

G. E. W. WOLSTENHOLME
O.B.E., M.A., M.B., B.Ch.

and

ELAINE C. P. MILLAR
A.H.W.C., A.R.I.C.

★

THE CITADEL PRESS · NEW YORK

THIRD PAPERBOUND EDITION, JANUARY 1969

PUBLISHED BY THE CITADEL PRESS
222 PARK AVENUE SOUTH, NEW YORK 3, N. Y.
BY ARRANGEMENT WITH LITTLE, BROWN AND COMPANY
COPYRIGHT © 1956 BY J. & A. CHURCHILL LTD.
MANUFACTURED IN THE UNITED STATES OF AMERICA

*Published in London by
J. & A. Churchill Ltd.
104 Gloucester Place, W.1*

First published 1956

THE CIBA FOUNDATION

for the Promotion of International Co-operation in Medical and Chemical Research
41 PORTLAND PLACE, LONDON, W.1.

PREFACE

WHEN Dr. Dingwall heard that one of the Ciba Foundation's small international conferences would be devoted to discussion of extrasensory perception, he exclaimed "incredible courage!". We did not feel particularly brave but had been easily persuaded by Dr. Parkes that there were matters arising from experimental work on communication other than by the known senses, which, if substantiated, would be of considerable importance in all branches of biological research. The time seemed ripe for an examination of the claims by a group composed of three categories of scientists: those engaged in such experimental work, those active in interpreting the findings, favourably or unfavourably in relation to extrasensory perception, and those to whom the problems were novel and disturbing, and therefore to be approached with even more than usual scientific caution. The Ciba Foundation is able to offer pleasantly informal conditions for discussions by small groups, and the circumstances appeared favourable for a friendly but critical review of the subject.

It would not have been possible to enlarge the group, but it was only afterwards that the Director learnt how widespread among scientists in many disciplines is the interest in experimental extrasensory perception. He can only hope that this volume of the proceedings may provide some compensation to those whom he neglected to invite.

As mentioned above, it was Dr. Parkes who initiated this symposium and it was, therefore, appropriate that he should preside over it. The Director is truly indebted to Dr. Parkes for his suggestion and for his chairmanship and also for great help in the organization of the meeting, based on much study of the relevant literature. Dr. Dingwall and Dr. Soal also very willingly provided invaluable expert advice.

To those to whom this book serves as an introduction to the activities of the Ciba Foundation it should be explained that it is an international centre, which is established as an educational and scientific charity under the laws of England, It owes its inception and support to its Founder, CIBA Ltd. of Switzerland, but is administered independently and exclusively by its distinguished British Trustees.

The Foundation provides accommodation for scientific workers who visit London from abroad, organizes and holds international conferences, conducts (in conjunction with the Institut National d'Hygiène) a postgraduate medical exchange scheme between England and France, arranges informal meetings for discussions, awards an annual lectureship, has initiated a scheme to encourage basic research relevant to the problems of ageing, assists international congresses and scientific societies, is building up a library service in special fields, and generally endeavours to give aid in all matters that may promote international co-operation in scientific research.

Leading research workers from different countries and in different disciplines are invited to attend the symposia or colloquia. The size of the group is, however, very strictly limited in order to obtain a free conversational manner of discussion—although the basic time-table of the programme is strictly observed. The smallness of the groups means the exclusion of many workers active and interested in the subjects discussed, and therefore the proceedings of these conferences are published and made available throughout the world.

It is hoped that the papers and discussions in this book will prove not only informative and stimulating, but will also give to readers a sense of participation in an informal and friendly occasion.

CONTENTS

List of those participating in or attending the Symposium on " Extrasensory Perception," 3rd–5th May 1955

R. AMADOU . . .	Inst. Métaphysique, Paris
G. SPENCER BROWN . .	Christ Church, Oxford
C. G. BUTLER . . .	Bee Department, Rothamsted Experimental Station, Herts.
SIR HENRY DALE . .	Wellcome Trust, London
E. J. DINGWALL . . .	London
J. H. GADDUM . . .	Pharmacological Laboratory, Edinburgh University
W. H. GILLESPIE . .	Maudsley Hospital, London
Mrs. K. M. GOLDNEY . .	London
A. C. HARDY . . .	Department of Zoology and Comparative Anatomy, Oxford
SIR CHARLES HARRINGTON .	National Institute for Medical Research, London
J. LANGDON-DAVIES . .	Gerona, Spain
A. J. LEWIS . . .	Institute of Psychiatry, Maudsley Hospital, London
R. A. McCONNELL . .	Department of Biophysics, Pittsburgh University
G. V. T. MATTHEWS . .	Wildfowl Trust, Slimbridge
J. FRASER NICOL . .	Cambridge, Massachusetts
A. S. PARKES . . .	National Institute for Medical Research, London
W. L. M. PERRY . .	National Institute for Medical Research, London
M. POBERS	Inst. for Clinical and Industrial Psychology, Rijks University, Utrecht
J. G. PRATT . . .	Parapsychology Laboratory, Duke University, Durham, North Carolina
J. SALVIN	London
S. G. SOAL	London
G. D. WASSERMANN . .	Department of Mathematics, King's College, Durham
D. J. WEST . . .	Society for Psychical Research, London

EXTRASENSORY
PERCEPTION

*Nous sommes si éloignés de connaître tous les agens de la nature,
qu'il serait peu philosophique de nier l'existence des phénomènes,
uniquement parcequ'ils sont inexplicables dans l'état actuel de nos
connaissances. Seulement nous devons les examiner avec une attention d'autant plus scrupuleuse qu'il paraît plus difficile de les
admettre: et c'est ici que l'analyse des probabilités devient indispensable pour déterminer jusqu'à quel point il faut multiplier les
observations ou les expériences pour avoir en faveur de l'existence
des agens qu'elles semblent indiquer une probabilité supérieure à
toutes les raisons que l'on peut avoir d'ailleurs de la rejeter.*

LAPLACE.

CHAIRMAN'S OPENING REMARKS

A. S. PARKES

National Institute for Medical Research, London

LEGENDS and reports of apparent telepathy or clairvoyance
must be as old as man, and the problem of whether the human
mind can perceive by any other means than the obvious
activity of the recognised senses has always intrigued people,
including many with scientific training. Unfortunately, over
the centuries, the subject has been confused with other, and
to my mind quite irrelevant issues, and has been bedevilled
by fraud, credulity and technical difficulties of investigation.

In the last 25 years or so, however, resolute efforts have
been made in several centres to apply to the problem under
laboratory conditions methods of investigation similar in
principle to those used in more ordinary branches of research.
Chief among these techniques is the one in which the subject
tries to ' perceive ' symbols on unseen cards, turned up one
by one behind a screen or in another room. Under carefully
controlled conditions of test, scores consistently and significantly in excess of probability are superficially suggestive of
telepathy or clairvoyance on the part of the subject, according to whether or not the experimenter was aware of the
nature of the card. Millions of such tests have now been
carried out and it seems clear that most people are able to
guess an unseen card only by chance. It seems equally clear,

however, that a small number of people among those investigated have been able to guess cards far in excess of probability over long periods. We are driven, therefore, to suppose either that these rare and anomalous subjects are able to perceive to a limited extent by some method not obviously attributable to the known senses, or else that current theories of probability are inadequate or in some way upset by guessing patterns and associations on the part of certain individuals. In other words, we are faced either with a major biological discovery, or else with the unpalatable conclusion that highly impressive results can arise as artifacts of the use of established methods. In either case there is here a challenge to modern science, whether it be to physiology, statistics or psychology. And, when I say modern science, that is exactly what I mean. Phenomena, vaguely and to my mind unfortunately known as ESP., if they exist, might or might not have some further implication, but the scientific problem is to decide whether or not they do in fact exist, and if so what biological mechanisms, known or unknown, may be involved. I need hardly say that the business of this symposium is to review and assess the experimental evidence relating to the scientific problem.

This brings me to the origin and aims of the present symposium. In common with many people working in various fields of research, I have been intrigued by the recurrent reports of positive results in card guessing and similar experiments, and have wondered which of the possible explanations was the most likely. About a couple of years ago, following a most instructive talk with Dr. Soal, and in my capacity as a member of the Advisory Panel, I suggested to Dr. Wolstenholme that the Ciba Foundation should organise a symposium at which a number of laboratory workers like myself could have the opportunity of meeting and listening to those with first-hand knowledge and experience of modern developments in ESP. Dr. Wolstenholme received this suggestion with his usual helpfulness, and that is how we come to be here today.

In conclusion I should like to add that we are extremely fortunate in being able to discuss a subject of this kind under the auspices of the Ciba Foundation. The Foundation has now held about thirty symposia over a period of five years, and in doing so has shown that even the most controversial problem can be discussed at a high level of scientific insight and in an atmosphere of friendly good humour. I have no doubt that the present meeting will maintain this tradition.

THE NATURE OF THE LABORATORY EVIDENCE FOR EXTRASENSORY PERCEPTION*

R. A. McCONNELL

Biophysics Department, University of Pittsburgh, Pennsylvania

Abstract

The experimental proof of the reality of a new scientific phenomenon must bear scrutiny from all relevant points of view. The meaningfulness of card-guessing tests of extrasensory perception depends upon the competence of the experimenter, upon a differentiation between ESP and the known mechanisms of physics, upon the technical adequacy of the data analysis, and upon the validity of the underlying statistical assumptions. Each of these aspects of an ESP experiment is examined in a preliminary fashion.

Statement of the problem

The beginnings of science are simple. The first experiments are usually derived from daily experience, and can be understood without special training. Later, when a theoretical structure has emerged, or when a complex technique has developed, only the specialist can comprehend. Parapsychology is still a young science, completely without theory (but see Dr. Wassermann's paper). It is a science with only the most primitive experimental techniques. In fact, its detractors say that it is not a science at all, but only the beginning of a science—and in this there is much truth. This primordial situation is our good fortune. For one need not be a parapsychologist, a mathematician, or a philosopher in order to be able to understand the nature of the laboratory evidence for extrasensory perception.

Today, I am going to talk about fundamental ideas from a

* This paper is listed as No. 35 in the Biophysics Department.

4

common sense point of view. I shall begin by describing a card-guessing experiment. Then I shall examine with you the interpretation of that experiment as evidence for ESP.

So that you can more easily follow what I am going to say, I shall break down our discussion of the interpretation of the experiment into four headings: (1) uncertainties about the competence and good faith of the experimenter, (2) decisions as to whether we can explain our data on the basis of some well-known phenomenon of nature, such as audible sound or X-ray transmission, (3) questions about the technical correctness of the mathematical analysis of the data, and (4) the validity of underlying statistical assumptions.

If I make the statement that extrasensory perception is a real phenomenon, you will ask: "What do you mean by 'extrasensory perception'?" In the back pages of every issue of the *Journal of Parapsychology*, ESP is defined as "response to an external event not presented to any known sense".

This is a good definition because it is what logical positivists like to call "operational". And if we can satisfy the logical positivists that ESP occurs, we ought to be able to satisfy any other group of present-day scientific philosophers. This definition is operational because it suggests the operations by which one establishes the occurrence of ESP.

An example experiment

Let me be more specific. I shall describe an experiment which might prove the existence of extrasensory perception. Suppose that two persons synchronize their watches, and then go to separate buildings, into rooms with no ordinary means of intercommunication. Suppose that the first person, whom we shall call the experimenter, carries with him a deck of cards, as well as pencil and paper. The other person, whom we shall call the percipient, carries only pencil and paper. After the experimenter has reached his room, he shuffles the card deck thoroughly, and, without looking at the card faces, takes the top card from the deck and places it, face down, on a table at a previously agreed-upon time. In accordance with the pre-arranged plan, the percipient in the other building writes down his guess as to the unknown card. This procedure is continued at the rate of one card per minute, until the entire deck has been gone through.

Next, the experimenter turns over the card deck, and copies down the order of the cards. Thus, there exist two, independently made records: the one describing the percipient's guesses, the other describing the cards in their actual order. These two records are brought together and carefully checked to find out how many successful guesses were made by the percipient. Suitable precautions are taken to prevent the loss or alteration of records until the experiment has been completed and the scores analysed. The question I wish to examine with you is whether or not such an experiment with its analysis could be said to prove the occurrence of ESP.

Before we look into this matter, perhaps I should mention that I have described an actual experiment, one performed by Dr. Gaither Pratt in 1933 and 1934 with a percipient who had previously demonstrated unusual card-guessing ability (Rhine and Pratt, 1954). Altogether, 1850 card guesses were made, at the rate of fifty cards a day. Although with the kind of card deck that he used, a total of 370 correct guesses would be mean chance expectation, the actual number of successful guesses was 558. Conservative computation indicates that a score this high or higher would be expected by chance on an average of less than once in 10^{22} such experiments.

Experimenter competence

What we wish to determine is whether this experiment is a case of ESP. Let us consider first the problem of experimenter competence and honesty.

Well-planned ESP experiments, such as the one I have described, are experimentally simple. The precautions to be observed in the handling of cards, in the recording of guesses, and in the avoidance of fraudulent interference, are all within the understanding of a child. Of course, there *can* be poorly planned experiments in which the situation may not be clear-cut. But in the kind of proof-of-occurrence experiment that is arranged so as to be of real scientific interest, all that we require of the experimenter is ordinary competence, sanity, and good faith. These things we may expect from most professional scientists. Indeed, by now, so many successful, well-planned experiments have been conducted by scientists of good repute, that we can cross off from our list the possibility that the best evidence for ESP is the result of fraud or incompetence. The idea that the experimenter is somehow at fault remains today a stumbling-block to the acceptance of ESP only among those who are uninformed as to what experiments have been done, or among those who wish to indulge in an unrealistic kind of cynicism as to the number of unrecognizable crackpots we harbour in our universities.

Ordinary physical explanations

Let us go on to the engineering questions that are raised by a card experiment of the sort I have described. ESP is defined as "response to an external event not presented to any known sense". To prove that ESP has occurred, it is necessary to examine separately every known form of energy or information transfer, and to decide that none of them will account for the experimental data. This may be very difficult to do in the case of tests with pigeons and other animals. But in a card test with human beings, the task can be relatively simple.

You may wonder how it can ever be simple to rule out *all* known forms of communication. How, for example, can we be sure that successful card guessing does not involve ordinary X-rays in some unexpected fashion?

There is a subtle point here that I want to dwell upon for a moment. In the expression "all known forms of communication", I would like to shift your attention from the word "all" to the word "known".

In so far as X-rays are *known*, they are known by their characteristics. It is a contradiction in terms to describe X-rays as a known form of radiation and then to talk about their disconnected, unknown properties. We know how X-rays originate, how they radiate, what they can penetrate, how they can be detected, and so on. If with a good engineering knowledge, we examine the conditions of our ESP experiment and find that our results cannot be explained by the known properties of X-rays, then it is semantic nonsense to say that this new mode of transferring information may be "some kind of X-ray".

Any purported connection between ESP and X-rays must match the sophistication of our present knowledge. The man-in-the-street will say that because X-rays penetrate walls of buildings and ESP also penetrates walls, therefore ESP might be a form of X-ray. The scientist knows many other characteristics of X-rays which ESP does not exhibit.

And so, to summarize this part of our problem: if we wish to rule out the known forms of communication, we must have it done on an individual basis for every kind of communication, and it must be done by qualified engineers or physicists. This has been done (Rush, 1943), and it is quite clear that none of the known radiations or force fields of physics can be used to explain the experimental results that have been obtained in any of the well-planned experiments with which we are concerned. Thus, in the case of our particular example experiment, we can conclude that after the shuffling of the cards, the order of the card deck was not presented to any known sense of the percipient until after he had recorded his guesses.

Statistical technique

The remainder of my talk relates to statistical matters. I have divided these into two categories, the first being concerned with correct statistical computation according to prevailing standards of good practice among experimental scientists. Then I have reserved for a separate category all those questions that seek to delve more deeply into statistical method, in search of unsuspected flaws by which one might explain away the ESP data.

In the utilization of statistics as a logical tool, there are certain well-known problems to be considered. I shall mention some of these:

1. The use of acceptable randomizing procedures, such as card shuffling or tables of random numbers.
2. The manner of choosing the stopping point of the experiment.
3. The control of data-recording errors.
4. The selection of data for analysis. (Some kinds of selection are permissible and others are not.)
5. The avoidance of *ad hoc* methods of analysis.
6. The overall suitability of the chosen method of analysis.

In this list of six items I am talking about prevailing standards of good practice. For example, the shuffling of cards as a randomizing procedure would never be questioned in any ordinary psychological experiment. Of course, it *can* be questioned; and when it is questioned, it must be investigated—as indeed it has been investigated. Here I shall just mention two important papers. Greenwood and Stuart (1937) did a cross-check of score and score-variance in which the percipient's guesses from our example experiment were scored, not against the intended cards, but against the card order that occurred at the following test session. Later, Greenwood (1938) did an empirical matching of half a million shuffled cards against call patterns of successful ESP percipients. The results in both of these papers conformed closely to chance expectation.

I shall not have time to examine these technical problems in detail, but I shall be glad to answer questions during the discussion period. All I want to say now is that the procedural standards in the better class of ESP experiment are far above those customarily observed in science.

Underlying logic

I have left to the end a most important topic, one that might occupy a great deal of our attention at this conference.

What about statistical method in general? Can it be trusted? Will a random number table really give random numbers? What does it mean when we calculate a probability of one in a hundred—or, for that matter, one in a hundred million?

From a philosophic point of view such questions have never been satisfactorily answered; and I do not think we shall succeed where many famous men have failed. But if our interest is scientific rather than philosophic, there is a simple manner of looking at these questions that will cut away their mysterious metaphysical integument.

Mathematical statistics is a tool, sometimes useful in scientific research. Yet often we forget that, as far as biological science is concerned, it is only a tool, and not even a universally necessary tool. We may misconceive statistical method to be a part of biological science, and we may overconcern ourselves with unanswerable questions about mathematical rigour and ultimate logical validity.

Statistical analysis is a tool in exactly the same sense that the hammer, the telescope and the art of writing are tools. We may use mathematics to improve our experimental discrimination, but we are foolish if we allow it to dictate our epistemology.

To establish a true perspective, we need only reflect that there are many tasks in which we do not use statistical theory at all. If we meet someone who is always able to guess every card that we hold in our hand, we do not need mathematical help to know that he has "information" and not just "good luck". Moreover, we can recognize the presence of an extrachance factor when the performance is somewhat less than perfect. We don't just shrug our shoulders if throughout an entire evening a new-found gambling friend knows correctly what die faces we are going to throw 75 per cent of the time.

Let us consider the equivalent situation in an ESP experiment. If a percipient is guessing cards from a deck with five different kinds of faces so that the odds for success are one in five, and if he makes an average of eighteen right out of a deck of twenty-five instead of the expected five out of twenty-five, and if he continues to do this for seventy-four card decks, we don't need a mathematical analysis to rule out chance.

These are the results, as many of you recognize, that were obtained by Professor Bernard Riess (1937, 1939) of Hunter College in New York City in a series of card-guessing sessions with a single percipient.

Let us look more closely at this process of "knowing without mathematical analysis". Our judgment of the significance of what we observe will always depend upon experience. If we say that in the given experimental situation a repeating-score average of eighteen out of twenty-five obviously implies causation as distinct from chance, we say so not only because we may have guessed a few card decks ourselves and averaged near five instead of eighteen. Principally we say so because we know that man has been drawing lots and throwing dice for several thousand years, and all of the history of these actions makes a consistent pattern that leads us to want to look behind any enormous deviation.

Thus far, so good. No amount of sophistry will destroy our faith in the extra-chance character of Dr. Riess' scores. But what shall we say about our example experiment by Dr. Pratt in which the percipient obtained a score of 558 where the expectation was 370?

Here is the point of my entire discussion. The Pratt case is no different in principle from the Riess case. We must decide on the basis of experience. Now the average scientist has not had statistical experience at this level of scoring, nor is he aware of exactly how much experience others have had. And so he is easily led astray. But anyone who is really familiar with statistical data, whether he be a professional gambler or a biophysicist, would be amused if someone suggested that Dr. Pratt's scores were anything but extremely improbable under the chance hypothesis.

If you were to press a statistically experienced scientist to justify this judgment without resorting to mathematical theory, he would do so by comparing the Pratt data with other similar data known to be of chance origin. This comparison involves only a counting process. And as far as I know, no one has yet suggested that the theory of ordinal enumeration is somehow defective.

I think it is obvious to anyone, mathematician or not, that if we expect to question the validity of standard statistical procedures, we must confine our attack to that marginal region below which their validity has never been adequately tested by experiment.

Recently, it has been proposed (Brown, 1953) that all otherwise convincing evidence for ESP might be an artifact resulting from defects in statistical procedures. It has been said that even such elementary operations as matching numbers from random number tables do not give the chance results predicted by binomial theory.

As far as ESP is concerned, the sole point at issue is whether such hypothetical defects in standard statistical procedures can be large enough to be relevant. It is my conviction that anyone who is familiar with the striking results obtained in the better ESP experiments, and who also knows how dependably binomial theory has proved itself in the orthodox branches of science, will unhesitatingly reject the idea that here is a feasible counter-explanation to extrasensory perception.

I do not mean to say that defects in standard probability procedures cannot exist. As an empiricist, I must admit that possibility, even while I am certain that such defects could never be large enough to impugn the reality of ESP.

Nor do I mean to imply that the discovery of such defects would not be of importance to science. On the contrary, the establishment of fundamental defects in probability would be of profound interest to science as a whole. To begin with— and it would be only a beginning—all statistical textbooks would need to be revised. At least from a short-range point of view, a mathematical discovery of the kind here contemplated would have a more revolutionary impact upon science than anything we parapsychologists have to offer.

If empirical data exist, showing that statistical theory is

wrong, or at least not applicable, in presumably chance situations where ESP and similar psychological effects cannot be expected to operate, such data should be submitted for publication, and preferably to a journal of mathematics. There, without the attention-getting benefit of appearing to be an attack upon ESP, they will receive professional consideration, prompt publication, and will bring lasting fame to their discoverer.

The subject I chose to discuss with you today is too big for more than a quick survey. We have seen how the evidential status of extrasensory perception depends upon several factors: upon the competence of the experimenter, upon the exclusion of ordinary physical explanation, upon the technical correctness of the analysis, and lastly upon the entirety of statistical experience against which the ESP data are to be judged.

There is one interesting byway that I wish we could have explored together. I have not said anything about the fact that ESP was so long undiscovered by scientists in their ordinary laboratory pursuits. Many people wonder how this fact can be reconciled with the claim that ESP is now established as a real phenomenon beyond all reasonable scientific doubt. Perhaps someone else will touch upon this subject. Or perhaps it will come up in the discussion period.

REFERENCES

BROWN, G. S. (1953). *Nature, Lond.,* **172,** 154.
GREENWOOD, J. A. (1938). *J. Parapsychol.,* **2,** 138.
GREENWOOD, J. A., and STUART, C. E. (1937). *J. Parapsychol.,* **1,** 206.
RHINE, J. B., and PRATT, J. G. (1954). *J. Parapsychol.,* **18,** 165.
RIESS, B. F. (1937). *J. Parapsychol.,* **1,** 260.
RIESS, B. F. (1939). *J. Parapsychol.,* **3,** 79.
RUSH, J. H. (1943). *J. Parapsychol.,* **7,** 44.

THE STRENGTH AND WEAKNESS OF THE AVAILABLE EVIDENCE FOR EXTRASENSORY PERCEPTION

D. J. WEST

Society for Psychical Research, London

THE evidence for extrasensory perception presents a curious paradox. On the one hand there are the well-nigh perfect experimental demonstrations by such workers as Pratt and Woodruff (1939) or Soal and Goldney (1943). No valid reason has ever been given for disbelieving the simple factual observations reported by these workers. In spite of many attempts at criticism, their experimental methods remain virtually unimpeachable. On the other hand, the majority of scientists retain an attitude of disbelief or indifference.

One possible explanation is that there is no real weakness at all, and that the reason why the evidence fails to carry conviction is simply that there is an irrational prejudice against the concept of extrasensory perception. Certainly the apparent implications of extrasensory perception are surprisingly at variance with orthodox scientific notions, but it is doubtful if this consideration weighs very heavily today. Scientists have witnessed so many revolutions in thought, brought about by the spectacular advance of physics, that theoretical orthodoxy no longer seems particularly sacred.

It has been suggested that non-acceptance of extrasensory perception is the result of an inherent unconscious bias of the human mind. Geared to deal with practical events of the immediate environment, the mind resists extraneous and irrelevant extrasensory impressions, which might interfere with the orderly stream of consciousness. This theory seems to me unnecessary, at least in the present context, for there are certain features of the evidence for extrasensory perception which suffice to explain the widespread lack of conviction, in spite of the seeming conclusiveness of the experimental work.

Other speakers will no doubt be giving detailed accounts of particular experiments, so I shall restrict myself to a few general remarks about the cogency of some of the experimental evidence, and then proceed to look at the other side of the coin and to examine the features that allow scepticism to prevail.

Extrasensory perception simply means information obtained other than through the normal channels of sense perception, and the card-calling method of demonstrating extrasensory perception possesses a really childish simplicity. A pack of cards is arranged in random order, and well concealed from view. The subject undergoing the test, having no information whatsoever to go upon, has to try to name the order of the cards. His calls are matched against the actual card order, and if he succeeds consistently in naming more cards correct than sheer guesswork would account for, this shows he has some capacity for obtaining information about the card order. So runs the argument.

Such an experiment would seem so simple to carry out, the results so easy to interpret, that it is puzzling why there should be so much doubt and controversy about it. Naturally, certain common sense precautions have to be taken before the experiment can be taken seriously. The cards must be absolutely concealed and entirely inaccessible to the subject, and, if the cards are anywhere in the same room, there must be a witness present to see the subject does not cheat. Soal and others have shown that if the backs of the cards are in view the subject may, knowingly or otherwise, pick up clues and be guided by them in his calling (Soal, 1937). Furthermore, it is obviously desirable that nobody present in the room with the subject should know the order of the cards, otherwise he may unwittingly give the subject clues by means of restless movements, intakes of breath, and so forth. At one time the possibility of involuntary, unconscious whispering of the names of the cards by experimenters or observers was a much discussed hypothesis (Pratt, Rhine, Smith, Stuart and

Greenwood, 1940). Another obvious precaution is to ensure that the person who records the subject's calls does not know the order of the cards, otherwise any errors he makes when recording may tend in the direction of changing the calls to correspond with the cards. Similarly, the card order must either be recorded in advance, or recorded by someone who does not know the subject's calls. Recently two American psychologists, Kaufmann and Sheffield (1952), claimed to have detected, by means of a hidden camera, gross motivated recording errors in a psychic experiment.

Such precautions may seem all very obvious, and hardly worthy of mention among a body of scientists who take thoroughness for granted, but unfortunately, in research on extrasensory perception, it has taken a very long time for these careful habits to become generally accepted as essential to an experiment. Even now, one all too often reads reports in which experimenters fail to make clear whether the right precautions were taken. In this respect, the researches which occasionally issue from psychological laboratories are apt to fall short just as often as the researches conducted by enthusiastic amateurs elsewhere. Nevertheless, there have been experiments, such as the two excellent series of tests previously mentioned, in which the precautions were adequate and the results were unquestionably positive.

There has been some questioning recently of the statistical basis of these card tests. I do not believe that the objections raised substantially affect the evidence, but I will not go into detail, because others better qualified to deal with the question will be talking about it later. It is sufficient to say that in the case of high-scoring subjects like Shackleton and Stewart (Soal and Bateman, 1954) the effect is so obvious that it is scarcely necessary to apply any statistical test in order to demonstrate its presence. I have recorded many thousands of card calls by subjects lacking Shackleton's flair, and their calls corresponded with the cards just about as often as one would expect according to probability. Shackleton, on the other hand, was able, week in and week out, to produce an obvious and consistent excess of correct guesses over chance expectation. Clearly he had some exceptional ability. That it was not in his case a fluke of chance is further proved by his consistent variation in scoring according to the conditions of the test. For instance, whenever Soal tried to do the experiment without an agent looking at the target cards Shackleton's calls ceased at once to show the extra-chance effect.

In my view, therefore, the Shackleton experiments, and others of like quality (of which there are not very many) constitute a perfectly good proof of extrasensory perception. Nevertheless, they fall short of the requirements for universal scientific conviction for several reasons, the chief one being that they are more in the nature of demonstrations than repeatable experiments.

This is the crux of the problem. No demonstration, however well done, can take the place of an experiment that can be repeated by anyone who cares to make the effort. The peculiar limitations of experiments with high-scoring subjects like Shackleton are twofold. First, such subjects are very rare and difficult to find. Second, their performances cannot be guaranteed to work with everybody who wants to do the test. These two limitations are present in all such work. Soal carried out experiments for many years, testing hundreds of subjects and becoming sceptical and discouraged in the process, before he eventually discovered Shackleton (Soal, 1940). Even when Shackleton was at the height of his powers, he only gave his best results with certain agents looking at the cards, and when, on one occasion, Soal was away and his colleague K. M. Goldney assumed the rôle of experimenter, Shackleton gave no significant results at all (Soal and Goldney, 1943).

These two factors—rarity, plus dependence upon the personnel of the test situation—combine to make it impossible to lay down any course of action whereby an interested outsider can be certain of obtaining for himself convincing evidence of extrasensory perception. Some perfectly open-minded investigators have searched literally for years without finding a successful high-scoring subject. It is not simply a question of rarity, otherwise routine card tests given to hundreds of subjects would inevitably lead sooner or later to the discovery of fresh high-scorers. Those without personal experience in the field might gather an erroneous impression on this point from reading reports of outstanding series. From a study of the research reports published from time to time in the Journals of the Society for Psychical Research and of the American Society for Psychical Research, and from an examination of the published reports of such workers as G. W. Fisk, it can be inferred that literally thousands of subjects may be tested and millions of card calls recorded without a single persistent high-scoring subject being discovered. Dr. Soal certainly worked hard to find his star subjects, but in comparison with some other workers he had the Midas touch.

Another way of demonstrating extrasensory perception is to use large numbers of unselected subjects, such as groups of students, to give each of them independently a small number of card trials, and to add their scores together to see if in the aggregate they give a positive result. If it is the case that a fair proportion of ordinary persons are capable of giving a slight positive effect over a short period, the effect should be cumulative and become apparent in the total score of large groups. This has been tried again and again, but whereas some experimenters have obtained positive results, others have achieved nothing, and others have had results only occasionally with particular groups. Since the results obtained from unselected groups are often null, or else small, inconsistent and unpredictable, it is difficult to disprove the theory that the positive scores are mere flukes of chance counterbalanced by the large numbers of tests that yield null results. The position would be made simpler for readers if parapsychological journals would keep to the policy of publishing summaries of all properly conducted and reported experiments, regardless of whether positive scores have been obtained.

The classic experiments by Pratt and Woodruff (1939), which have already been mentioned, involved (in Series B) the testing of thirty-two unselected subjects under most careful experimental conditions. There were 60,000 card calls, which produced a deviation of 489 correct calls in excess of chance expectation. ($t = 4 \cdot 99$, odds against chance being of the order of three million to one.) At least a quarter of the subjects tested appeared to have contributed substantially to the production of this surprising score. (See Table IIB in the original report.) That was in 1939. Neither experimenter has reported since any comparable results either with unselected groups or with special individuals. Their Midas touch was lost. If it was not a fluke of chance, which is unlikely in the extreme, it would seem that some unknown but essential factor was present in their classic series which they have never been able to reproduce.

It may be that reproducibility depends as much on the experimenter as on the subject. In some recent experiments in London, G. W. Fisk, who had previously not been particularly successful, began to use a new type of card test with which he reported obtaining significant results with unselected subjects. I took the opportunity to collaborate in the following manner. His method of testing was to prepare randomized packs of cards, enclose them in sealed envelopes, and post them to his subjects. Together with the packets of cards he also sent record sheets on which the subjects recorded their impressions of the order from top to bottom of the cards inside the envelopes. They then returned the cards, still sealed and unopened, and Fisk checked their guesses. In our joint experiment, without telling the subjects, Fisk continued to send out sealed packs as before, but included among them packs containing cards randomized by myself the order of which he had never seen. The results with the Fisk target cards continued significantly positive, the results with my cards were not (West and Fisk, 1953).

Although it is difficult, in the absence of repeatable results, to exclude chance completely as an explanation of the irregular scores produced by unselected subjects, the theory seems to me implausible for the following reason.

Several workers, notably Humphrey, Nicol and Schmeidler (Nicol and Humphrey, 1953; Schmeidler, 1949), in tests with unselected groups of subjects, have demonstrated that positive scoring is correlated with certain personality traits and attitudes in the subjects. If this work can be further developed, it may become possible to use personality tests to select groups of subjects who can be guaranteed to produce in the aggregate a significantly positive score under specified conditions. One difficulty is that the factors favouring positive scoring are probably more closely correlated with experimenter-subject relationship than with the subject's personality in isolation. All the same, this work comes nearer than any other to defining the conditions of an experiment with predictable outcome.

To summarize, the position regarding the evidence for extrasensory perception appears to be this. Excellently conducted demonstrations have been reported by various workers, but because the conditions which produce good scores are not understood and not reproducible, these experiments are not repeatable in the strict, scientific meaning of repeatability. It is still open to the sceptic to doubt the competence and integrity of those who claim positive results.

The situation is rendered still more unfortunate by the dubious history and background of extrasensory experimentation. As everyone knows, the concept of extrasensory perception arose before card tests were heard of; it arose out of the activities of spiritualists and psychical researchers. Certain mediums and so-called "psychic" persons are said to receive extrasensory impressions which enable them to predict the future and to give their clients personal, factual messages apparently received from spirits of the dead. Most of these claims are not susceptible to scientific testing, and can only be judged by personal experience. Without going into the question of whether there is a substratum of truth, it is quite obvious that this is a highly emotion-laden subject, and one that attracts cranks, dupes and charlatans in embarrassing numbers. And it is from this unsavoury crowd that the extrasensory experimenters have emerged. The field of extrasensory research remains a no man's land between the lunatic fringe on the one hand and the academically unorthodox on the other. The emotional and controversial nature of the phenomenon under investigation, and its unfortunate elusiveness, call for exceptionally level-headed, patient investigators. But some persons are attracted to the subject on account of the scope for controversy and easy notoriety. This is a serious matter, because, lacking university or financial backing, research into extrasensory perception, especially in Great Britain, is carried on chiefly by enthusiastic amateurs working in semi-isolation. All the serious work is done by a handful of people who could easily be swamped by cranks. Indeed, the field is so small that any fool can make a name for himself in it. There are no courses of training, no recognized qualifications. Anyone can set up as an authority with the assurance that his reports will be widely boosted in newspapers and popular books. Knowing these facts only too well, parapsychologists tend to look upon each other with a distrust far exceeding the distruct of scientists in general. I have been present on occasions when persons who have worked in the field for years have seriously discussed whether the whole of the evidence for extrasensory perception might not be a worthless conglomeration of fraud and fallacy. The introduction of an easily repeatable experiment would, I believe, attract the immediate attention of many scientists, and cause these suspicions to evaporate.

Besides creating an atmosphere of suspicion, the unpredictability and elusiveness of extrasensory effects hinders research at every turn. Experimenters have had to concentrate on demonstrating the presence of the effect instead of seeking to discover its nature. So long as the effect is uncontrolled and variable, and conclusive results incredibly difficult to obtain, it is virtually impossible to answer with certitude even the simplest questions about the nature of extrasensory perception.

Here is an illustration. We know that there are a few well

conducted experiments in which an extrasensory effect has been demonstrated with a subject separated from the cards by a distance of the order of a mile or more. But we cannot say for certain that distance is irrelevant to the scoring of most subjects. By present methods such a conclusion could only be arrived at by testing numbers of high-scoring subjects over various distances (and there is not even a single high-scoring subject available for testing), or by carrying out masses of group tests which might occupy all the workers in the field for years to come. The situation is even more uncertain when one comes to discuss precognition. There are a few experiments which are strongly suggestive of a precognitive effect. For instance, in one section of the Shackleton series, positive scoring of the usual order still took place when he was asked to predict the card two ahead in tests in which the selection was made by picking counters out of a bag. Under these conditions it seemed that Shackleton was making his calls a second before the target card was selected. But this is a far cry from precognizing the distant future. Moreover, all subjects who achieve success in ordinary extrasensory perception tests are certainly not equally successful in tests of precognition. These formidable difficulties are glossed over in popular writings in which glib assertions are made about extrasensory perception being independent of space and time. Perhaps that will ultimately prove to be the case, but the truth is that no sweeping generalizations about extrasensory perception can be made with any confidence until better controlled and predictable results become available.

REFERENCES

KAUFMAN, R. S., and SHEFFIELD, F. (1952). *J. Amer. Soc. psych. Res.*, **46**, 111.

NICOL, J. F., and HUMPHREY, B. M. (1953). *J. Amer. Soc. psych. Res.*, **47**, 133.

PRATT, J. G., and WOODRUFF, J. L. (1939). *J. Parapsychol.*, **3**, 121.

PRATT, J. G., RHINE, J. B., SMITH, B. M., STUART, C. E., and GREENWOOD, J. A. (1940). "Extra-sensory perception after sixty years." New York: Henry Holt.

SCHMEIDLER, G. (1949). *J. Parapsychol.*, **13**, 23.

SOAL, S. G. (1937). Univ. of London Council for Psychical Investigation, Bull. 3.

SOAL, S. G. (1940). *Proc. Soc. psych. Res., Lond.*, **46**, 152.

SOAL, S. G., and BATEMAN, F. (1954). "Modern Experiments in Telepathy." London : Faber & Faber.

SOAL, S. G., and GOLDNEY, K. M. (1943). *Proc. Soc. psych. Res., Lond.*, **47**, 21.

WEST, D. J., and FISK, G. W. (1953). *J. Soc. psych. Res.*, **37**, 185.

SOME DIFFICULTIES IN THE WAY OF SCIENTIFIC RECOGNITION OF EXTRASENSORY PERCEPTION

J. Fraser Nicol

Cambridge, Massachusetts

ALMOST three-quarters of a century have elapsed since the first, and still continuing, attempts were made to study that obscure group of phenomena commonly called "psychical", in a "spirit of exact and unimpassioned enquiry". The words were those of the founders of the Society for Psychical Research, and the date was 1882. Few societies in any field of knowledge have obtained such strong support from men and women accustomed to other scientific and scholarly disciplines. It is sufficient to name only a few—Richet, Crookes, Lodge, J. J. Thomson, W. Bateson, Freud, Jung, Barrett, W. James, and Professor and Mrs. Henry Sidgwick. The list could be extended indefinitely.

The evidence studied by the founders of the Society and by their successors can be conveniently considered under four categories. Extensive accounts of the relevant material are readily obtainable in the literature. The four categories are:

1. *Spontaneous cases*, such as those collated and closely analysed by Gurney, Myers and Podmore (1886), and by Mrs. Sidgwick (1922). An example of a spontaneous psychical experience, fairly well authenticated as such cases go, is that of Mrs. Jeanie Gwynne-Bettany, who reported that in her childhood, "I was walking in a country lane at A., the place where my parents then resided. I was reading geometry as I walked along . . . when, in a moment, I saw a bedroom known as the White Room, and upon the floor lay my mother, to all appearances dead. . . . I could not doubt that what I had seen was real, so, instead of going home, I went at once to the house

of our medical man. . . . He at once set out with me for my home, on the way putting questions I could not answer, as my mother was to all appearances well when I left home. I led the doctor straight to the White Room, where we found my mother actually lying as in my vision. . . . She had been seized suddenly by an attack at the heart."

2. *Mediumistic material*, such as that obtained in the investigations of Piper (Lodge, 1890), Leonard (Radclyffe-Hall and Troubridge, 1919) and Cooper (Soal, 1925). The mention of mediumistic utterances at this symposium should be taken to imply *only* paranormal cognition (i.e. telepathy and clairvoyance) involving only living persons. The best of the evidence is impressive and not easy to dismiss.

3. *Qualitative experiments*. These differ from the two preceding categories in the fact that the *material* for study or transmission is prepared by the researcher in advance of the experiment. The weakness of such investigations is that the material, generally drawings, solid objects, verses of poetry and the like, is inaccessible to statistical evaluation. Some important accounts of such work were prepared by Guthrie and Birchall (1883), Guthrie (1885) and Miles and Ramsden (1907 and 1914).

4. *Quantitative experiments*. These appear to have been initiated by the physiologist Charles Richet (1884). Quantitative research forms the main subject matter of this symposium. The leading experiments have been summarized and discussed by J. G. Pratt and others (1940) and by S. G. Soal and F. Bateman (1954).

Within these four categories the printed evidence is ample and sufficient, I believe, to sustain a strong case for the reality of paranormal cognition ("extrasensory perception"). This is common ground to most psychical researchers, though they differ extremely in their judgment as to the quality of individual cases. It is also commonly held by psychical researchers that the facts deserve greater recognition from practitioners in other fields of scientific work than they have thus far been accorded.

Scientific recognition is a term not easy to define. Scientific societies do not adopt resolutions of approval of new discoveries, for this might be the road to scientific dogmatism. Rather, new research findings grow into acceptance gradually, in most instances. This must be especially so if the claims are of a highly novel character. Such widely different things as the anaesthetic use of chloroform and G. Cantor's theory of infinite numbers were accepted only after prolonged and bitter struggle. On the question of psychical research, after three-quarters of a century the disapproval, indifference or apathy of scientific men seem "unconscionably long a-dying".

Psychology is the field in which one would expect to find the greatest amount of interest and study of this subject. In 1938 and again in 1952 L. Warner (Warner and Clark, 1938; Warner, 1952) sought by means of a questionnaire which he issued to several hundred Fellows of the American Psychological Association to obtain information about that question and some others. He found, in both cases, that of those who offered their opinions on extrasensory perception, only one-fifth arrived at their views after reading the published experimental reports. He found also that over the period of fourteen years there was very little change favourable to belief in extrasensory perception. In both surveys, three-quarters of the respondents believed no more than that extrasensory perception was either "a remote possibility" or "merely an unknown".

Having given some indication of the strength and high quality of the evidence in psychical research, I now turn to the reasons why members of other scientific professions appear to react to the subject with feelings of doubt, indifference or aversion. I shall divide the reasons into four classes:

1. The seeming irrelevance of the subject to other sciences.
2. The lack of any repeatable experiment.
3. Disagreement among psychical researchers as to the quality of much of the evidence.
4. Claims made that are unsupportable by the published evidence.

1. The seeming irrelevance of the subject to other sciences

Few scientific men can find any meaningful place for paranormal cognition in their own fields. Sir Oliver Lodge supposed there might be a link between the physical and psychical worlds by means of what was then known as the ether of space. His conjectures have obtained little support. Dr. J. B. Rhine has spoken of extrasensory perception and psychokinesis as giving new meaning to the study of biology, medicine, psychology, "the government of man", "the freedom of the individual" and the struggle against physical-istic Communism. He has also projected a new "Copernican revolution" as a logical consequence of the experiments in psychokinesis (dice-throwing). Those views are perhaps a little speculative. More instructive and interesting are the cautious conjectures of A. C. Hardy (1953) in respect of pos-sible relations between the findings of psychical research and evolutionary theory. Some psychiatrists have written of the significance of paranormal occurrences to their own studies. Something may come of this, but the evidence from this source is slight and often ambiguous. It has been said—but the reference has evaded recent research—that the first mention of Freud in any English writing appeared in a paper by a psychical researcher, Frederic Myers, in the Proceedings of the Society for Psychical Research.

The name of Myers recalls to us that the main title of his classic of psychical investigation was *Human Personality* (Myers, 1903). Psychical research is the study of personality, though this fact is sometimes lost sight of. If we try to look forward, it may seem very probable that the interrelations of paranormal cognition with other factors of personality such as extraversion-introversion, dominance-submission, intelli-gence, neurotic tendencies and the like, will form the main line of advance in psychical research in the coming years. We may learn something.

Yet by and large it is difficult not to feel some sympathy with those engaged in experimental and applied psychology who have thus far detected little of interest in our work that has any bearing on theirs. No doubt time will change the scene, but progress is slow. In brief the subject at the present stage of its difficult history seems to have no immediate relevance to the subject matter of other sciences.

2. Failure to produce a repeatable experiment

The major difficulty of qualitative research—that of estimating the chance factor—was overcome in quantitative research by application of the calculus of probability. This was an important step forward.

The second advantage, characteristic of all scientific work in which quantitative methods are used, is the opportunity they give to create repeatable experimentation. By this is meant the designing of an experimental set-up which, found in practice to produce a significant effect, can be repeated by any competent person at any time in the foreseeable future with approximately similar significant results. After thirty years, psychical researchers have failed to produce one repeatable experiment. Yet more than sixteen years have passed since R. A. Fisher (1938) made the following comment on extrasensory perception experiments: "Perhaps I may say, with respect to the use of statements of very long odds, that I have before now, criticised their cogency on the grounds, not only that the procedure of calculation is often questionable, but that they are much less relevant to the establishment of the facts of nature than would be a demonstration of *the reliable reproducibility of the phenomena*".

The failure of psychical research to meet the fundamental inductive principle of science was bound to lead to embarrassing questions. Mr. Spencer Brown has raised one such question. There may be others. I shall return to the pressing need for repeatability at the close of this paper.

3. Disagreement on the quality of the printed evidence

It might be supposed by the friendly inquiring scientist that even if psychical researchers are unable to obtain repetition of their experimental phenomena, at any rate they presumably agree on the validity of those experiments that have not been susceptible to repetition. By this I mean that there are perhaps certain experiments reported in the literature, call them A, B, C, D, E, etc., on which psychical researchers are of the unanimous opinion that *those* experiments certainly cannot be explained away on "normal" hypotheses. It is the purpose of this section of the paper to point to the discouraging fact that psychical researchers of undoubted authority do not agree among themselves as to whether some of the leading experiments are conclusive evidence for paranormality.

To show how real this disagreement is it is necessary only to consider part of the contents of the two most important surveys of the evidence published in recent times. The first is *Extrasensory Perception After Sixty Years* (J. G. Pratt and others, 1940), written by five members of the Parapsychology Laboratory at Duke University. In further references I shall abridge the title of this book to *ESP Sixty* The other important work is *Modern Experiments in Telepathy* (S. G. Soal and F. Bateman, 1954). This title will be abridged hereafter to *Modern Experiments*.

In *ESP Sixty* the authors discussed thirty-five "counter-hypotheses" which they rightly held must be met before the results of an ostensibly psychical experiment could be accepted as valid evidence for paranormal cognition. Those counter-hypotheses included such contingencies as non-random shuffling of cards, sensory leakage in the experimental room, incompetence of the experimenters, errors of recording the targets and calls, dubious statistical methods and so on.

The authors examined 142 published reports, and of these only six survived the counter-hypotheses. The claims made for those six experiments will now be compared with the opinions on the same experiments presented in *Modern Experiments*, a book which it is necessary to note is described by the authors as "a fairly detailed account of the better class of experiments in extrasensory perception which have been carried out in the past thirty-five years". The six experiments of *ESP Sixty* all happen to be covered by the time period mentioned. We may now turn to them.

(i) *Pratt-Woodruff*, the title (being the experimenters' names) by which it is widely known in the field, was a test of sixty-six subjects by a procedure known as "screened-touch-matching". There were about 60,000 trials, the total score was measurably above chance, χ, the normal deviate, being 4·99, representing odds against the null hypothesis of the order of a million to one. I should regard this research as an example of experimental rigour applied to the last degree of scientific necessity. But the authors of *Modern Experiments* judge it to be only "a fairly good series", an unexpected comment that has "surprised" Dr. McConnell (1954). Hence, we have here four opinions, three unreservedly favourable to the research, one (from a most distinguished source) not so favourable.

(ii) *Lucien Warner's "A Test Case"*. This was a series of 250 trials. The subject, a woman, was accommodated in a ground-floor room. The two experimenters (described as "psychologically trained") were in a locked room on the first floor and in the opposite wing of the house to that in which the subject was placed. The cards were drawn singly from a pack which was shuffled after each trial. There was no conversation between the experimenters, and the signalling system was one-way; from subject to experimenters only. The average score was 9·3 per run, a remarkable result if genuine; mean chance expectation being the usual 5·0 per run. The normal deviate was 6·8, and the odds against the null hypothesis too astronomically remote to be worth computing. This truly astonishing result obtained under seemingly impeccable conditions is treated by Soal and Bateman with total silence, for it is nowhere mentioned in their most thorough survey of thirty-five years' research.

(iii) *Pearce-Pratt*. This well-known clairvoyance investigation was carried out with the principal experimenter, J. G. Pratt, and the subject, Hubert Pearce, accommodated in separate buildings at two distances apart, 340 feet and 740 feet. The number of trials was 1850, the average score per run was 7·53, and the normal deviate was 10·87, which has an associated probability of 10^{-20}.

The Pearce-Pratt series is warmly commended in *Modern Experiments*.

(iv) *Turner-Ownbey*. This was a short series of telepathy experiments in which the agent, Miss Ownbey, and the subject, Miss Turner, were at first 250 miles and later 300 miles apart. Each day's work comprised twenty-five trials, and (what is important to note) it was arranged that they would despatch their records to J. B. Rhine at the end of each day's work. For the first three days, however, Miss Turner failed to carry out this instruction, sending her records instead to Miss Ownbey. The results claimed under those regrettable conditions were phenomenal, the scores for the three runs being 19, 16 and 16. In the subsequent experiments, in which Miss Turner faithfully followed the prescribed rule, her scores were in close accord with mean chance expectation.

Modern Experiments, if I understand the authors correctly, is on the whole, favourable to the Turner-Ownbey affair, though some doubt is expressed. The authors say, "we shall have to accept the results of the experiment, or assume that the two experimenters were in collusion ".

(v) *Riess*. The experimenter, Dr. B. F. Riess, was a psychologist. The subject (name not disclosed) was a young woman music teacher. Whilst Riess exposed the cards in his home, the subject wrote down her guesses at her own residence more than quarter of a mile away. There were seventy-four runs (of the customary twenty-five trials per run). The average score per run was the extraordinary figure of 18·24, which is the largest average score in the history of the subject. In one spell of nine runs all the scores were more than 20. The normal deviate works out at 53·57, which is the largest on record for a single series. The probability against the null hypothesis appears to be about 10^{-700}.

The case is accepted by the Duke group as one of the six most conclusive series in history, but in *Modern Experiments* it is dismissed as one of "the questionable experiments . . . which in the present book we have scarcely considered to be worthy of mention. . . ."

(vi) *Murphy and Taves.* This was a long and careful piece of research involving many subjects. All the necessary precautions were taken. For each subject there were several kinds of tests, the experimental material consisting of playing-cards and various forms of ESP cards. The number of trials was 175,000. The total scores were not significantly above chance expectation, but significant correlations were found between certain of the ESP tasks. These correlations had not been foreseen in the experimental design, and hence their statistical quality is only that of *ad hoc* hypotheses.

As indicated, in *ESP Sixty* the experiment and its outcome are judged to be one of the six most impressive cases on record. In *Modern Experiments* the case is not mentioned.

Summary. Six out of 142 researches were judged by the first group of authors to surmount all plausible counter-hypotheses. Of these cases, the second group of (two) authors assent unhesitatingly to their predecessors' views on one research (or two if the Turner-Ownbey matter be included), are not completely satisfied with a third research, reject a fourth, and ignore the existence of the two remaining researches.

Clearly, there is no unity of opinion among leading psychical researchers as to what constitutes valid evidence.

4. Unsubstantiated Claims

This is the fourth, and last, of the factors which appear to be operating against the scientific recognition of parapsychology. The question now refers to certain exaggerated and unsubstantiated claims that appear with uncomfortable frequency in the literature of parapsychology. To deal with the problem comprehensively would call for the writing of several papers. Here I shall try only to illustrate the gravity of the matter by taking examples from several pages of one book.

The subject of discourse is psychokinesis, a word that is

commonly abridged to "PK". Psychokinesis has been formally defined as: "The direct influence exerted on a physical system by a subject without any known intermediate physical energy or instrumentation", or, very colloquially, "the power of mind over matter". The physical objects commonly used in the many reported experiments are ordinary commercial dice. These are caused to be thrown whilst the subject "wills" which face will turn up, and the results are assessed statistically. Dice throwing raises a host of awkward problems, which will not be discussed now; but it is necessary to recognise that all dice are in varying degrees biased, or must be assumed so.

That extrasensory perception is a well-established fact of nature, few who have studied the literature with care and without prejudice will doubt. The evidence for psychokinesis is less satisfactory. It is interesting to note, however, that according to one important authority (Rhine, 1947), "PK implies ESP, and ESP implies PK. . . . Each phenomenon follows from and leads into the other; each derives confirmatory support from the work which established the other." This passage is from *The Reach of the Mind* by J. B. Rhine. The book is not easy to classify. It was regarded as sufficiently suitable for the general public to be published in an abridged form in *Readers Digest*. On the other hand, its pretensions to being classified as a scientific statement may be gleaned from the fact that the author recommended it to the attention of the New York Academy of Sciences (Rhine, 1950). On meeting scientists engaged in other fields of work one commonly discovers that they rarely have time to read the original reports in our subject. So it is convenient for them to have available in a couple of hundred pages a summary of the facts —or the supposed facts. In this book a large number of the pronouncements of claims with respect to psychokinesis evidence are misleading, sometimes they are contrary to the evidence presented in the original reports, and in some places formidable claims are made on the basis of evidence that has never been reported in any scientific paper.

To take one case, it is remarked in the book that two students, H. Hilton and G. Baer, obtained "significantly high scoring in high dice tests". This claim sags somewhat when it is found in the original report that a control series of throws was made to determine the bias of the dice, and that the "high dice" totals in this case were of precisely the same order as in the putatively PK throws. The probability of observed difference between control and supposed PK is a modest 0·27.

With regard to PK work comparing the effect of throwing different numbers of dice at a time, the author of the book endeavours to present evidence (here and elsewhere) that PK is more effective on many dice thrown together than on one or two. For example, in the book it is observed that "the tests with six dice scored higher than those with two dice. The rate with two dice was not much above 'chance', but the results with six were highly significant. This finding is obviously not what one would expect from a physical viewpoint."

These statements are at variance with the experimental facts. In the PK literature two experimental papers cite comparisons of this type. One is the work of Frank Smith (Rhine, 1944), the other is part of the first E. P. Gibson research (Gibson and Rhine, 1943). The results were:

No. of dice thrown	SMITH Average per run	χ	GIBSON Average per run	χ
2	4·33	3·56	4·80	2·40
6	4·31	2·56	4·07	0·82

(A "run" is twenty-four throws of one die, twelve throws of two, or four throws of six. The expected average, other things being equal, is therefore always 4·00.)

The results for both Smith and Gibson are plainly the exact opposite of those so confidently announced in the book. Moreover, since there was no control on the bias, and the "target" was almost consistently chosen as face 6, the normal deviates computed can have no bearing on the PK hypothesis. One searches the literature in vain for any comparison fitting the book's claim that "tests with six scored higher than those with two dice ".

The belief that in psychokinesis experiments the dice do not obey physical laws is constantly urged. H. L. Frick investigated his own psychokinetic powers by throwing at the same time twelve dice described as of medium size and twelve described as small, the former being "approximately twice as large cubically" as the small ones. But, according to the book, "the larger dice gave almost twice as many *hits* above chance average" as compared with the small ones, and therefore "the results obtained were just the opposite of what one might expect from a physical theory ".

In face of this seeming modification of the Laws of Motion, a scientific reader might be tempted to consult the original report. With the aid of elementary statistics he would easily find that the discovery reported in the book is dangerously misleading. So closely similar are the scores for the two kinds of dice that the probability of their observed difference is 0·40. Yet the tone of the book is such as to leave the reader to infer that the difference is significant and real. On the basis of such data, and others of little better quality, it is seriously stated on a subsequent page that "the indifference of PK to the physical law of gravity is surely something to ponder ".

A factor of distance in relation to psychokinesis is reported to have been introduced in experiments at the Parapsychology Laboratory. "When ", observed the author of the book, "the subject was assured that he could do better from the more distant position, the results obtained at twenty-five feet were much better than when he stood close to the dice. After this point was demonstrated, the advantage of distance was played down and that of being close to the dice was emphasized. As a result the relation between the two scoring averages was reversed so that proximity was favoured." These supposed findings, which are later described as "more than suggestive ", are clearly of great importance to the scientific world, indicating as they do the abrogation or modification of gravitational law and the existence of a force that can operate invisibly at a distance of twenty-five feet from its source. When the PK reports are searched for further details, we come away empty-handed. No such report exists.

On the strength of dice throwing said to have been performed at Duke University, it is recorded elsewhere that the psychokinetic force is more effective on heavy metal dice than on wooden ones; and also, from the same source, that the shape of the dice—sharp corners, rounded corners, or extremely rounded corners—makes no difference to the power of the human psychic force. Neither of these strange claims can be validated in any of the published reports on psychokinesis. It is mainly on the basis of these and similar unverifiable assertions that the author concludes that "the finding that *mass, number, and form* [of dice] *are not determining conditions in PK tests*, takes its place, then, alongside the discovery that time and space were not limiting factors in ESP". The italics are mine.

Only a few of these rash pronouncements have been quoted in the above paragraphs. Many others could be cited. One wonders what the more objective but friendly type of scientist must think when he is confronted with such highly adorned claims. He might, one surmises, rather easily turn away from psychical research, moved by the uncomfortable realization that a subject in which scientific method and the need for careful reporting are so casually pushed out of the way, is not a field of study in which he would care to indulge.

General summary and conclusions

Four factors operating to produce indifference or hostility to psychical research have been adduced. These are the apparent irrelevance of psychical research to other scientific fields, the failure of psychical researchers to obtain reproducible phenomena, discordant views on the validity of evidence, and inflated claims to discoveries.

These factors are not of equal importance, and it seems clear to me that the most pressing need is that of obtaining repetition of results. Given the discovery of one experimental design with repeatability qualities, however simple and modest it might be, one would expect others to follow in its steps. The conflicts of belief amongst psychical researchers (to say nothing of the scientific world in general) would presumably lose significance, and the temptation to make inflated claims ought to decline. Results that could be predicted, at least to a fair degree of precision, are by definition, *science*, and therefore "respectable", and deserving of recognition. This desirable consummation would be nearer in that situation than it has been in the past. A preceding speaker has expressed the urgent need for experimental repeatability. I can only add my support to that view, and express the hope that the whole strength of research should now be devoted to that end.

REFERENCES

Fisher, R. A. (1938). *J. Parapsychol.*, **2**, 267.

Gibson, E. P., and Rhine, J. B. (1943). *J. Parapsychol.*, **7**, 118.

Gurney, E., Myers, F. W. H., and Podmore, F. (1886). Phantasms of the Living (2 vols.). London: Trübner.

Guthrie, M. (1885). *Proc. Soc. psych. Res., Lond.*, **3**, 424.

Guthrie, M., and Birchall, J. (1883). *Proc. Soc. psych. Res., Lond.*, **1**, 263.

Hardy, A. C. (1953). *Proc. Soc. psych. Res., Lond.*, **50**, 96.

Lodge, O. J. (1890). *Proc. Soc. psych. Res., Lond.*, **6**, 443.

McConnell, R. A. (1954). *J. Parapsychol.*, **18**, 252.

Miles, C., and Ramsden, H. (1907). *Proc. Soc. psych. Res., Lond.*, **21**, 60.

Miles, C., and Ramsden, H. (1914). *Proc. Soc. psych. Res., Lond.*, **27**, 279.

Myers, F. W. H. (1903). Human Personality and Its Survival of Bodily Death (2 vols.). London: Longmans, Green.

Pratt, J. G., Rhine, J. B., Smith, B. M., Stuart, C. E., and Greenwood, J. A. (1940). Extra-sensory Perception After Sixty Years. New York: Henry Holt.

Radclyffe-Hall and Una, Lady Troubridge (1919). *Proc. Soc. psych. Res., Lond.*, **30**, 339.

Rhine, J. B. (1944). *J. Parapsychol.*, **8**, 287.

Rhine, J. B. (1947). The Reach of the Mind. New York: Wm. Sloane.

Rhine, J. B. (1950). *Trans. N.Y. Acad. Sci.*, Series II, Vol. 12, 164.

RICHET, C. (1884). *Rev. Philos.*, Dec.

SIDGWICK, E. H. (1922). *Proc. Soc. psych. Res., Lond.*, 33, 1.

SOAL, S. G. (1925). *Proc. Soc. psych. Res., Lond.*, 35, 471.

SOAL, S. G., and BATEMAN, F. (1954). Modern Experiments in Telepathy. London: Faber & Faber.

WARNER, L. (1952). *J. Parapsychol.*, 16, 284.

WARNER, L., and CLARK, C. C. (1938). *J. Parapsychol.*, 2, 296.

DISCUSSION

Gaddum: I am afraid I feel like Dr. Parkes on this subject—ignorant but interested. I have a subconscious prejudice against believing in anything at all. I do not know why I have that prejudice and I am grateful to Mr. Fraser Nicol for telling me something about my reasons. It is always difficult to analyse your own reasons, and when you do, you are apt to rationalize them wrongly. Fifty years ago I would have been the kind of person who said that it was all coincidence, and when eventually convinced that perhaps the statistics were all right, I would have said that it was incompetence, and finally I would have been driven back to saying that it was all fraud. But I am not going to say any of those things now, because I know that some of you people here would turn on me and rend me, being much better informed than I am about the facts. But I have a sort of hope that you will turn on one another, because I would like not to believe it.

All the same, I do not believe that scientists today have as strong a sales resistance as you people say. I think that they were very resistant fifty years ago, and that they are now much more credulous. Physicists have always been rather credulous and even the biologists are ready to believe quite a lot. It is the physicists who have taught us to be less dogmatic. When Michelson and Morley did the experiment which seemed to show that the velocity of light relative to all observers was always the same, even when the observers were moving rapidly relative to one another, it was a very surprising thing indeed. If I had been alive at that time and somebody had explained it to me and made me understand the significance of it, I imagine I should have been incredulous, and certainly would have shown a lot of sales resistance; I would have had indifference and aversion of the kind which you have accused scientists of having now. It was a completely bewildering thing which eventually became credible because Einstein thought it out and saw what it meant. Newton's laws were a very good first approximation which worked for all practical purposes, but under special circumstances, if you got the right observer and you had the right apparatus, you could detect small divergences from Newton's laws. And I should like to know whether you people think that we are in the same position now with regard to extrasensory perception.

Another reason why people have less resistance than they used to have is, I think, because they are better informed. A lot of popular and semi-popular books have been written. I have read some of them

myself and it is clear that there is a great deal of evidence which it would
be very difficult to upset. I must confess that I have not studied the
original papers, and I hope that those who have will be able to find
flaws in the arguments advanced by their colleagues.

One kind of evidence that I feel is really convincing is that some
people can do it and some cannot. I mean, if it was the sort of thing
that anybody might do sometimes, I should not believe in it so readily
as in the fact that once you have got a man like Shackleton, you can
apparently make repeatable experiments with him. I do not understand why it is suggested that it is not a repeatable experiment, if day
after day you can always get significant scores. That seems to me a
convincing experiment and the important thing is to find some more
experimental material of that kind. In biology we often have trouble
getting the appropriate experimental animal in good supply. We have
been having trouble lately over the supply of a mollusc, which was
working very well and then suddenly became unobtainable, because of
the winter, and supplies are only just coming in again now. I think that
is the same sort of problem that you people have in connection with
these percipients.

Another kind of evidence that convinces me is the kind in which the
controls are contained in the experiment itself. When you compare the
guesses in one experiment with the cards which have been laid down
before and after, or two before and two after, sometimes you find percipients showing precognition or postcognition; it seems to be particularly convincing when it is something you did not expect. When you
can see a row of figures, as reported in Dr. Soal's book for one of the
experiments with Shackleton, in which there is a row of smaller figures
and then there is a score of 325, when he is guessing one ahead, it
produces the sort of graph which is convincing to a biologist. I rather
wish that there had been more cases in which you, Dr. Soal, had actually
quoted the control observations which were not significant, instead of
just saying that they were not significant.

Another case which seemed striking to me was the experiment in
which Shackleton was tested alternately for telepathy and clairvoyance,
without being told which it was, and one worked and the other did not.
That has also got the control results and the main results inside the
same experiment and it seems convincing to me.

The important thing is to find more experimental animals and to be
able to find them often. I do not know how much has been done in big
surveys in the way of selecting the people who do well the first time
and then trying them again, and gradually selecting out sensitive subjects by repeated tests. Perhaps somebody will tell us about that later.

Another thing which I have wondered about, is how much has been
done with drugs. I have heard of experiments in which people have
used drugs which stimulate the central nervous system, like caffeine,
and experiments with drugs which depress the central nervous system,
like barbiturates. There are a lot of drugs which have specific effects on
different parts of the central nervous system, like mescaline, lysergic
acid diethylamide, morphine, and cocaine. It seems to me possible that

if more experiments were done with those drugs, it might be possible to find one which put the percipient in the right state of mind for perceiving. It may be that I am ignorant of work that has actually been done in this field, but I would like to hear more about it.

Then, how much have we to believe ? I gather that there is quite good evidence for telepathy and perhaps for clairvoyance, and precognition. I hope that it will become apparent how many of these and other things we must believe, and particularly what the general opinion here is on the subject of psychokinesis.

The eventual object, I imagine, of this meeting, is to form some sort of theory which will fulfil the function fulfilled by the theory of relativity in connection with the Michelson-Morley experiment. It seems to me that no such theory can really be of much use until we know how much ground it has to cover, and for that reason I should like to know how much we are now to believe.

Pratt: It seems to me that what we have had in the three papers thus far is an excellent sequence of appetisers, but the main course, the actual results that the parapsychologists *might* present as evidence for extrasensory perception, has not been reached. I am sure that some of the topics still lying ahead will offer us something more in the way of actual results, but it is scarcely to be expected that this symposium can, in the course of two and a half days, summarize fully the evidence that ESP occurs in the human species. I do not lament that situation, I just face it. And I think it is indeed a good thing to have had such good appetisers.

A concept that has been emphasized by all three of the previous speakers, if I remember correctly, is the one of repeatability, and there I need only say "Amen" to what Prof. Gaddum has said. I cannot see how there is any serious question to be raised regarding the repeatability of an experiment when Dr. Soal and Mrs. Goldney, for example, working with their selected subjects week after week, were able to get results and were able to do so with visitors brought in to witness and even to take charge of their experiments. Dr. Soal actually started out with the intention of seeing if he could repeat the earlier ESP experiments done at Duke University ; and while he thought he was failing over a number of years, when he finally found two high scoring subjects I am sure, that to his way of thinking, he had successfully repeated the Duke work. The thing to keep in mind, it seems to me, is the *essential* nature or the *essential* feature of the experiment, and if similar results are obtained by a number of people working in different places, then I think that in every real meaning of the term the results are repeatable.

I noticed Mr. Nicol's emphasis upon the differences of opinion, and it seems to me that this emphasis might be carried too far. If we go to the books which have been written, as many of the books cited have been written, to interpret and present to the intelligent lay reader the basic principles and the basic findings of the subject, naturally we can find differences when we compare one book with another. I had the pleasure on the boat over of reading Dr. West's book, and I think I could cite from his book and from what he said here today a few instances in which he even differs with himself! These differences on small points are not so important as the basic agreements among people who have been devoting a great deal of time to this subject. And I suspect that before we get through we will find that on the truly basic matters the agreements stand out.

Wassermann: I should like to take up two points about repeatability mentioned by Dr. West and Mr. Fraser Nicol. Perhaps I might first say that although I disagree with them on this particular problem, I agree with them on more problems than I disagree. It would be a serious misconception to think that because there are slight differences of opinion that parapsychologists are at loggerheads on a large scale.

It has been said that repeatability is a very important thing and one which convinces people that there is something in an experiment. But I do not think that we can use the word 'repeatable' without caution, because, as Prof. Gaddum said correctly, there are two types of repeatability. There is first of all repeatability *within* a single experiment, such as that found in the Soal-Goldney experiments and the Soal and Bateman series. Then there is repeatability between different experiments, and these two types of repeatability are entirely different things.

Let me also discuss what repeatability *at will* means. Supposing I said: "I shall take Mr. Smith from the street and ask him to sit for a hundred controlled card-guessing sessions to see if I get something positive! If I do not get anything I can say that the experiment was not repeatable at will, because Smith has not done what Shackleton did in similar experiments." Well, there is no logical reason why Smith should perform like Shackleton. Looking for such a type of repeatability is looking for a mare's nest. Take, for instance, experiments in cosmic ray physics. Sometimes you find a meson track, sometimes you do not. You can set out with iron determination to find a track and come home empty handed. Nevertheless, physicists agree that these tracks, even if rarely found, are important. In other words, if we have a rare event we cannot expect it to be repeatable at will. We must simply distinguish between high and low inductive probabilities, and this, I think, Mr. Fraser Nicol does not seem to appreciate.

Meteorites, for example, occur rarely and therefore have a low inductive probability. It would be silly, therefore, to demand that they should be observable just when it suits us. Nature does not always bend to our demands.

Another difficulty in achieving repeatability is that different people or different animals will not respond similarly in similar situations. If you take twenty rats each of a different strain there is no reason why they should respond in the same way in the same experiment; they may have different genetical equipment. In parapsychological experiments the things that can vary are very numerous, and none of the speakers, Dr. West, Dr. McConnell and Mr. Fraser Nicol, has stated this. In such an experiment you often have an agent who looks at cards, you may have one or more percipients (as in the Schmeidler and Humphrey experiments), and finally you may have experimenters and witnesses present. A large number of experiments by McFarland, Soal, and many others, show us only too clearly that the personality structure of the agent, percipient and the others present may all matter. In other words, you have an interrelation between a large number of personalities which Dr. Gardner Murphy calls an interpersonality field (incidentally this has nothing to do with the field theory I am going to talk about tomorrow). It is something like the topological 'fields' which Kurt Lewin has described. The interpersonality relations introduce, of course, a large number of parameters. Now, you cannot demand that all the parameters of all people are exactly the same. They may be similar or different, you cannot be sure. Genetical differences, learning and other things may differ from case to case. We have, for example, Riess' subject who, after a few hundred highly successful ESP trials, developed thyroid trouble and after an operation failed completely in further tests. To suggest, therefore, that all people must always behave alike in similar experiments, or that different people should behave alike, is a monstrous demand which just cannot be fulfilled. We must be grateful if a limited amount of repetition occurs within a single set of experiments with the same people.

Let us ask: what makes an experiment acceptable ? I think that a parapsychological experiment will be accepted provided there occurs a consistent change of behaviour of the subject when the experimental conditions are changed. We know that this happened in the Soal-Goldney experiments. This is comparable to what you do in physical experiments. If in a gas you measure pressure against volume at constant temperatures, you get different curves when you change the temperatures. If you return to the original temperature you get your original curve back, at least near enough. Something similar happened in the Soal-Goldney experiments. When they went back to the same conditions they usually obtained the same type of results. Soal's subjects showed repeatable behaviour within these series. It would be too much to ask that other subjects should behave likewise.

Finally, Mr. Fraser Nicol's remarks that parapsychology may not have any relation to other fields seem to me unjustifiable—I may be misquoting him but I think he said something of the sort—because I think that parapsychology when isolated has little or no meaning at all. No scientific facts by themselves have much meaning unless they are correlated within a theory to other facts of other fields of science. It is vital for this reason to find generalizations and to put these within a united system, so that one set of facts supports another one, as Braithwaite has pointed out in his recent book.

L.-Davies: May I say one further word about repeatability ? It seems to me, a lunatic-fringe amateur, as Dr. West might describe me, rather interesting that the parapsychologists all fall over backwards and say, "We must have repeatability," but the biologists at this symposium say that that does not impress them as a primary necessity. Within the field of normal biological research, the whole problem is very much easier, because the biologist, experimenting on an experimental animal, at least knows which is the experimenter and which is the experimental animal. But in the field of extrasensory perception, we have not even yet found out whether any true data can be arrived at by regarding the experimental animal alone, or whether we must, as the last speaker said, consider the immediate Gestalt, and when trying to find out why sometimes we get results and why sometimes we do not perhaps several other Gestalts too, historical and geographical.

The situation is even more difficult, because in most ordinary biological work, it is possible to work out how many variables there are in the experiment, and to reduce their number or treat them by various techniques, so that you know which variable you are testing. But the variables in ESP are at present so many, and so unknown, that we are nowhere near the stage where we can say: "Well, we will pin that variable down and deal with that and then go on to the next variable". For example, the whole question of telepathy and clairvoyance is at present obscure, because some experimenters, like Dr. Soal, cannot get their guinea pig to work at all in a clairvoyant experiment, whereas in my own case I found that it did not matter in the least whether I or anyone else looked at the cards, one got exactly the same results whether the cards were seen or unseen by an agent before Maria guessed them. In short, we are right back at the very beginning, because we have not yet been able to discover what the variables are with which we are dealing. Until we can do that, we cannot get anything more than the kind of repeatability which consists in some facts happening, and then next day, if we are lucky, the same facts happening again. That we can do. Dr. Soal did it year after year. Other people have done the same.

The next stage will surely be when we have got enough of these repeated facts in any one piece of material to ask why on Wednesday things were different from Tuesday. But of course we cannot do that until we have more material.

Brown: I want to continue this discussion of repeatability, but I should like first to refer to two things which Dr. McConnell said in his paper. McConnell talked about the shuffling of cards, saying that this was a well-known randomizing procedure, and he referred to two cases. One of the cases was the Greenwood experiment which is so often cited as a control experiment for ESP. I think there are some misconceptions about this experiment, and with permission I shall read you part of a letter which I sent to Rhine about it.

"The Greenwood check was undertaken primarily to see if successful subjects' calling patterns showed a general tendency to score higher than average against shuffled decks of ESP cards. As was to be expected, no such tendency was found. In no other respect does this remarkable series constitute a control experiment in ESP. The reason is as follows: in the experiment, a hundred runs of guesses were taken from the best scoring subjects and matched against shuffled decks of ESP cards until a total of 500,000 matching operations had been carried out. Thus, the same series of guesses were matched again and again against different shuffled decks. A simple calculation shows that each run of guesses must have been matched 200 times, and I know of no ESP experiment in which a subject has been asked to try to make one series of guesses do for 200 different packs of cards at once."

Thus the Greenwood experiment, whatever else it may be, cannot be taken as a control experiment for ESP. We have, in fact, a deficiency of a number of control experiments which have been carried out, because the Greenwood one can only be counted as a control in a very special way.

The other comment I wish to make is in reply to his rather pointed reference to my not having yet published my random number counts. But this is no longer an urgent matter since A. T. Oram has now done a very large experiment, rather larger than any of mine, on Babington Smith's random numbers in which he has obtained a significance (which he failed to notice) in the matching scores in the $+ 1$ position of $P <$ 1/7000th. And this significance was obtained in a quarter distribution test, which is standard in parapsychology. McConnell said that such effects as have been found in random number experiments were certainly not large enough to impugn the reality of the evidence for ESP, and yet he himself quotes a significance of 1/500th in his own psychokinesis experiment as reliable evidence for the existence of a psi effect. So he is not being consistent.

Now I should like to get back to the general discussion on repeatability. It does seem that there has been some confusion on this point, because repeatability means so many different things. As some one pointed out, we can get repeatability within a single experiment, but that is not what is meant by repeatability in science. We want results which are not only consistent in one experiment, but which can be observed to recur in further experiments. This does not necessarily mean that they must be repeatable at will. A total eclipse of the sun is not repeatable at will; nevertheless it is demonstrably repeatable—we can give the recipe for its repetition. And this is the minimum we look for in science. We must be able to give a recipe. Until then we may say only that something is happening; but we may not say what it is.

West: I should like to enter this discussion on the question of what exactly I meant by saying that the experiments were not strictly repeatable. Prof. Gaddum has said that he thought that the situation was rather similar to what might be found in other sciences where the material available is rare; one may have to wait until one finds a particular subject before one can do the experiment, but once having found the subject one can repeat the experiment at will. I think that in the field of ESP experiments the difficulty goes further than that. We do not even know that everybody can find a good subject. Dr. Soal spent a very long time before he found his subject. Other people failed to find even one subject. If it is true that success depends upon a combination of experimenter and subject, then, of course, it is not simply a question of going on searching until you find a subject. If that were so, then one could say that the experiments were reproducible. As it is one must face up to the fact that they are, strictly speaking, not repeatable.

I should like to illustrate what I mean by referring again to the joint experiment by Mr. G. W. Fisk and myself. I had for a very long time failed get any results at all, but, Mr. Fisk, using a new card method, had recently produced successful results with a group of unselected subjects, and I thought that this would be an opportunity to find out whether

I, personally, could obtain results similar to those obtained by Mr. Fisk. So we arranged that we would send to a group of subjects some target cards, packed up in sealed envelopes which they could not open, the order of which they had to guess. Half the target cards were arranged by Mr. Fisk, the experimenter who had been successful on previous occasions, and half the cards were made up by me. With one exception, it was found that the subjects continued to guess successfully Mr. Fisk's cards, whereas they were not successful with mine. This appears to suggest that some experimenters may be incapable of repeating the results which other experimenters are able to obtain. That is what I meant by factors of repeatability.

Goldney: I think you have not made it clear, Dr. West, that the people who received the cards were under the impression that they all came from Mr. Fisk; that was the essential thing, wasn't it?

West: In all cases, the outer wrappers were put on and the packets posted by the one experimenter, Mr. Fisk.

Pratt: Mr. Spencer Brown referred to a Greenwood control check as the one mentioned by Dr. McConnell, but I do not think he was speaking of the same control series of Dr. Greenwood's as that which Dr. McConnell mentioned. Dr. McConnell's reference was to a cross-check of the sort that Prof. Gaddum referred to, in which the subject's calls intended for one sequence of cards, are compared on a purely arbitrary basis with a later sequence of cards.

Brown: He mentioned that also.

Pratt: I think there is a further point of interest regarding the large Greenwood control check, namely that Greenwood did not carry out this mammoth series of comparing sequences of subjects' calls with actual sequences of shuffled orders of cards, with the purpose of finding out whether the cross-check would give a significant deviation from the expected average. Rather his intention was to see what the variance and what the other statistical moments of this series would be. At that time, we were considering whether it was appropriate to use the bi-nominal variance as opposed to the normal variance or the matching variance, each one applicable to a series in which you compare orders of shuffled cards with packs of a particular composition. I think it misses the point to emphasize the *average* obtained in the Greenwood series as though that was the main focus of interest in this project.

Brown: I am not criticizing Greenwood's experiment as such. I see what his purpose was, and he achieved it magnificently. What I think is unfair is that this experiment should be referred to by my critics as a valid control for ESP experiments.

Pratt: We have no need to refer to that as a valid control, as we can find in the literature of parapsychology a great abundance of valid controls. It might, in the minds of some people, have been classified as a control experiment, but I think we could get past that issue by just saying that this is a misconception, and just leave it at that.

Lewis: I would like to say a word about repeatability. Normally an experimenter can be regarded as outside the experiment, so that, if the experiment is exactly repeated by another competent experimenter, the results should be the same. But in these experiments there is a relationship, a social interplay between the experimenter and the percipient. The experimenter is in a dual rôle; he designs the experiment, and makes the observations; but he also acts as one of the participants, one of the subjects of the experiment. It would be better if the experimenter who observes could keep outside the actual experiment. Some of the difficulties in reproducing the conditions of such experiments are due to the fact that the experimenter has functioned in two capacities, as investigator and as participant.

Parkes: It could be argued that all agents ought to be tried with all subjects.

Wassermann: I think Mr. Spencer Brown is in error on one point. Scientists, in my opinion, must distinguish between two types of statement. First of all, there are inductive statements which refer to what is going to happen. They start by saying something has happened and from that induce what is likely to happen: secondly, there are statements about what has happened in the past, i.e. historical statements. For instance, the theory of evolution deals with past statements, and I dare say that many statements in parapsychology are also essentially historical scientific statements; they deal with what has happened to a subject, but they do not necessarily say that it must happen to all subjects in the future or ever again to any particular subject. Now, science essentially deals with both types of statement, and I think that is a crucial point not to overlook this. There are many examples you can take. For instance, again in meson theory, you can say a certain type of meson track was very unlikely to happen within 1,000 generations of people observing these tracks, but that does not mean that such a track has never been observed. In other words, this is a historical statement, and such a statement is important when we come to formulate theories. I think much confusion has arisen from the unjustified demand that all statements must be simple inductive statements which involve high inductive probabilities. They are not. Mr. Spencer Brown seems to assume this. In other words, he seems to think there is some logical necessity for all statements being of one type, and I don't believe there is.

Brown: Not at all. This is the very point I made at the British Association last year in your presence, when I said that the results of psychical research were not science but history.

Wassermann: Even then I do not agree completely.

Brown: What I do say is that if you maintain that there is communication going on, you step out of history into informative theory, which is science in the proper inductive sense.

Wassermann: For practical purposes it is important to distinguish between inductive and historical statements. However, a historical statement may be represented as an induction, namely, an inductive posit, which would have been appropriate before the event happened. A statement about a communication may be of either type. A communication which happened twenty years ago may have been important then, but need not have inductive value any longer.

Parkes: I am a bit puzzled about this problem of reproducibility. One is familiar with biological variation, where a group, say, of 20 rats will each respond slightly differently quantitatively to a given stimulus. But that variability in response follows quite well-known laws. The kind of variability scatter seen in such cases seems to me entirely different from that seen with ESP subjects, where perhaps one in 200 may respond and the rest all show nothing. I think, Gaddum, you will agree that that is an unusual biological variation, wouldn't you?

Perry: Is it unusual in vestigial remnants or things of that sort?

Parkes: I think even vestigial remnants might show a normal variability.

Wassermann: What about in morphogenesis? You get a good many cases of freaks coming up which are extremely rare.

Parkes: Yes, but that is not normal biological variation.

Wassermann: Yes, but even under experimental conditions you get some extremely rare freaks produced, because if you carry out an experiment in which you use an artificial induction, you may sometimes get a particular Gestalt effect, but in another 50,000 trials you may not get it, I believe.

Parkes: If you are going to analogize the perceptive subjects with entirely abnormal freaks, can you draw any regular conclusions?

Wassermann: Yes, you can, because within a particular series, you get constancy of the facts just as you do in certain biological experiments. You can say that in Dr. Soal's experiments, for instance, for tens of thousands of guesses there was repeatability within the series, which is an historical statement but refers only to that particular person, and you cannot generalize to others. You can say that certain people have shown such and such things—you can also say that in meson track theory, certain specific meson tracks have been found and have never been found again. But if you can fit these isolated results together within a theory and they make sense, then you are all right.

Parkes: I quite agree that even one isolated phenomenon, even if of a positive nature, has to be explained.

Gaddum: Do you not think that it may be that we are dealing with the threshold of detectability, right on the tail of the curve? It might easily be that people have different powers of perception and that only the very sensitive ones can given significant results.

Parkes: You mean that this is a tremendously skew curve and the perceptive ones are right on one end of it?

Gaddum: Not a skew curve, but very near the tail.

Wassermann: Take genius, for instance. That is a thing which occurs very rarely. You can say that a Mozart is only born once in every hundred generations; such a great composer, for instance, provides a typical example which seems historically repeatable though only extremely rarely.

Parkes: Yes, but that is continuous biological variability. Genius comes in many shapes, doesn't it?

Wassermann: Yes, but perhaps you get parapsychological gifts in all shapes. In many experiments very slight gifts are found in most people, but it doesn't happen on the scale shown by a parapsychological genius like Shackleton, say, if you can call him a genius, you only get that rarely. It is the same, I think.

Pratt: Is the gift of absolute pitch comparable? Musicians sometimes have it.

Brown: Genius and absolute pitch, when they occur, can be shown to everyone, but not everyone can see telepathy. I, for example, have never seen it.

Pratt: Have you seen anyone with absolute pitch?

Brown: I have it.

Nicol: Most of this discussion has been on repeatability. My doubts ought to have been allayed by Dr. Wasserman's assurance that this consummation of all our labours has in fact been achieved. But Dr. Wasserman is clearly giving the word a meaning and definition that are not usually attached to it in scientific thought. Dr. West apparently, and certainly I, were unaware that the repeatability problem, which has defeated many years of effort, has in fact been solved and we did not notice it. With regard to the repetition of results like those of Shackleton, my understanding is—I cannot quote the figures accurately but I think there were rather more than 40 experimental sessions—that with one or two exceptions, those experimental sessions were all significant. Eventually, Shackleton failed. So that the phenomenon was repeated many times, and thereafter it ceased to show. This is no disparagement of Shackleton, who was a most distinguished exponent of telepathy. Then there was Mrs. Stewart. As I recall, there were about 130, maybe 131 experiments with her, and for most of 120 of those experiments Mrs. Stewart repeated her results, week in, week out, but thereafter there was no repetition. And so on with the others. I am not sure but I think Pearce ultimately ceased to repeat too. Now, those cases do not constitute repetition as I understand it. I mean by repetition—and I am rather under the impression that in the physical and other sciences this is also the understanding—that you design an experiment which any competent person can repeat with approximately the same results, and now come the essential words, *at any time, in the foreseeable future.*

If we persuade ourselves that repeatability has arrived and has been in front of us for a long time, we are going to do nothing to convince scientists of our scientific soundness. Several people have tried to produce repeatable experiments, of whom the most distinguished and persistent, I think, was the late Whately Carington. He designed an experiment in which drawings were exhibited, say, once every night for ten nights, to be reproduced by his subjects. Now he believed that on half a dozen occasions, he got the repetition, with himself as experimenter. Then he more or less farmed out the experiment to psychologists in this country and in America, and taking their results together there was repetition. But Dr. West and others in this country tried to repeat it, and got nothing. At the American Society for Psychical Research, I think they tried it three times over, and the results were at best ambiguous.

About three years ago, my colleague, Dr. Betty Humphrey, and I did an experiment in which we tried to correlate certain variables of personality with the individual scores of the subjects, quite ordinary subjects. The main variable was extraversion and introversion, in this case sometimes called self-confidence; and in this experiment the correlation with clairvoyance was found to be high. Subjects who were high in self-confidence got high scores; those who were low in that measure, got small scores; none of them was particularly striking in demonstrating clairvoyance alone. The correlation, however, was 0·55 and the result was highly significant. We tried to reproduce the effect with about the same number of subjects, about 36, the following year. The correlation was found to be still positive, but it was 0·16; this was not significant, and the experiment, however much I might try to persuade myself to the contrary, was not a duplication of the earlier effect. That is the kind of thing I mean by repetition and the failure of repetition. If by using a personality variable or some other factor, you can get a result repeated over and over again, then you have only to describe it to any other competent person, psychologist, physicist, medical man or anyone else, invite him to do it for himself and he will get the same results. When you can do that successfully you will have won half the battle for recognition.

West: I should just like to take up one point that was raised by Prof. Lewis, who suggested that the difficulty might be that we were not tackling the problem correctly, that the experiment was a social situation and that the experimenter was becoming involved in that social situation. If I understand rightly, Prof. Lewis was suggesting that the designer of the experiment should stand back altogether from the actual performance of the tests. Now, I believe that the influence of the experimenter on the results is not a simple matter of being present in the social setting. To illustrate what I mean, I will take the same example that I mentioned before. In the experiment which Fisk and I did, neither of us was present with the subjects, Mr. Fisk has had contact with the subjects, mainly by correspondence. I did not even know who the subjects were, and the subjects themselves did not know of my part in the experiment, which was exclusively that of a designer and evaluator of the results when they were sent to me. And yet I appeared to have an effect upon those subjects. Of course, that is an experiment which needs to be tried by other people. But it certainly seems to me that the problem is much more mysterious than merely a matter of social influence between the experimenter and the subjects taking part in the experiment.

McConnell: First, I should answer Mr. Langdon-Davies' question regarding the Pierce-Pratt series which I described. Dr. Pratt did not look at the cards. Therefore, at least from a naive point of view, this was a clairvoyance experiment. Personally, I do not believe that any attempt to distinguish between such things as clairvoyance and telepathy is very important right now—important, that is, for science as a whole.

Mr. Spencer Brown raised a question concerning the reference I made to the paper by Greenwood. I cited it in connection with whether the shuffling of cards in an ordinary fashion could be expected to be an adequate randomization process. I believe that for that purpose Greenwood's paper is an adequate control. I do not know if Mr. Brown, with that understanding, would agree with me or not (See *J. Parapsychol.*, 1955, **19**, 58).

Brown: I think you are quite right; there is no evidence in that experiment for absence of randomness in the shuffle.

McConnell: The recently published work of Oram (*J. Soc. psych. Res.*, 1953, **37**, 369) has been cited and Mr. Spencer Brown believes, I think, that this might in some way invalidate statistical methods in a basic sense. Now, one does not invalidate statistical method by performing an experiment, which one would expect to yield chance results, and by getting instead one very odd result. If one wishes to investigate the soundness of statistical method, one is going to have to perform a large number of experiments, and for that reason I think it is particularly relevant to bring to your attention an article which appeared in *Nature* (1953, **172**, 154), by Mr. Spencer Brown. He says: "It is therefore incumbent upon us to try the hypothesis that the results which are the best designed and most rigorously observed experiments in psyʌhical research, are chance results after all, and that the concept of chance can cover a wider natural field than we have previously suspected." I cite this sentence to show the general tenor of his thinking: that what is under question here is not really shuffling of cards or random number tables, but something much deeper. Are we up against something basically wrong in statistical theory? Well, just a little further down he says: "In addition, I have evidence, also to be published shortly, that statistically significant results, similar to those of psychical research, are obtainable simply by making selections in published tables of random numbers, as if the tables were themselves the data of a psychical research experiment."

The reason I raise this—as far as I know these results have not been published—is not to harass Mr. Brown, but to make clear the point that one must examine a large number of experiments; one cannot take one result and draw a conclusion, if one is concerned with the basic validity of statistics. Therefore, I think it is vital that these empirical results should be published, especially since this particular article, in this eminent journal, has been picked up repeatedly in the United States. It has been published in *Science*, the journal equivalent to *Nature* in the States, and in other important journals. As a matter of fact, it has also come to me from private sources in the form: "this explains all of ESP, we can now forget about it". It is, I think, an unfortunate thing that we should not yet have had a publication of these data.

One might raise at this point, a different type of question. If we would need a lot of experiments in order to test whether statistical theory is good, why are people always citing single control experiments, and saying "This shows that we can go ahead; our ESP experiment was significant?" I should like to say just a word about the purpose of a control experiment, because I think there has been some confusion in that connection. Ordinarily, a person performs a scientific experiment, an ESP experiment, let us say, and gets a result which is surprising and probably not a chance result; and then he wonders whether he has over-looked something in the experimental conditions, some systematic error, which he does not see but which might be there. In order to test that hypothesis, he performs another experiment, like the first experiment, but changing it just the minimum amount that is necessary to eliminate the ESP effect. If in this control experiment the results are chance, he draws the conclusion that there were not, in the original ESP experi-ment, any systematic errors of the class that could be eliminated by this type of control experiment. What one really should calculate in this situation is the probability of the *difference* between the two experi-ments. On that basis, one is not questioning the basic validity of statistical theory. One is assuming, in such a control series, that the underlying mathematical theory is all right; and one is using it to try to eliminate other experimental factors which may not have been recognized.

A final point about which I want to say something is that, at least in the United States in my own experience, a certain class of critic, who is in a related field and who might be presumed by his colleagues to have some opinion about ESP—I am thinking particularly of certain psychologists—has managed to confuse the thinking of the scientific fraternity as a whole by a very simple procedure. Whenever the ques-tion comes up as to what is wrong with the ESP experiments that have been performed, the tactic which has been followed—and I can only conclude it has been followed consciously—is to describe the weaknesses in those experiments which are not the best experiments; to point out all the things that are wrong with the poor experiments and quietly to ignore the experiments which cannot be explained away.

Now, it seems to me that Mr. Brown, in raising the question of psychokinesis, is giving us just a new variation of this old tactic. We are concerned at this symposium with one question, ESP. PK is a different phenomenon, although those who believe in PK, also believe that it is probably related to ESP. So I do not think that the citations of PK of which we have had several already, are really pertinent to the central question of this symposium. Let me hasten to say that I think that the question of whether PK is real is of great scientific importance and of great philosophical importance; and yet for several reasons I would be unhappy to see it discussed in detail at this symposium. First of all, we have not come prepared to discuss it; but more than that, it is a very difficult subject to assess. The evidence—I think everyone would agree—is not as clear-cut and is much more difficult to evaluate than that for ESP. Whilst I, on the basis of my own study of the papers which have been published and, to a lesser extent, of some unpublished work of my own to which Mr. Brown referred, do believe that there is rather good evidence for PK, I know of other people who have studied the papers and who have come to a different conclusion. I think the thing is just too complicated to try to assess in a symposium of this sort, at this time.

I am much more interested from a general scientific point of view in whether any psi phenomena exist? Does ESP occur? If ESP does occur, we need not worry whether it is clairvoyance or telepathy; we need not worry whether some other things, such as PK, also occur, because if any one of these phenomena occurs, then we have thrown down the challenge, which society and science must accept. This is the thing to be decided. The lesser questions can be ironed out in the laboratory.

AN OUTLINE OF A FIELD THEORY OF ORGANISMIC FORM AND BEHAVIOUR

G. D. WASSERMANN

University of Durham

1. Introduction

THEORETICAL physicists have succeeded in deducing many known empirical generalizations of physics from a single set of field theoretical class relations. This deductive scheme postulates as initial hypotheses a class of fields each of which is defined by means of a Lagrange function that satisfies a variational principle (Wentzel, 1949). The theoretical constructs of modern physics such as electrons, protons, neutrons, neutrinos, positrons, electro-magnetic fields, meson fields, etc., can all be defined in terms of field equations which are derived from such a variational principle, each construct having an appropriate Lorentz-invariant Lagrange function associated with it. In addition, field theory defines a "Hamiltonian" in terms of the Lagrange function and then provides rules of quantization for each field (Heisenberg and Pauli, 1929; Heitler, 1954; Wentzel, 1949). This quantization scheme leads to a set of important results which apply to all fields of the class considered irrespective of structural peculiarities.

1. Fields if undisturbed will remain permanently in one of a number of possible *stationary states*. Fields are therefore, according to this theory, not genuinely created out of nothing but have permanent existence, and unless disturbed will remain in a stationary state, the most stable of these states being the *ground state* (of lowest energy). Each stationary state has a specific energy level associated with it, and the energy levels may form either one or more continuous bands or a set of discretely spaced levels, or a mixed spectrum.

2. Any two fields may, circumstances permitting, interact and exchange their energy in such a manner that the total energy is being conserved. For example, when the field of the valency electron of a hydrogen atom (described by a Dirac equation (see Wentzel, 1949)) changes from an excited state to the ground state it gives off its energy to an electro-magnetic "radiation" field which thereby goes into an excited state. Whether two fields which are coupled may or may not exchange energy depends on the quantum mechanical selection rules which are based on the study of transition probabilities. In quantum mechanics only certain types of transitions are allowed and others are forbidden. In this way the selection rules produce a directivity of transitions between stationary states, which has no analogue in Newtonian physics.

3. Quantum mechanics predicts that for any two fields there may in suitable circumstances exist *bound states*. If a bound state exists it has lower energy than the two fields would have if they existed in isolation in corresponding stationary states (Coulson, 1953). The theory of bound states has already permitted a complete deductive interpretation of chemical bonding.

4. There is much indirect evidence which suggests that there exist "duplication" processes for fields. One set of fields may arrange itself so as to be in one-one correspondence with another set of fields and thus produce an isomorphic (but not necessarily identical) copy of the second set. For example, a photographic negative and the print of the corresponding photo, although not identical copies, give a unique isomorphic representation of one set of molecular matter fields (those of the negative) by another set of molecular matter fields (the print). Similarly, enzymes like trypsin and pepsin, which are self-reproducing in the presence of their precursors trypsinogen and pepsinogen (Pirie, 1938), suggest that one set of mutually bound matter fields (namely the molecular fields which build up the enzyme) may become duplicated so as to form another similar set of mutually bound fields. It is possible on principle to interpret such duplication

processes systematically in terms of the quantum theory of bound states.

The preceding results of quantum mechanics when systematically applied to combinations of fields which belong to the Lorentz-invariant class permit on principle the deduction of almost all the well known empirical "laws" in physics. For example, the equations of state for solids, liquids and gases and the transport equations for kinetic processes (see Born and Green, 1949) follow as purely formal deductions from the basic assumptions of the field theory of "fundamental particles" and "interaction fields".

The success of physicists in deriving empirical "laws" from a very small set of initial class relations (which provide an Ockham's razor) raises the question whether empirical generalizations which refer to the behaviour and form of organisms may not also be deducted from the same field theoretical class relations. That previous writers, for example Köhler (1940), Hebb (1949), Katz and Halstead (1950), McCulloch and Pitts (1943, 1947) and Rashevsky (1948) among others (see Gomulicki, 1953), have failed to provide a consistent deductive theory of learning, perception and motivation in terms of the constructs of theoretical physics only, should not deter us from looking for such a theory. In a book which is nearly completed I have attempted to show that the empirical generalizations of experimental embryology, psychology and parapsychology can all be deduced from the same initial field theoretical class relations and rules of quantization as the empirical "laws" of physics. The present paper, being restricted in length, can only provide a very superficial sketch of the new theory. A detailed discussion of the relation of the new theories to other theories and to the vast number of available experimental papers will be left to the book.

2. Field theory of morphogenesis

In order to account for the processes of molecular organization in morphogenesis Gurwitsch (1921), Spemann (1921) and Weiss (1922, 1924, 1926, 1926a, 1928b) have introduced the concept of a "morphogenetic field". Needham (1950), Costello (1949) and others have repeatedly emphasized the lack of precision which is inherent in the term "morphogenetic field" as defined by Gurwitsch, Spemann and Weiss. It was neither made clear whether a "morphogenetic field" designated a construct which could in principle be deduced from a Lagrangian, nor whether this "field" obeyed any of the rules which are obeyed by other physical fields.

If a deductive physical theory of morphogenesis is at all possible along the same lines as the already existing deductive physical theories about the physical state of "inanimate" systems, then we should expect that either (1) fields derived from already familiar Lagrange functions should suffice as basic hypotheses for a deductive theory, or (2) some fields derived from Lagrangians not hitherto considered, which belong to the same class as the already familiar ones, may have to be chosen as a basis of the deductive theory. A careful discussion of the empirical evidence, which for lack of space cannot be given here, and which involves use of Boltzmann's H-theorem, has led me to favour the second alternative. Wigglesworth (1948) has favoured the first alternative, but, as I shall show elsewhere, his theory seems to be contradicted by various empirical data. I suggest therefore that the morphogenetic fields belong to the same class of fields as the already familiar energy fields of physics (electron fields, neutron fields, proton fields, electro-magnetic fields, meson fields, etc.) but are not identical with any of these or with any combination of these. The introduction of new fields by considering new Lagrangians is no longer startling, since physicists have in recent years postulated many new types of fields which are all members of the same Lorentz-invariant class and which obey a variational principle. The newly postulated Lorentz-invariant morphogenetic fields will be called "M-fields" for short. *Since M-fields belong to the same class as the other postulated energy fields of physics, they will have the typical properties of this class, namely, those listed in the Introduction.*

The relation between M-fields and the molecular matter fields of the organism will be assumed to be similar to that which exists between an electro-magnetic radiation field of visible light range frequencies and the molecular matter fields of a photographic plate on which the radiation field "impinges". The electromagnetic field changes the molecular states of the matter fields of the plate; and similarly the M-field will be assumed to produce a change of molecular patterning by changing the molecular states of the organismic matter fields according to the quantum mechanical selection rules which govern the energy exchange.* I shall assume that the amount of energy exchanged between an M-field and a molecular matter field is extremely small. There are two ways in which an M-field can influence changes of state of the molecular matter field. The first way is by passive presence, namely, by influencing the transition probabilities of transitions of the molecular fields owing to the fact that the M-field is coupled to these fields and thus influences their quantum mechanical eigen-state functions and thus the transition probabilities. The second way is by active energy exchange. It seems possible to establish a satisfactory theory by using both possibilities. According to this the M-field "steers" the transitions of molecular fields much as a powerful motor-car may be steered by a controlling system of relatively small energy. In other words, an M-field may act as a slight perturbation field which changes the transition probabilities of the molecular fields and also changes their energies slightly through active transitions. The main energy for molecular changes comes from the energy stored in the molecular matter fields and the molecular environment of the organism. I shall assume that M-fields successively absorb energy from the matter fields and thus run up a "ladder" of energy levels. Which of these transitions is permitted depends again on the

* Another, perhaps slightly less appropriate analogy is that of a wireless receiver and a transmission field, the wireless receiver corresponding to the molecular matter fields of the organism and the "received" transmission fields to the M-fields. Selectivity is obtained by "tuning" which corresponds to the automatic quantum mechanical selectivity in the present case.

selection rules. Thus the selection rules act as directive quantum mechanical factors which according to this theory decide the selective course of patterning in morphogenesis. In fact, each energy level of an M-field, by hypothesis, is associated with a specific stationary state which has a specific pattern in its co-ordinate configuration space, and this pattern decides the "polarity" of the development pattern. Energy transitions between M-fields and molecular matter fields will occur until the joint system reaches an equilibrium state which is conditioned by quantum-kinematical (i.e. statistical) considerations (Boltzmann's H-theorem). The steady state which is reached in this way (or the nearly steady state) represents the "goal" or organismic development and the process of reaching an almost steady state between M-field and molecular matter fields is therefore "goal directed". The present theory can thus dispense with vitalistic "purposes" or "vital forces" or Bergson's "élan vital" and similar mysterious non-physical constructs. It is noteworthy that M-fields, like electromagnetic fields, can only have observable consequences through changes which they cause in matter fields.

It will be assumed that M-fields and the matter fields of the organism can exist in mutually bound states, so that M-fields can be "carried" by the matter fields. Moreover, M-fields are assumed to have the properties given in (1) of the introduction and thus to exist always latently, ready to enter into bound states with suitable matter fields as soon as these matter fields become available. Which out of the multitude of latently existing M-fields becomes bound to a particular molecular field depends entirely on the molecular structure of the organismic system—the egg—concerned, that is on the structure of its gene-complex and of its cytoplasm. Presence or absence of a specific gene will result in binding or absence of binding of a specific latently present M-field. It is suggested that "living" systems differ from "inanimate" ones primarily in their power of binding M-fields. Only when a specific molecular complexity has arisen can M-fields and these molecular fields go into bound states.

In quantum mechanical field theory cases are known where two field systems which can normally exchange energy may exist in states in which they can no longer exchange energy. Superconducting states of metals provide well-known examples of this principle. I suggest that M-fields and matter fields can exist in states in which they cannot exchange energy. For example, inanimate systems are assumed to be unable to exchange energy with M-fields. Similarly, prior to fertilization (or parthenogenesis) the molecular system of an egg is assumed to be in a state in which it cannot exchange energy with an M-field. The molecules of the sperm then act as a "trigger" in changing the quantum state of the molecular field of the ovum, which can then commence to interact with the "steering" M-fields. In fact, I suggest that a morphogenetic inductor acts likewise as a "trigger" which enables previously "forbidden" transitions between M-fields and matter fields of the egg to occur and which leads to a bonding between an M-field and a molecular matter field.

Pluripotency in morphogenesis means according to the present theory that the molecular fields of different parts of an egg are potentially capable of entering the same energy states. For a particular monad of an egg the choice of quantum states from among the large number of possible states depends on the actual states of the other parts of the egg and on the states of the M-fields. If any matter fields are transplanted prior to induction into a region to which a specific M-field has already become bound* they will then become steered by that M-field and hence develop "neighbourwise" (see Needham, 1950). If, on the other hand, the transplant has already an M-field attached to it prior to transplantation, its molecular system will be determined according to its place of origin, namely, according to the M-fields which became attached at the place of origin, provided that this M-field dominates the transition probabilities in competition with M-fields in the region into which the transplant is grafted. It will be observed

---

* The present theory assumes that morphogenetic induction, apart from a triggering action, helps to bind specific M-fields.

that the reversibility of self-differentiation found in *Clavellina* (Needham, 1950) is just the kind of reversibility which the present quantum mechanical field theory with its possibilities of reverse transitions would lead us to expect as a possibility.

Finally, some brief remarks about the concept of competence in morphogenesis. The molecular field of a regulation egg does not usually respond to an inductor except during a specific time interval. This means, according to field theory, that energy transitions between M-fields and molecular fields of the egg are only possible while the molecular fields are in any one of a set of possible energy states which lie within fairly narrow limits. Outside that range of energy states transitions are effectively "forbidden".

The present field theory permits also an interpretation of recapitulation phenomena (see De Beer, 1951) in terms of quantum mechanical principles. I shall assume that throughout evolution very stable multiple bonds between M-fields became gradually formed. Each organism forms germ cells subject to its M-fields, and as soon as these germ cells are formed, I suggest, some of the M-fields of the parent organism are "duplicated" onto the latter by the field duplication process mentioned in the introduction. In the duplication process these fields become bound by the appropriate genes. Other M-fields become bound to the egg during subsequent development. The M-fields which are bound to the egg at the germ cell stage may be called "primitive" M-fields. Thus the present field theory suggests that both genes and primitive M-fields are inherited (i.e. "passed on" to the germ cell from the parent organism). It is further suggested that the M-fields themselves affect the mutation scheme of the gene-complex of the germ cells by causing changes in transition probabilities of the transitions which could occur during mutation. Any change which the environment could cause in the very stable M-fields of the parent organism would thus react back on the M-fields of the germ cells, which again would affect the mutations. Thus, in addition to random mutations there could occur directed mutations caused by changes in the M-field.

Similarly, any change of the gene-complex, owing to mutations induced by M-fields or through random events, would react back on the M-fields which are bound to the gene-complex of the germ cell. Thus new M-fields may become bound and existing bonds between the gene-complex and M-fields may become weakened. This change of bond strength could affect in turn the transition probabilities and hence the rate at which transitions are proceeding. Such a change of rates could result exactly in the various distortions observed in the "recapitulation phenomena".

Regeneration according to the present theory is a consequence of the fact that similar molecular systems will selectively bind similar M-fields, and hence similar selective "steering" transitions tend to occur, provided the environment remains roughly the same. In a regeneration process such as morphallaxis (Needham, 1952) M-fields would adjust themselves to the boundaries of existing molecular fields in a way similar to that in which electro-magnetic fields in optics adjust themselves to the boundaries of the matter fields which consist of a selective optical lens system.

3. Field theory of animal behaviour

Since the behaviour of animals starts during morphogenesis, there exists a complete continuity between animal behaviour and morphogenetic processes. The similarity of many laws of animal behaviour and those of morphogenesis has been noted by Spemann (1938), Weiss (1951) and other authorities. Hence we may expect that fields similar to the postulated M-fields might play an important part in a deductive theory of animal behaviour. I suggest that the fields which "steer" the molecular systems of the post-embryonic animal, so as to give rise to observable "animal behaviour", are of the M-field type, and they will be called behaviour fields, or B-fields for short. B-fields are those M-fields which interact with neural matter fields after the morphogenetic M-fields have led to the structuring of the nervous system, if there is a nervous system. In view of the fact that typical learned behaviour, namely classical conditioning, can already occur in infusoria (see Hilgard and Marquis, 1940), B-fields could interact also with protoplasmic molecular organizations which are not nerve cells. Like M-fields, of which they are a special case, B-fields can only absorb very small energy quanta and emit only such small quanta when interacting with other fields. Similarly, B-fields and neural matter fields can go into mutually bound states as soon as the neural matter fields become formed during embryogenesis. Again, which particular type of B-field, among the latently present ones, will become bound to a neural matter field will depend uniquely on the chemo-structure of the tissue concerned, and this in turn is genetically determined.

We expect therefore, according to the present theory, that chemically different neurons will bind different B-fields, whereas chemically similar neurons will bind the same type of B-fields. This is in good agreement with Lashley's (1950) numerous experiments. If, for example, in that area of the rat's cerebral cortex which is concerned with vision almost 59/60ths is arbitrarily extirpated, the power of recognizing certain simple shapes (and of remembering them) remains unimpaired. This would mean that the B-fields which are concerned with sensory perception do not depend for their function on specifically located neurons but can be activated by any suitable combination of those neurons to which they are bound and which are chemically equipotential. Lashley's hypothesis of the equipotentiality of cortical cells within a particular histologically homogeneous functional area is therefore in good agreement with the present binding hypothesis of field theory. According to this hypothesis it is only the number of chemically similar neurons, but not their precise position, which should determine the bond strength between B-fields and neural matter fields, at least in the first approximation. We might then expect that the more cells are being destroyed in a given experiment (or operation), the weaker the bonds become and, hence, the weaker the effective interaction between B-fields and neural matter fields. Thus the theory leads us to expect that functional deficit following extirpation increases with the amount of neural tissue destroyed in a given functional area, which is in good agreement with Lashley's (1929) well-known law of mass-action.

B-fields will not only interact with neural matter fields but, like M-fields, they can interact with each other and exchange energy. Animal behaviour is postulated to be the consequence of such mutual interaction of B-fields and of their interaction with neural matter fields. The selectivity of behaviour, that is, its directivity, is again a consequence of the quantum-mechanical selection rules for the interaction of B-fields with each other and with neural matter fields. Suppose, in particular, that an ablation of some neural tissue is performed. This would weaken the bond strength between the B-fields which were bound to that tissue and other tissues, and this could cause a change of state of the bound B-field. This change would react on the other B-fields, since the selection rules for the exchange of energy between any two B-fields depend on the state of all the other B-fields (and neural matter fields) which are sufficiently strongly coupled to those two B-fields. This could account for Goldstein's (1939) and Lashley's (1950) discoveries that ablation in one cortical area could result in disturbances of functions which are normally associated with other cortical areas, since ablation in one area would react indirectly, as suggested, on the B-fields bound to other areas.

During morphogenesis the "innate" B-fields become bound to neurons as soon as the neural matter fields have become structured; and these B-fields are responsible for innate behaviour patterns. Learning occurs when later B-fields become bound to the already existing complexes of B-fields. Memory, according to the present theory, is the result of the formation of systems of mutually bound B-fields which can exist in stable bound stationary states. The selectivity of recall is then a consequence of the quantum-mechanical selectivity for the exchange of energy between B-fields. The memory "trace" in the present theory is represented by bound states of a "complex" of mutually bound B-fields, and ablation of neural tissues does not dissolve this system of bonds but only bonds between neural matter fields and B-fields. If certain bonds are particularly strong—and such a strengthening of bonds could be brought about quantum-mechanically through repetition of the learning (conditioning) process—then transitions between such strongly bound fields may become more probable than transitions between weakly bound fields, and this selective probability determines the serial order (Lashley, 1951) of excitation of B-fields in the recall process. Thus quantum-mechanical field principles could automatically produce the selectivity and permanence of memory and learning.*

It has already been stressed that the state of all B-fields is decisive in determining the selection rules between any two B-fields. This influence of the total set of B-fields which are bound to the cortex and to each other may then lead to a specific selectivity which expresses itself in "attitude" and "attention" in which certain B-fields would show markedly greater transition probabilities as compared with others. "Attention" would mean simply that a strong change of quantum-mechanical selectivity had occurred which favoured a few fields and selective serial orders for excitation between these fields.

The present theory can also apparently give a satisfactory interpretation of classical conditioning, trial and error learning, and the constancies in perception as well as of goal-directed activity. These and other topics will be fully discussed in my book. I shall only illustrate the theory by referring to the experiments of Weiss (1950) and Sperry (1951). In numerous experiments Sperry found that if in certain amphibia the afferent nerve fibres were severed between the eye and the central projection area and permitted to regenerate at random, normal central peripheral connections were retained in spite of apparent random connections (similar

* The present discussion of learning theory is very superficial and is only meant to indicate the nature of the new theory. A fuller discussion to be given in my book will require an examination of reinforcement and motivation in terms of field theory (see Spence, 1951).

experiments were performed earlier by Weiss for efferent connections). The present theory suggests that there exists a unique link between centre and periphery via B-fields. When a light signal reaches the retina it excites both the photo-receptor neurons and a set of peripheral B-fields which are bound to these neurons. The peripheral B-fields are linked by intermediate B-fields to the central B-fields which are bound to the cortex. The function of the peripheral and central neurons, according to the present theory, is that of releasers or "triggers" of B-fields. Thus, the peripheral neurons send pulses to the central neurons and these centrally arriving pulses help to excite central B-fields. However, the central B-fields are not only excited by the pulses arriving from the periphery but also by the B-fields which link the central B-fields with the peripheral B-fields, and the selection of central B-fields for excitation depends uniquely on the state of excitation of the B-fields which link centre and periphery. Hence, a random connection of nerve fibres between centre and periphery does not matter, since the unique B-field linkage between centre and periphery is not affected by a random linkage of neurons. Owing to the postulated one-one correspondence between central and peripheral B-field states there occurs in the present theory a unique central representation of unique retinal figures. Since on the retina there occurs a unique topographical representation of figures, a corresponding unique central representation will be given by the B-fields. The present theory, therefore, does not meet the notorious difficulties of neural network theories noted by Polyak (1941) and Hebb (1949, p. 52), who observed that the central neural projection of a retinal excitation pattern fails to give a unique topographical representation of simple figures such as squares, circles, equilateral triangles, etc.

4. Field Theory of Parapsychology

Vitalist philosophers and biologists have maintained that parapsychological phenomena could not possibly be interpreted in terms of the theoretical constructs of physics. By constructing a purely physical theory, in which mental experiences occur only as epiphenomena of B-field transitions, I shall attempt to show that the vitalist arguments (Hardy, 1953; Rhine, 1953) are unwarranted. It will be assumed that parapsychological phenomena may be interpreted in terms of Lorentz-invariant energy fields which have properties similar to B-fields and other fields of the class of Lorentz-invariant fields considered in the introduction. The postulated fields, which will be called "psi-fields", will be assumed to have very narrowly spaced energy levels and to be able to occupy wide regions of space. The selection rules for interaction between psi-fields and matter fields will be assumed to be such that psi-fields can only make transitions between neighbouring energy levels. Hence the psi-fields could only accept extremely small quanta of energy or give off such extremely small quanta. If these quanta are smaller than the quanta which can be absorbed by matter fields or given off by matter fields to psi-fields, matter fields and psi-fields could not interact.* Consequently psi-fields could radiate their energy over long distances without it becoming absorbed by matter fields. Hence the argument by Rhine (1953) and others that energy fields could not be responsible for telepathy, since their energy would become absorbed, falls to the ground. Of course there will be attenuation of the psi-fields as we proceed from the excitation source. However, such attenuation could be locally compensated by B-field reinforcement and neural amplification.†

I suggest that in telepathy a central B-field‡ of an agent excites selectively a specific psi-field, and that this psi-field excites selectively in turn a corresponding B-field of the

---

*An alternative assumption, which is even simpler, is to stipulate that the interaction term in the Hamiltonians between matter fields and psi-fields is so small that no effective interaction can occur.

† Since this paper was written I have shown that it is possible to construct a simple cascade process of fields in which no attenuation with distance occurs.

‡ In the detailed development of the theory in book form I have distinguished between sensory B-fields, motor B-fields, B-fields concerned with emotions and B-fields concerned with meaning patterns, etc. But for the present purpose such a distinction is not vital.

percipient. The selectivity follows as usual from the quantum mechanical selection rules. The percipient's B-fields, even if weakly excited by the psi-fields, could become fully excited by absorbing energy from other reinforcing B-fields (which would correspond to "unconscious motivation") or from neural matter fields. If a time series of agent B-fields become excited, a correlated time series of B-fields of the percipient would become excited by the action of the intermediate psi-fields. There may be a long time-delay in the excitation of the percipient's B-fields (a similar time-delay occurs in post-hypnotic suggestions) which could be due to the fact that the excited B-field has to wait until suitable circumstances arise for it to give off its energy to other B-fields, since transitions are not always permitted. Whether a psi-field can excite a B-field and whether the excited B-field can make transitions* depends on the total state of all the other B-fields, that is, according to the present theory (see section 3), on the "attitude" of the percipient. It is also seen that the present theory does not require a coding of "information" since the B-fields remain correlated via psi-fields and the B-fields *are* the carriers of "information." This defeats another argument of the vitalists, who thought that a specific "coding" mechanism would be required if any field theory were to be possible. Moreover, the present theory does not require a specific sender or receiver of "signals", since B-fields act as their own senders and receivers. Hence another argument against a field theory of parapsychology breaks down. The reader of Tyrrell's (1938, 1948) and Rhine's (1948, 1953) books will recall that such arguments were used to suggest that physical interpretations of parapsychological phenomena would be "impossible" on principle.

I shall now attempt to provide a theory of clairvoyance. It will be assumed that every matter field can bind a specific energy field called a P-field. Consequently, the P-fields bound

---

* It may be assumed by subjectivists that B-field transitions and mental experiences are isomorphically related. Behaviourists may disregard this piece of metaphysics.

to molecular fields will give an isomorphic representation of the molecular fields comparable to the isomorphic representation which a photographic negative gives of the printed photo. The assumption that every molecular field binds a specific B-field is a generalization of the previous hypothesis that neural matter fields bind specific B-fields. (B-fields and M-fields may be regarded as special cases of P-fields.)

In visual perception there exists, according to the theory developed in section 3, the following chain of processes between the perceived object and the B-fields bound to the cortex:

1. The matter fields of the object excite electro-magnetic fields or absorb and re-emit such fields. The spectral structure of the absorbed and emitted light depends uniquely on the reflecting, transmitting or emitting substance.

2. The electro-magnetic fields coming from the object excite the retinal receptors and the peripheral B-fields. The retinal receptors send pulses to the centre, and the peripheral B-fields excite B-fields which link centre and periphery and these in turn jointly with the central neurons excite a unique set of central B-fields. *The centrally excited B-fields are therefore in one-one correspondence with** *the states of the object's matter fields* which gave rise to the emission of light or which helped to change selectively the transmitted or reflected light.

I suggest that in clairvoyance there exists a one-one correspondence between the P-fields which are bound to an object and the B-fields bound to the cortex of the percipient via intermediate psi-fields. Since the P-field states of the object are in one-one correspondence with the states of its matter fields, the psi-fields which are excited by these P-fields will have states excited which are in one-one correspondence with the excited states of the object's matter fields. Finally, the excited psi-fields will excite B-fields of the percipient so as to

---

* This one-one correspondence may be destroyed by subsequent excitation of specific types of B-fields which in my book I have called B_m-fields and which are concerned (epiphenomenally) with meaning. However, these B_m-fields are independent of the sensory fields which are excited and thus will not be introduced into the present more restricted account of the general theory. These B_m-fields play a vital part in the fuller development of the theory, as do fields (called B_e-need fields) which are concerned with "needs".

be in one-one correspondence with the matter field states of the object. Hence, it is seen that the present field theory of clairvoyance establishes, like the field processes of ordinary visual perception, a one-one relation between the state transitions of the matter fields of the object and those of the central B-fields. The formation of the percepts is subsequently carried out by special B-fields (the B_m-fields, see footnote *, p. 68) which selectively become excited by the primary sensory B-fields. I cannot fully discuss in this short paper the many complexities which require analysis, namely, the part played by reinforcement (motivation) and by preformed concepts and schemata (see Vernon, 1952) which can all be interpreted in terms of field theory and which play a vital part in clairvoyant and ordinary perception. It is evident that in ordinary visual perception, as well as in clairvoyant perception, what is perceived is very different from what is received, at least in many cases, and a fuller analysis of this will follow in the book to be published.

It is important to notice that because of quantum-mechanical selection rules only specific P-fields can absorb energy from any particular psi-field, so that in general the energy of psi-fields may not be absorbed by P-fields unless the P-fields are of an appropriate type and in appropriate states. The present theory, it should be noticed, avoids the difficulties which the philosopher C. D. Broad thought would make any physical field theory of clairvoyance *a priori* impossible (Broad, 1935, 1949).

Finally, let me outline a field theory of precognition. According to the present theory all observable events in the universe are deducible from changes of states of fields and mutual interactions of fields (including mutually bound states). Suppose now that a set of energy fields are in a specific state. Let us also suppose that these fields (which may include matter fields, radiation fields, B-fields, M-fields, P-fields and psi-fields) become duplicated so as to form a corresponding complex of mutually bound and interacting fields which are ''copies'' (though not necessarily identical ones) of the first set of fields.

The copy fields are then in unique correspondence with the "originals". Let us suppose that the copy fields can make transitions more rapidly than the originals and that their transitions are such as to be in one-one correspondence with the transitions which the "original" fields will make. The copy fields will then "imitate" the behaviour of the originals.

Perhaps the nearest analogy to such "copying" processes occurs in the development of monozygotic twins from cleaved egg cells. There one system of fields independently makes transitions which closely resemble the transitions of another similar set of fields. It is suggested that in nature there exist similar processes of one set of fields imitating (isomorphically) the behaviour of another set of fields (and vast numbers of fields may be involved). If the copies make transitions more rapidly than the originals, they could give an advanced representation of field events which will happen later to the originals. If the copying fields could also excite psi-fields and hence specific B-fields of suitable percipients a precognition could occur, provided the B-fields of the percipient are excited in a serial order which corresponds to the serial order of the copying fields. This, I think, lays the ghost of the vitalist assumption that a physical interpretation of precognition is "impossible" (see Price 1949).

Psychokinesis and object reading can similarly be interpreted in terms of P-field and psi-field interactions and bound states, but I shall leave this to the book. It will be noticed that the present theory, like that of Spencer Brown (1953), provides an Ockham's razor for interpreting parapsychological data in terms of a few simple hypotheses. The difference between his theory and the present one is the following. He attempted to show that the observed data are statistical illusions, whereas the present theory suggests that these phenomena are no such illusions but fit well into the deductive framework of theoretical physics. Brown's theory has the disadvantage that it clashes with experimental data (see Wassermann 1955), which does not seem to apply to the present work.

REFERENCES

BORN, M. and GREEN, H. S. (1949). A General Kinetic Theory of Liquids. Cambridge University Press.

BROAD, C. D. (1935). *Proc. Soc. psych. Res., Lond.*, **43**, 412.

BROAD, C. D. (1949). *Philosophy*, **24**, 291.

COULSON, C. A. (1953). Valence. Oxford University Press.

COSTELLO, D. P. (1949). *In* Survey of Biological Progress, Ed. G. S. Avery, vol. I. New York: Academic Press.

DE BEER, G. R. (1951). Embryos and Ancestors. Oxford University Press.

GOLDSTEIN, K. (1939). The Organism: A Holistic Approach to Biology. New York: American Book Co.

GOMULICKI, B. R. (1953). *Brit. J. Psychol. Monogr.*, Suppl. 29.

GURWITSCH, A. (1921). *Arch. EntwMech. Org.*, **52**, 383.

HARDY, A. C. (1953). *Proc. Soc. psych. Res., Lond.*, **50**, 96.

HEBB, D. O. (1949). The Organization of Behavior. New York: Wiley & Sons.

HEISENBERG, W., and PAULI, W. (1929). *Z. Phys.*, **56**, 1.

HEITLER, W. (1954). The Quantum Theory of Radiation, 3rd edn. Oxford University Press.

HILGARD, E. R., and MARQUIS, D. G. (1940). Conditioning and Learning. New York: Appleton-Century Co.

KATZ, J. J., and HALSTEAD, W. C. (1950). *Comp. Psychol. Monogr.*, **20**, 1.

KOHLER, W. (1940). Dynamics in Psychology. New York: Liveright.

LASHLEY, K. S. (1929). Brain Mechanisms and Intelligence: a Quantitative Study of Injuries to the Brain. Chicago: University Press.

LASHLEY, K. S. (1950). *Symp. Soc. exp. Biol.*, **4**, 454.

LASHLEY, K. S. (1951). *In* Cerebral Mechanisms in Behavior. Hixon Symposium, Ed. L. A. Jeffres, p. 112. New York: Wiley and Sons.

McCULLOCH, W. S., and PITTS, W. (1943). *Bull. math. Biophys.*, **5**, 115.

McCULLOCH, W. S., and PITTS, W. (1947). *Bull. math. Biophys.*, **9**, 127.

NEEDHAM, A. E. (1952). Regeneration and Wound Healing. London: Methuen and Co.

NEEDHAM, J. (1950). Biochemistry and Morphogenesis. Cambridge University Press.

PIRIE, N. W. (1938). *In* Perspectives in Biochemistry, Ed. Needham and Green. Cambridge University Press.

PRICE, H. H. (1949). *Hibberts Journal*, **47**, 105.

POLYAK, S. L. (1941). The Retina. Chicago: University Press.

RASHEVSKY, N. (1948). Mathematical Biophysics: Physicomathematical Foundations of Biology, 2nd edn., Chicago: University Press.

RHINE, J. B. (1948). The Reach of the Mind. London: Faber & Faber.

RHINE, J. B. (1953). New Worlds of the Mind. New York: William Sloan.

SPEMANN, H. (1921). *Arch. EntwMech. Org.* **48**, 533.

SPEMANN, H. (1938). Embryonic Development and Induction. Yale University Press.

SPENCE, K. W. (1951). *In* Handbook of Experimental Psychology, Ed. Stevens, p. 690. New York: Wiley & Sons.

SPENCER BROWN, G. (1953). *Nature, Lond.*, **177**, 154.

SPERRY, R. W. (1951). *In* Handbook of Experimental Psychology, Ed. Stevens, p. 236. New York: Wiley & Sons.

TYRRELL, G. N. M. (1938). Science and Psychical Phenomena. London: Methuen.

TYRRELL, G. N. M. (1948). The Personality of Man. London: Penguin Books (Long).

VERNON, M. D. (1952). A Further Study of Visual Perception. Cambridge University Press.

WASSERMANN, G. D. (1955). *Brit. J. Phil. Sci.*, in press.

WEISS, P. (1922). *Jber. ges. Physiol.*, p. 65.

WEISS, P. (1924). *Jber ges. Physiol.*, p. 77.

WEISS, P. (1926a). Morphodynamik. Berlin: Borntrager.

WEISS, P. (1926b). *Jber. ges. Physiol.*, p. 107.

WEISS, P. (1928). *Jber. Physiol. exp. Pharm.*, p. 70.

WEISS, P. (1950). *Symp. Soc. exper. Biol.*, **4**, 92.

WEISS, P. (1951). *In* Discussion in Cerebral Mechanisms in Behavior. Hixon Symposium, Ed. Jeffres. New York: Wiley & Sons.

WENTZEL, G. (1949). Quantum Theory of Fields. New York: Interscience.

WIGGLESWORTH, V. B. (1948). *Symp. Soc. exper. Biol.*, **2**, 1.

THE DATA OF PSYCHICAL RESEARCH:
A STUDY OF THREE HYPOTHESES

G. Spencer Brown
Christ Church, Oxford

The Society for Psychical Research officially defines its task as the study of "those faculties of man, real or supposed, which appear inexplicable on any generally recognized hypothesis". One of the most interesting features of this definition is that it makes the subject suicidal. For as soon as any faculty of man becomes familiar enough to be explained by a generally recognized hypothesis, it at once ceases to be a part of psychical research, and comes under some less esoteric discipline. Hypnotism, for example, was once a part of psychical research, but is now within the field of experimental psychology and medicine.

Hypotheses of extrasensory perception having so far escaped general recognition, the study of their plausibility or, failing this, of their necessity, still remains a task for psychical research. But here again, the very concept of perception that is without senses suggests a further suicide within a suicidal field. Extrasensory perception, we have already been told, is "response to an external event not presented to any known sense". If such response occurs often enough, must not the sense through which it occurs eventually become known? Is it possible for a reaction to occur to a stimulus which does not come through any sense organ? I think the nearest we can at present get to proven extrasensory perception is in a case such as this. If we open the skull of a man and paint his visual cortex with a strychnine solution, the man reacts by saying he sees things. What is the sense by which he reacts? Unless we are to say his visual cortex is a sense organ, his perception of the strychnine must be extrasensory. Yet we do not feel happy about saying so, because we know what is going on; and for the purposes of the experiment, we should rather say that the subject's visual cortex had in fact become a sense organ. Thus the study of extrasensory perception logically reduces to the study of so far unknown or unexplained forms of sensory perception. It remains for us, therefore, to examine the data which have been supposed to be relevant to perception of this kind.

The earliest evidence obtainable is in what are called spontaneous cases. Almost everyone has his own story of events which seem to indicate telepathy or clairvoyance. I will cite two which aroused my own interest in the subject. I was performing the fairly common experiment of inducing hallucinations in a hypnotic subject; I had a blank sheet of paper in a photograph frame, and I suggested that the subject saw in it the picture of a house. Upon asking him then to describe what he saw, he surprised me by saying he saw a portrait, going on to describe in some detail a photograph of one of my cousins whose picture happened to be behind the blank sheet within the frame. Interested by this, I tried the subject with other pictures hidden behind the same blank sheet, but all without success. This looked like clairvoyance, but of course its unrepeatability made it impossible to preclude other explanations. For example, it is possible that the subject had on some other occasion seen the photograph in the frame, and the suggestion produced by the association of the frame had been stronger than my own counter-suggestion. On the other occasion, I had hypnotized a subject in my rooms in Cambridge, telling him that I was going to another set of rooms and that while I was gone he was to describe to his observer what I was doing. I then went away with an observer who recorded my own actions. Later the two record sheets were compared and a remarkable correspondence was discovered between what I had done and what the subject said I had done. Another experiment of the same kind was done later, but it had no success.

Now these results seem typical of all the evidence we have

for extrasensory perception: suggestive but not conclusive. New oddities are always occurring, but we hardly ever seem to get the same thing twice. Because of the difficulty of assessing results of this kind, attention was turned to the design of the experiments, and statistical techniques were brought in.

The statistical experiments, as we all know, soon produced results of undoubted significance. But although significance occurred under more and more different conditions and in more and more different forms, the results were similar to those of the old qualitative experiments in that it was just as difficult to repeat a specific result. Throughout the literature, with one or two exceptions, we have new phenomena only— not confirmation of the old ones. But it was considered that the criterion of statistical significance somehow gave these results a respectability which the old qualitative results lacked.

This respectability is a delusion. Statistical significance cannot by itself prove a natural law; at best it is a pointer, signalling where such a law might be found. The term "significant" is an unfinished term. It does not help us to say results are "significant" until we can say what they are significant of. From reading some of the criticisms of my work, it would appear that critics think that I have maintained that psychical research data are not significant of anything. But in fact all I have said is that most of the results, though significant, do not, as is commonly supposed, appear to be significant of telepathy, clairvoyance, etc.

The fashionable hypothesis, then, that significance in psychical research is significance of a kind of communication, I take to be, even on the most lenient view, not proven. Statistical significance is simply a tool indicating where we might find inductive repeatability. If it seems to lead us to the wrong places, we have two courses open to us: we can examine our interpretations of the indications given us, or we can examine the validity of the indicators themselves. There seems to be evidence to show that the adoption of either of these courses will be more fruitful than continued dogged adherence to an inflexible communication hypothesis.

In my paper in *Nature* (Spencer Brown, 1953), I supposed that the calculus from which we derive our criterion of statistical significance might be not only inapplicable in some of the psychical research experiments, but also might be itself doubtful because of certain internal contradictions. Some of the evidence in psychical research seems to bear this out, because the modern psychical research experiment, supposed to be a biological experiment in communication, has in most cases degenerated into an experiment in pure probability. For experiments in pure probability consist of operations such as throwing dice, tossing coins, and shuffling cards, and matching the orders produced thus against a given order and this procedure is now typical of experiments in psychical research. The only factor which might be said to constitute a relevant difference is that the psychical research experiments involve some sort of effort on the part of a person called the subject. Yet is this effort in fact relevant to the result? Nigel Richmond (1952), in his experiment with *Paramecium*, obtained highly significant results in his control series where he was making no effort whatever. Similarly, more than half the examples of probability experiments cited by Keynes (1921) gave results well outside chance expectation, and later experiments seem to have fared no better. Fisher's random numbers (Fisher and Yates, 1949), obtained in a specified way from logarithm tables, were found by Yates to contain too many sixes. Some of the sixes therefore had to be removed. Similarly, ten thousand of the random digits produced by the Kendall and Babington Smith machine (1951) were found to be so unrandom that, although originally meant for publication, they had to be left out (Kendall and Babington, 1939). Thus the significant results discovered in matching columns of published random numbers by myself (Spencer Brown, 1955), and later by Oram (1955), were certainly not new; they were merely found in a new context.

But there is yet a third factor which might act to give the

significant scores which have occurred in physical research. This is centred in the ultimate analysability of the randomizing procedure basic to the test.

It is possible to refine Poincaré's description (1912) of a randomizer as a machine where a very small cause leads to a very big result. On this view a randomizer may be called a machine for magnifying uncontrollable errors. Let us take, for example, the Kendall and Babington Smith randomizer. Here a rapidly revolving wheel with figures 0 to 9 on the circumference was illuminated periodically by flashes of light under the hand control of the operator. The number appearing at a particular point on the circumference was noted at each flash and written down. Now it is assumed that in this machine the size of the human error from regularity in the flashes has been magnified so as to cover many repetitions of the stochastic series on the circumference of the wheel. Only in such circumstances is it by definition impossible for the operator to determine what number his next flash will illuminate. But although this set-up logically admits of no control over what number is to appear next, it by no means prevents a periodicity occurring within the numerical sequence and dependent upon the unconscious repetition of motor patterns by the operator. Such periodicities would of course tend to be destroyed if the operator noticed them, but would tend to remain where he did not. Furthermore, we have no reason to suppose that all natural "random" series are not periodic in this way.

Now when we match two periodic series against one another, the result will itself be periodic. This, in terms of matching scores, would mean periods of significantly successful matching followed by periods of equally significant failure to match. Further, there is nothing to show that a series produced by ordinary guessing is not subject to the laws of the Poincaré machine. Thus unconsciously produced periodicity in a random series and a guessing series might, albeit but rarely, produce a quite startling synchronicity as evinced by matching scores. Furthermore, once such synchronicity had started,

it would be destroyed by a relatively slight interference with
one of the other of the series-producers. Just as, in the
Babington Smith machine, an unconscious pattern produced
by the operator will disappear as soon as he becomes conscious
of it, so, in the case of a subject who happens to be unconsciously producing a period closely matching that of the series
which he is guessing, will the guesser's pattern be automatically modified if he is informed of this fact.

This is indeed borne out in practice. In general, when a
subject begins to score above the chance expectation, the
best means of keeping up his score is to leave everything as
it is, and especially not to disturb the subject with information about his success. Thouless and others have noticed that
once such information reaches the subject, his scores tend to
fall dramatically. In addition, the personality tests carried
out by Dr. Humphrey and Mr. Fraser Nicol (1953) bear out
this view. For it is the extraverts, who have the greater internal stability in their reaction patterns, who tend to produce
large deviations in matching scores.

Thus we have discussed three possible meanings of the data
of psychical research. First there is the possibility that these
data are, as was originally supposed, evidence of some odd
sort of communication. There are a few experiments bearing
out this view, but they are now many years old and their
results are not typical. Secondly, we have briefly discussed
the view which I first put forward in 1953 that there might
be internal contradictions in the axioms of the calculus of
probabilities itself which could lead to statistically significant
deviations which nevertheless possessed no conventional
inductive significance. And finally we have mentioned the
possibility that some of the results have been obtained by
applying the calculus of probabilities in situations which are
open to a more definite analysis than was originally supposed.

I am quite sure the last two factors have been operative
in producing statistically significant results both in psychical
research and elsewhere. It remains to be shown whether there
is evidence of communication occurring as well. The evidence

for communication is, I think, smaller than we have hitherto supposed, but it may not be entirely negligible. In any case it seems to be this mixture of possible interpretations, none of which excludes any of the others, that makes the task of the psychical research worker so difficult and sometimes so unrewarding.

REFERENCES

FISHER, R. A., and YATES F. (1949). Statistical Tables for Biological, Agricultural and Medical Research. London: Oliver and Boyd.

FRASER NICOL, J., and HUMPHREY, BETTY M. (1953). *J. Amer. Soc. psych. Res.*, **47**, 133.

KENDALL, M. G., and BABINGTON SMITH, B. (1939). *Supp. J. R. statist. Soc.*, **6**, 51.

KENDALL, M. G., and BABINGTON SMITH, B. (1951). Tables of Random Sampling Numbers. Cambridge University Press.

KEYNES, J. M. (1921). A Treatise on Probability, Ch. XXIX. London: MacMillan.

ORAM, A. T. (1955). *J. Soc. psych. Res.*, **38**, 40.

PONCAIRÉ, H. (1912). Calcul des Probabilités, 2nd édition. Paris.

RICHMOND, N. (1952). *J. Soc. psych. Res.*, **36**, 577.

SPENCER BROWN, G. (1953). *Nature, Lond.*, **172**, 154.

SPENCER BROWN, G. (1955). *J. Soc. psych. Res.*, **38**, 38.

SOME STATISTICAL ASPECTS OF ESP

S. G. SOAL

London

I HAVE been asked especially to include in my paper some account of my own work on extrasensory cognition and of the positive findings. Although, therefore, this work has now been published in detail (Soal and Bateman, 1954), I am beginning with a very short account of some of our main findings.

Throughout, we have employed what might be termed the "differential" method of experiment. That is to say, we have observed the effects on the subject's rate of scoring when one of the physical or psychological conditions of the experiment is varied, with the others remaining as far as possible constant. For instance, we found that both Shackleton and Mrs. Stewart scored consistently high above chance expectation when an agent or sender looked at the figures on the cards and failed as consistently when he or she was not allowed to see the cards until the finish of the experiment. The differential method is easy to employ with consistent scorers such as Shackleton or Mrs. Stewart. But it would be rather difficult with such a subject as that of Mr. Langdon-Davies, whose scores appear to fall to the chance level and remain there for a considerable period after every slight change in the experimental set-up.

With Shackleton, the most interesting results obtained followed upon changes in the rate of guessing. At the normal speed of calling (i.e. about one minute for twenty-five guesses), Shackleton guessed correctly over a period of two years, and in a series of 11,000-odd trials the card one ahead of that which was being looked at by the agent. But when the speed of calling was doubled (i.e. when twenty-five cards were guessed in about thirty-five seconds), Shackleton ceased to score significantly on the card one ahead but made highly significant scores on the card two ahead. This was what happened when the agent Miss Elliott was employed. But when Mr. J. Aldred was substituted for Miss Elliott, Shackleton reverted to the same type of scoring as he had shown in 1936, when working with this same agent. That is, he scored significantly on both the ($+$ 1) and ($-$ 1) cards as he had done six years earlier, when Aldred was the principal agent. Still more interesting, when the speed of calling was quickened to about double the normal rate, with Aldred as agent, the ($+$ 1) and ($-$ 1) scores disappeared and were replaced by very significant scores on the ($+2$) and ($-$ 2) cards.

When numbers taken from tables were replaced by an experimenter drawing counters from a bag or bowl the phenomena obtained with Miss Elliott as agent showed the same consistent characteristics with little or no change in the degree of success. It appeared to make no difference whether we used coloured counters drawn from a bag or random numbers to decide the card to be looked at by the agent.

When Mrs. Stewart, with whom I first experimented in 1936, was retested in 1945, she maintained over a period of more than four years and in a series of some 50,000 trials a very consistent average score under telepathy conditions of nearly seven hits per twenty-five trials. She succeeded, moreover, in reaching three standard deviations or more with fifteen of the thirty persons who worked with her as agent.

Among the many interesting features of her work was the experiment carried out with Mrs. Stewart guessing the cards at Merksem near Antwerp and the agents looking at the cards in London or Richmond. In this test at a distance of 200 miles she maintained the same high rate of scoring which she was accustomed to produce when separated from the agent by one solid wall at a distance of 18–20 feet.

In other series of experiments in which two agents focused on different cards at every trial it was found that she scored significantly with the person whom she thought was the agent and obtained only chance results with the other agent of whose participation she was unaware.

We discovered also that when two or three agents focused on the *same* card at every trial, Mrs. Stewart appeared to establish telepathic contact with one only of these agents; with the others she obtained only chance results.

Perhaps the most interesting experiment of all was that in which two agents in different rooms each contributed an essential fragment of the message to be transmitted. One agent saw the numbers presented at the aperture in the screen and the other knew only the order of the five target cards. Apparently by putting these two pieces of information together Mrs. Stewart was able to identify the card it was intended to transmit.

In the year 1936 Mrs. Stewart produced significant scores not only on the card contemporaneously focused on by the agent but also on the $(+ 1)$ and $(- 1)$ cards. Nine years later, when working with different agents, her principal score was consistently on the target or "O" card. We were unable to try her in 1945 with Mrs. Johnstone and Miss Johnstone, with whom she had previously obtained the $(+ 1)$ and $(- 1)$ scores. We found in 1946 that when the rate of calling was approximately doubled Mrs. Stewart consistently displaced her "O" hits on to the $(- 1)$ card, i.e. the card which the agent had just looked at. This effect, however, may have been due to a psychological lag and not to a true temporal displacement.

These are only a few of the many remarkable features exhibited by these two subjects and established by the use of the differential method. As a rule, batches of fifty trials under one experimental condition were alternated with other batches of fifty in which there was a change in the condition.

Briefly we may say that there are two methods available for the investigation of extrasensory cognition. We may work with a group of unselected persons in the hope that though individual contributions to positive scoring may be almost negligible, yet the group may contain enough persons with a slight ESP capacity to result in an overall modest significance in the total score. The method is not a hopeful one and few experimenters would employ it who had access to a high-scoring subject whose gifts can be studied over a long period.

As regards the statistical evidence for ESP itself, repeatability of high scores over a reasonable period of time is the acid test. It is not of course necessary that this repeatability should be permanent in the case of any one individual. A person may exhibit certain medical symptoms for a period of two years and after that his condition may change and the symptoms completely disappear. ESP is probably a phase in the life of certain individuals and not a permanent ability such as the ability to play the piano or do mathematics. It is well known that the extraordinary abilities of certain calculating boys have faded out as they grew older.

Now I would like to say something about high odds against chance in ESP experiments. Some people have said that they are not impressed by odds of say 10^{35} to 1 obtained by persons like Shackleton and seem to distrust them. But it is surely obvious that astronomical odds are the necessary consequence of a steady above-chance rate of scoring which may not in itself be very high. If a subject goes on scoring an average of seven hits per twenty-five instead of five hits per twenty-five week after week and month after month as Mrs. Stewart did, he or she will reach after, say, 37,000 trials, odds which certainly exceed 10^{70} to 1. The high odds are only important in themselves as a consequence of a steady consistent rate of extra-chance scoring. The importance lies in the consistency of the scoring. If, on the other hand, a guesser obtains on a single run of twenty-five cards a score of 18 and produces afterwards nothing but chance scores for the next ten thousand trials, his achievement is far less impressive than that of the man whose score for twenty-five seldom reached 12 but who kept up an average of 7 for 30,000 trials. We should indeed begin to suspect that the man with the odd score of 18 cheated in some way or obtained glimpses of the faces of the cards.

Some critics have said that ESP cannot be a fact, since, if it were, gamblers would make fortunes on the Stock Exchange or at Monte Carlo. This of course is nonsense. When we remember that even the best subjects are able to cognize by ESP only two or three cards in twenty-five and that they usually fail with agents with whom they have no previous acquaintance, and that such subjects constitute only an infinitesimal fraction of the population, it will be obvious that the advantage over normal people bestowed on them by their gift is quite negligible.

There are certain scientists who have questioned the applicability of the probability model to ESP experiments. I am quite certain, however, that on the whole the probability model works excellently in practice. Anyone who, like myself, has over a period of years tested several hundred people with five-symbol cards will find that, except possibly in the case of one or two outstanding individuals, the mean score and observed standard deviation are close to those predicted by the binomial formulae. But once one has discovered one of these outstanding scorers there is as much difference between his or her performance and that of the ordinary guesser as between chalk and cheese. The genuine ESP subject cannot be mistaken. Not only does his critical ratio keep going up and up but we soon find conditions under which his powers consistently fail or certain agents or experimenters with whom he consistently fails to score above chance expectation. This differential method of experimentation at once renders the demonstration of ESP independent of the probability model. In our experimentation with Mrs. Stewart, as with Shackleton, we found very early the peculiarity that while high scores were produced when an agent knew the order of the five cards in the box, only scores at chance level were registered when the agent was kept ignorant of this order. Thus we have the two following sets of scores (Table I). In row T an agent looked at the cards; in row C no one knew the order until the end of each fifty trials. Series of fifty trials done under the T (telepathy) condition were alternated or randomly mixed with series of fifty trials done under condition C (clairvoyance). Each score is on a series of 200 trials, and mean expectation is forty hits.

Table I

	Hits in 200 trials												Totals
	1945					1947			1948		1949		
T	67	58	62	58	60	54	55	65	39	56	49	51	33	707
C	51	42	29	47	38	35	36	31	38	43	40	37	42	509

In row C not a single score reaches even an excess of two standard deviations, while the majority of those in row T have deviations which exceed three standard deviations. Comment on the enormous difference between the totals in the two conditions is superfluous.

Our book, *Modern Experiments in Telepathy* (Soal and Bateman, 1954), abounds with such examples. It is a pity that so many experimenters in the past have made little attempt to compare one experimental condition with another. They have been content to go on piling up quite unnecessary odds against chance. A typical case is that of the experimenters Martin and Stribic (1938–1940), who carried out more than 300,000 trials with, for the most part, only trivial variations in the experimental procedure such as making the subjects guess upwards instead of downwards through the pack (Martin and Stribic, 1938; 1940).

In a foreword to the American edition (Yale University Press) of *Modern Experiments in Telepathy* Professor Evelyn Hutchinson warns ordinary scientists and psychologists to read works on parapsychology with care before attacking them. But in a recent review of the book by Professor E. G. Boring of Harvard University, which is on the whole eminently fair and sympathetic, the reviewer says that his preference would be to get away from the probability model and that it would be better to have scientific controls. "In a good experiment", he says, "you would turn telepathy on and note the number of hits. Then you would turn it off—the control experiment—and note the number. If the difference were large enough to show that you are probably not in the two series dealing with the same populations of guesses then you have ESP and also an indication of how surely you have it." Now this is just what we were constantly doing with Mrs. Stewart and Shackleton—"turning off the telepathy tap". Professor Boring later apologized to me for having entirely missed all the scientific controls of this sort with which the book abounds, but this is an example of Hutchinson's contention that scientists review books on parapsychology without careful study.

Regarding the vexed question of the use of random tables in the ordering of the target symbols in ESP experiments, I was the first experimenter to select targets from mathematical tables, and I did this as far back as 1934. I fully agree with Dr. R. H. Thouless that in statistics we are more concerned with random processes or random selectors than with so-called random series.

To adapt an illustration in *Modern Experiments in Telepathy*, suppose we have an electronic device which prints in a row some one of the four letters A, B, C, and D, repeats of the same letter being possible. Suppose further that we print sequences of 100 trials. The total number of different arrangements we could obtain is 4^{100}. If in the long run the machine turns up each of these 4^{100} permutations approximately an equal number of times, it would be reasonable to say that the machine was a random selector. A direct verification would of course be extremely laborious. Now, by supposition, all the arrangements are equally probable and the permutation consisting of 100 A's is just as likely to turn up as any other specified arrangement. It is clear then that this particular arrangement is just as "random" as any other and we ought to be no more surprised if it turns up than if any other specified arrangement appears. It is of course very improbable that it will turn up, but not more improbable than any other. Nevertheless, we should be very embarrassed if we had to use it in a card-guessing experiment for a target-sequence, especially with a subject whose previous guessing had shown an habitual preference for the letter A. But even if we did use it for a hundred trials, any advantage gained by the subject would soon be washed out if we made him carry out a large number of other sets of 100 chosen by the selector. Now the mathematical model for a random series is the Bernoulli distribution and from this distribution we can calculate the mean expectation of various patterns such as AA, AAA, etc. Most compilers of random number tables apply three or four tests of this kind, and if the actual distribution agrees fairly well with the mathematical model they feel satisfied that their distribution is a random one, i.e. one produced as the result of a random process. But there are obviously millions of different patterns that could be tested and we have no guarantee whatever that for many of these patterns the observed values might not differ wildly from their chance expectations. It is therefore quite impossible to be sure if a series really agrees with the mathematical model, since it would be impracticable to try out all the patterns. Statements about a series being random are therefore based on ignorance and it is quite absurd for experimenters to make a fetish of the matter. All that is really necessary in a card-guessing experiment is that there should be no real correlation between the target series and the guessing habits of the subject. Suppose for instance that the target series contains an excess of one symbol—say the circle. If the guesser has a preference for calling circles this will artificially augment his total score. But we are able to deal with even this case by employing Stevens' formula which allows for the inequality of the numbers of the various target symbols. Stevens' target distribution is certainly not a Bernoulli distribution but it has been found to work in practice both with shuffled packs of cards and with numbers taken from tables.

Another example of a real correlation which might occur

between a person's guessing habits and a target sequence is afforded by a defective experiment to test pure telepathy. Suppose that an agent thinks of a series of symbols A, B, C, D, E, making them up in his head in groups of five, and that another person guesses at these symbols. Then it might easily happen that both agent and percipient had a common preference for choosing a particular symbol, say A, for the central place in the group. This would of course be a fatal flaw in the experiment. But while it is easy to imagine a real correlation between the guessing habits of two human beings, it is incredible that there should be any persistent correlation between numbers taken from a table and the guessing habits of a human being. There might be a brief accidental synchronization lasting over a hundred or perhaps two hundred guesses. All who have had much practical experience of card-guessing will have noticed that occasionally some subject appears to be scoring well above chance for about 200 trials or so but that he does not keep it up. This is probably due to such an accidental synchronization. But chance synchronization between numbers taken from tables and a person's guessing habits which went on for thousands of trials is unthinkable. In our own experiments, even if there existed a synchronization between a person's number habits and a series of numbers taken from tables, it would be upset by the fact that the subject is not guessing numbers but five animals whose relation to the numbers 1, 2, 3, 4, 5 is not fixed but is changed after every fifty guesses by the agent's shuffling of the five cards in the box.

My main point is that the use of tables of so-called random numbers rests more on empirical than on any logical justification, since it is hard even to define a random finite series in such a way that an actual series can be put to any comprehensive test. The use of such tables is really based on the fact that for the past thirty years they have worked quite well in practice. Here and there discrepancies are to be found, as was pointed out by Karl Pearson in his introduction to Tippetts' tables, but the discrepancies are trivial compared with those that are observed with a high-scoring ESP subject and not in the same class with them at all.

Actually much less than perfect randomness (whatever that may mean!) is required for a satisfactory card-guessing experiment, as Thouless has very clearly pointed out. Provided that a number of packs of cards are used, ordinary shuffling is quite adequate if followed by a random cut. This was shown conclusively by the statistician Greenwood, who made 500,000 matchings of shuffled packs of cards against the guesses of high-scoring subjects. The targets had no connection with those at which the guesses were originally aimed. Both the observed mean, 4·9743 per 25, and the observed standard deviation 2·0058 were extremely close to the theoretical values based on a Bernoulli series, namely 5 and 2.

If there is any doubt as to whether the binomial formulae are applicable to a given target distribution it is generally possible to substitute in place of the theoretical binomial standard deviation the observed standard deviation from the theoretical mean. This has been done for both the Shackleton and Stewart series and in each case the results are still overwhelmingly significant.

Again there is the evidence from cross-checks. By a cross-check is meant a systematic comparison in which each column of a subject's guesses is compared with a target column *of the same series* for which the column of guesses was not originally intended. The total score for the cross-check is then compared with that for the original series. Thus we might compare Guess Col. 1(a) with Target Col. 1(b), and Target Col. 1(a) with Guess Col. 1(b). Now clearly if the Shackleton or Stewart series gave for the cross-check results which were in reasonable agreement with the binomial expectation we could infer from this two things. In the first place there could be no systematic relation between the guessing habits of the subject and the patterns of the number table from which the targets were compiled, whether this table was really random or not. Further, it would show that whatever patterns there were in the target series whose frequencies differed seriously from those of the Bernoulli model, such patterns were not of such a nature as to affect seriously the score expectation or the variance.

Now the 3,789 guesses with Shackleton as percipient and Miss Elliott as agent gave on the actual targets 1,101 (+ 1) hits and the corresponding critical ratio was a bit over 13. But the number of hits on the targets chosen for the cross-check was 798, with a critical ratio of 1·6. Using the Stevens expectation the critical ratio is less than 1. As Professor Broad has remarked, comment is superfluous. In support of the thesis that ESP is an artifact of statistics, Mr. Spencer Brown in a broadcast talk said that "every new experimental design, provided that it is statistical, seems to give similar results ". *Modern Experiments in Telepathy* is full of examples which refute this statement. For instance, at a time when Hubert Pearce was averaging about eight hits per twenty-five in a telepathy test he was asked to aim consciously àt low scores during a batch of 275 trials. His average per twenty-five for this series was only 1·81 and the drop in the scoring is tremendously significant. There are many such cases quite outside my own work, and there would have been many more had not so many experimenters fallen into a senseless routine of never changing the conditions for fear that their high-scoring subject would slump to chance level and not recover.

Acknowledgement

Much of the information contained in this paper has been published in the volume entitled "Modern Experiments in Telepathy" by S. G. Soal and F. Bateman, published by Faber and Faber, Ltd. and in the U.S.A. by Yale University Press.

REFERENCES

MARTIN, D. R., and STRIBIC, F. P. (1938). *J. Parapsychol.*, 2, 23.
MARTIN, D. R., and STRIBIC, F. P. (1940). *J. Parapsychol.*, 4, 159.
SOAL, S. G., and BATEMAN, F. (1954). Modern Experiments in Telepathy. London: Faber and Faber Ltd.

DISCUSSION

Perry: I think I ought to start by saying that I agree very much with what Prof. Gaddum said yesterday. I would dearly like to find an explanation which would not involve extrasensory perception. But like Prof. Gaddum, I find Dr. Soal's evidence very difficult to get round; especially difficult to get round is the direct type of test, where the subject scores significantly over and over again in the telepathy tests and not at all significantly in the clairvoyance tests. Dr. McConnell yesterday began this conference by summing up the various ways in which he thought the data of ESP could be explained. He put forward much of what I planned to put forward, but I think it is worthwhile my going ahead in any case, in spite of the similarities of our views.

I have tried to summarize in Table I the possible explanations of the results of ESP experiments. The first three explanations would discount

Table I

POSSIBLE EXPLANATIONS OF RESULTS

A. ESP IS A FALLACY

    It is created by :
            1. Deliberate Fraud
            2. Methodological Errors :
                        (*a*) Experimental
                        (*b*) Recording
                        (*c*) Analytical
            3. Theoretical Errors—statistical

B. ESP IS A REAL PHENOMENON

    It occurs because :
            1. ESP really is Extraordinary SP.
            2. Materialistic philosophy is a fallacy.

ESP as an artifact. I think that we are all agreed now that we can exclude No. 1, but when we come to Nos. 2 and 3, there is considerable controversy. I would myself instinctively reject data which are of borderline significance, based on statistical theory. I would reject them for two reasons: firstly, with the best will in the world, even with independent recording, you can have an error simply in writing the thing down. That is not likely to happen over and over again, but it might well happen once in 50 times, which would be enough to give you a result of $5 \cdot 5$, instead of 5 out of 25. The other reason is the sort that Mr. Spencer Brown has put forward; the fact that an apparently random series may not be truly random, and that you may thus get apparently significant results, which are in fact due to chance alone. I was sorry that Mr. Spencer Brown did not enlarge on PK; as far as I know, all the results of PK experiments fall into the category that I would call borderline, but that does not apply to some of the better experiments in telepathy. I was very impressed by Mr. Spencer Brown's *reductio ad absurdum* in his abstract, in which he pointed out that if PK is a real thing, then there is no reason to suppose that someone doing an experiment cannot influence the order in which the cards are going to appear in the pack; consequently the cards will cease to be in a random order, and will be in an order determined by the subject and, therefore, you cannot analyse the results on a statistical basis. My own views, having heard all the papers in the last two sessions, would be to reject the evidence for PK altogether, which would make the *reductio ad absurdum* not applicable, and that would leave me in the same position, having certain experiments in ESP which I find very difficult to reject.

That brings us to the last two explanations (Table I). I think that most intelligent laymen, and certainly most scientists would very much rather think of the first of these as being the real explanation. In other words, one would like to read for extrasensory perception "extra-ordinary sensory perception", and think of some influence on the central nervous system explicable in terms of neurophysiology, rather than become mystical about the subject. That is one of the reasons why I found Dr. Wassermann's theory of such interest. It is the sort of theory that I had hoped would come forward in time to explain some of these otherwise apparently inexplicable data. On the other hand, to my simple mind, it is a theory which in its present form is still incomprehensible—in spite of Dr. Wassermann's valiant attempts to make it easy. There are a number of questions I should like to put about this. In so far as I can analyse the theory from a neurophysiological point of view, it seems to me that the net end result is that the subject's muscles are activated, and he writes, he makes marks on a piece of paper. One must therefore assume that certain of his motoneurones are activated in a given pattern, and this, in turn, implies that energy is provided. There is an input. Something triggers those motoneurones. Now, the only known way to trigger them, without using unnatural machines, is through other neurones in the central nervous system. One thing that strikes me, that has not been mentioned yet in this meeting, is that this ESP faculty, that certain people would appear to have, seems to be a purely subconscious phenomenon; the subjects are not consciously aware of any influence being exerted upon them. Shackleton did not know whether the agent was looking at the cards or not, but yet when the agent was looking at the cards he appeared to guess more accurately. Therefore, any effect that occurs presumably occurs in the subconscious. That merely excludes some of the cortical neurones associated with consciousness, and puts the activators of the motoneurones one stage down in the central nervous system.

The point I am trying to lead up to, is that Dr. Wassermann says that a psi field, as he calls it, need not necessarily interact with a matter field, but only with a B field, which presumably in turn would interact with a matter field. Now, he also says that these fields exist all the time, in equilibrium, at a certain stationary energy state, and that the equilibrium is upset by some input, and it is only at that point that energy is transferred from one field to another according to selected patterns. Well, since the matter fields of the neurones react in a pattern to produce the movement of writing the name of the selected card, those neurones must themselves receive energy before they are activated. And to my simple mind, it seems that the theory must stand or fall by the production of evidence that, in fact, energy is fed into those moto-neurones, which is a thing which should be detectable.

Where does the energy come from? What sort of energy is it? How can we measure it? On what neurones is it exerted? Is it exerted directly on the motoneurones, so that it produces the pattern of writing? Or is the influence primarily on the correlation centres which determine this pattern or writing, even if it is at a subconscious level? Finally, is it really an influence on some sensory afferent fibres, which themselves interact with the correlation centre; in other words, is it an extra-ordinary sensory perception; or does it bypass the afferent side of the central nervous system, and affect either inter-neurones or motoneurones directly?

Eccles in his Waynflete lectures, attempted to explain ESP by describing how the delicately poised equilibrium of the neuronal chains in the central nervous system might be affected by the slightest modulus. To my mind any modulus is theoretically a measurable event and we have then a physical and scientific explanation of the phenomena of ESP; the slightness of the modulus does not aid the argument in favour of a psychic or "non-physical" explanation. Dr. Wassermann has a more physical explanation, and I welcome any attempts to provide one, even though it is still incomprehensible to me.

Gaddum: It seems likely that the central nervous system is sensitive to very small amounts of energy. I think it is true that the amount of light that is necessary to produce an effect on the retina is of the order of a quantum, and it is quite possible that there is something in the central nervous system which is sensitive to very small amounts of energy, which could not be detected by any ordinary physical apparatus. I should like to know, in that connection, how good the evidence really is that ESP is independent of distance. It is possible that there are forms of energy which are also independent of distance, but very small so that they may be undetectable by physical apparatus.

Soal: I can't answer why or how ESP is independent of distance. I think Gray Walters' theory was that the energy output of the brain is so small that it could not be detected about a millimetre from the head, which rather disputed the theory that you could get ESP at 400 miles, if it were due to physical radiation of any recognised kind.

Parkes: But it is a fact in your opinion, is it, that ESP is more or less independent of distance?

Soal: I would not say it is independent of distance. I don't think there have been nearly enough experiments to establish that. I merely say that we have got it at 200 miles—I am quite sure of that.

Parkes: Of the same order of significance as at close range?

Soal: Yes. There was no significant difference in the scores obtained at 20 feet and at 200 miles.

McConnell: I should be inclined to respond to Prof. Gaddum's question by agreeing with Dr. Wassermann, that such ideas as inverse-square laws applying here or there are, from the physicist's point of view, rather unimportant. I mean that this is not a line of thinking that would be likely to be fruitful, and I think one can even go further and say that, while questions of distance relationship would be very interesting and important, we are unable at this stage to make a specific argument of a mathematical nature.

I might say, too, that I was very pleased with Dr. Wassermann's presentation, more so than I expected to be, and I shall look forward with great interest to the book that he has promised.

I have two comments upon what Dr. Perry said. My own feeling is that a distinction is unjustified between the two final alternatives that he proposed, namely that ESP is either extraordinary sensory perception or that it supports a spiritual philosophy. When you beat these things down into experimental terms, from what one might call an operational point of view, it will probably be found that there is not any difference and that the distinction is more of a verbal one than anything else.

The other thing that I would like to mention is that he has discussed something which he found in the abstract of Mr. Brown, which Mr. Brown did not discuss himself, presumably because I discouraged him yesterday with my remarks about the undesirability of discussing PK. The only thing that I would like to say here, is that from what I know of the *reductio ad absurdum* argument, which has been mentioned and which I think Mr. Brown has given in the *Nature* article to which I referred yesterday, it is not a sound argument against PK. I think it derives from a logical difficulty, a verbal difficulty, which has as its basis the assumption that PK and ESP are absolute phenomena of some sort, and have qualities which they may not in fact have. These things can exist as partially effective phenomena, and still both be real.

Perry: My argument was not based on a logical difficulty but on the fact that I would reject the evidence for PK on totally different grounds.

Parkes: Being border-line?

Perry: Yes.

McConnell: But you were glad to find that the evidence was inadequate; because otherwise you feared you would invalidate the evidence for ESP, if PK existed. This is the point which I say I don't believe follows at all, unless one treats this thing as a purely logical problem in which one assumes absolute qualities for both of these phenomena. I think that one proceeds in science by a series of successive approximations, and that one can have a little bit of PK, and a little ESP, and not assume that PK will interfere with every ESP experiment so as to completely destroy the effectiveness of statistical argument.

Wassermann: If I am not mistaken, an article has just been published giving a very significant series of results. I am not an expert on PK but the author established something very similar to Dr. Soal, namely a differential response which was highly significant. When he intended a low target, he obtained a corresponding hit; when he intended a high target, he obtained a high hit. Now this shows something remarkably like Dr. Soal's work and suggests for the first time that one has here a very genuine effect dependent on human intentions, intentions of the subject, and intentions, I dare say, have nothing to do with statistical artifacts.

A more serious point, Mr. Brown, has rather surprised me. I feel it is rather sad, for I had already taken up this issue a year ago at Oxford, in a paper which Mr. Brown has seen and which is coming out in the *British Journal of Philosophy of Science* in the August issue. It concerns the question of control, which Mr. Brown mentioned. Mr. Brown has brought it up again and again, and I thought I had sufficiently answered it. He seems to be at pains to point out that in Richmond's experiments and certain other experiments, there was nothing we could call control experiments, because both of them showed something positive. In other words, one only took things as evidence for the statistical model, if there were no results at all.

What matters, of course, is that one obtains a differential response. Scientists are not really only interested in the magnitude of absolute differences. Take, for instance, a person measuring the pressure-volume curve at different temperatures. He has a whole series of curves for different temperatures. What he is interested in is, if he changes the temperature, do the curves change persistently? Now, much the same happens here. In Richmond's experiments, there were persistent scores when he willed the *Paramecia* to go on the target, they were positive; and when he did not will them to do so, they were persistently negative. In other words, you have a differential response. Now, such a differential response was persistent throughout the whole experiment, and I think this is very significant. One does not require a zero result in the experiment.

Again, for instance, the argument I have put forward in my paper is the question of people smoking; if a person smokes a lot, it has been suggested that he may develop lung cancer. But this does not mean that people who do not smoke could not develop lung cancer from the same causes. You could not say that they have never been in touch with smoke; they may have been in cinemas which are full of smoke and you can never be sure as to what precisely happened. It is extremely difficult in any scientific experiment to be sure that a particular effect, which you are measuring, is not present. That is the point I wish to make.

Pobers: I wonder whether Dr. Wassermann's principle of restricted selectivity in the bonded fields would explain, for instance, the fact that telepathic communications are so frequently observed among people belonging to the same family or to a closed society, a tribe or a social unit? Dr. Wassermann's theory would be very close to the Jungian hypothesis of telepathy, as an archaic means of communication inside a closed community.

L.-Davies: May I make one specific point with regard to Mr. Brown's paper? I confess that I did not expect to understand very much of Mr. Brown, and I did not expect to agree with anything, whether I understood it or not! He was so lucid, however, that I think I do understand nearly everything he had to say. There was one thing that he said which was admirably summed up in even more colloquial language by our Chairman. It was, that if you have a good result, you know it; and if you have a bad result, you forget it.

Now, with regard to the whole of this discussion of statistics and ESP, I feel that one of the points that has not been sufficiently emphasized, is that those who have done ESP experiments are very often impressed by, what shall I say, the 'fine structure' of the results, which may not come out in the overall statistical evaluation. For example, you may have a result of guessing on 25 cards, showing no particular importance statistically, yet within that guessing there may be an incident, an episode, which it is very hard to explain in terms of mere chance. I should like to give an example of what sometimes happens. You have a subject sitting at a table. In front of her (it is usually a her), there are the five symbols, the five cards. She is looking at those cards. A pack of 25 cards is placed between her and the agent; in this particular case that I am describing, each is covered with a heavy card-index card, and she has never seen what card is under what cover. And in this case, moreover, the agent has not seen the cards. She begins guessing. Of the first ten cards, she gets one right, and three of these ten she puts against the symbol "square". Though neither she nor the agent knows as yet, they are all wrong. Cards number eleven, twelve, thirteen and fourteen she puts one after the other all on "square", and then finishes the pack. When the cards are examined by the agent he finds that she has six right in all, of which four are the four consecutive "squares". Now the overall score of six correct guesses is not in any way impressive, but within the guessing there is the very remarkable fact that she guessed all four cards right when there were four cards running of the same symbol. I don't know how often there is a sequence of four with properly randomized cards, but I can only say that with carefully shuffled cards, it does not happen very often—it has only happened on one occasion in my experience. You have your four cards running. The normal person, having already guessed three, and not knowing that they are wrong, mind you, on one symbol, is exceedingly unlikely to guess four more on that symbol in any case; they are even more unlikely to guess four more running, and if they do, it is surely very unlikely indeed that the result will be right.

I don't know how you would evaluate that episode statistically, but the point that I want to make is, that when you count up her results using ordinary statistical methods, she has got six cards right, which proves nothing at all. And you may never hear, when you look at the results afterwards, of this extremely remarkable fact that she has guessed four cards running on the right suit. Incidents such as that, are quite common. I don't say the same incident, but if you run through a large number of scores of a subject who is really showing ESP, you will find a number of curious incidents of one kind or another. The people who have experimented know of the existence of those incidents, and the people who merely read the reports do not know of them. They form their judgement from the overall statistical evaluation, and perhaps that is one reason why so few people believe in ESP until they have experienced it. But having once seen it, one has that unpleasant and very unscientific thing, a change of heart or a sudden conversion. Your new certainty is largely due to your always coming across little episodes like that, which are lost in the statistical evaluation.

Soal: I admit that there are points of fine structure, but I am not particularly impressed by that example, because after all, the chance of getting 5 running in a single block of 5 is only 5^4, that is 1 in 625, and when you are doing thousands of trials you should surely come across it occasionally.

McConnell: But, Dr. Soal, two of the features here are of particular interest. One, this occurred in a case where there were already several guesses on the square, so that it was rather unusual that the subject should have proceeded to make more responses on the square; and also, this occurred in the unusual case where there was a sequence of four correct guesses. There was the unusual aspect of the response as well as the unusual aspect of the cards. For several reasons one cannot assess this mathematically, but surely it is not as simple as you state it.

L.-Davies: That is exactly the point. I don't know what the likelihood of a sequence of four is, and you have the anomaly that the girl suddenly guesses those four right on the right symbol, after having already made three guesses on that symbol. And this when her symbol habit is to guess more or less five to each symbol. So that she has guessed seven on that symbol and she has guessed the right ones. And she has guessed the same symbol four times running, which very few people ever do; in fact, I don't ever remember her guessing four times running on the same symbol on any other occasion.

Parkes: What are the odds involved ? Can anybody tell us ?

Soal: That is quite a common thing to happen in card-guessing experiments. I have seen it over and over again with people who just get chance results. It is just a run of four successes.

Gaddum: To calculate the overall probability, you would have to take into account all other equally remarkable phenomena which might have occurred, and it is rather difficult.

Pratt: I think you will find more scepticism expressed in the writings of the people who have been doing the research than you will in the writings of the people who have been critical of it. That is as it should be. I was wondering, as I heard Mr. Brown talk, just what he would have the people who are working on the ESP problem do. It seems to me that his attitude sums up to this: since the investigators do not have perfect understanding of and perfect control over their phenomena, they should not be investigating them.

Brown: I have said no such thing.

Pratt: No, I am saying that that is my interpretation of the way you put it, because the examples you cited are cases in which things did not happen exactly as the experimenters expected at the start. That, to my mind, is simply an indication of the fact that the experimenters did not know all about their phenomena at that stage. I think we still do not know all about our phenomena.

I was wondering if Mr. Spencer Brown was going to get around to proposing a positive programme for investigators. We could just say: "Let us drop it all and forget that it happened." In that case, I should think the programme would call for government action to provide pensions for those of us who have reached the point where we cannot easily shift to another career (all of which is not intended to be taken too seriously).

In connection with Dr. Perry's remarks, it seems to me that he referred to various points of emphasis as "mystical." Then he represented the alternatives, if ESP occurs, as lying between "extraordinary perception" or the rejection of the materialistic philosophy. This point has already been touched on by Dr. McConnell, and there is little more that I can add to what he said, except to say that I think it is a little early to take our position so sharply as lying between two mutually exclusive alternatives. It seems to me that we may well be cautious about assuming that all of the shades of interpretation have been fully stated and understood. I suspect that there are developments yet ahead of us which will really surprise us.

West: Mr. Spencer Brown has said that the definition of parapsychology, or psychical research, is suicidal. I don't think this matters in the least. We have got a puzzling phenomenon, and we are trying to reduce it to some sort of order. It is true that the definition in the Society for Psychical Research's manifesto is suicidal, but that is in a sense constructive because ultimately one hopes these phenomena will be incorporated in the general work of psychology or physiology or some other branch of science, in which case, the Society would have fulfilled its function.

On the question of controlling experiments, I am sorry to go back to the question of PK, which we are not really discussing, but I think it is important to note that, in stating that one had obtained apparently significant results in control experiments, Mr. Spencer Brown had to turn to PK research. Now, I think that one of the main reasons why people are sceptical of PK research is that certain control series have produced statistically significant results. I don't think the same can be said of controls in ESP research, such as the cross-check controls described by Dr. Soal. That is a very important distinction to keep in mind.

A last point, I just want to pick up something that Dr. Perry said when he was speaking about marginal statistical significance. One of the reasons why he didn't believe in ESP was the possibility of recording errors, that is, that if only one mistake in fifteen records was made, it would account for the significance of the overall result. But I don't think that is true when the recording is made independently, as it was in Dr. Soal's experiment, because one has to assume a consistent tendency in the error, correlating with the targets. Such a correlation could only come about by ESP, or by a defect in the experimental technique whereby the recorder had knowledge of the targets. But perhaps I have misunderstood what Dr. Perry said.

Perry: I gave the recording error as one possible way in which a small effect could be produced. I was not trying to indicate that I thought it was the only way. I think that anyone who has worked in biology knows that errors of methodology or of recording can often be biased without there being any apparent reason for such bias. If, in a purely physiological experiment, there were a reflex that activated the muscles of my fingers, we could make an hypothesis that there was an equal chance for each finger to move. If I record 25 trials of the reflex and 5 times my thumb moves and 5 times each of my fingers moves, then I assume that my hypothesis is right. If, on the other hand, my thumb moved 18 times out of 25, I would be convinced on purely biological grounds that that was a more likely event than was movement of any other finger and I would not repeat the experiment more than once. On the other hand, if my thumb moved 6 times instead of 5, over a limited number—say 10 or 20 runs—I do not think I would be very convinced. I would be more inclined to suspect the apparatus or the arithmetic.

Soal: Regarding this question of recording errors: if you have the subject's own record of his guesses, and there is no question of somebody else writing them down and making mistakes, there is no question about that record, you have got it. If you make records of the target symbols before the experiment, you have got that. Therefore, the only errors that can be made are in comparing the two. Now, in the Shackleton experiment, Mrs. Goldney and I compared and counted up our hits. After the entire experiment was done, that is after 11,000 guesses, we sent our records to different people, for example, different members of the Society for Psychical Research, who made independent comparisons, and we found altogether 12 errors in 11,000 guesses. Not one of those, however, was in the particular kind of thing we were interested in, i.e. the plus one displacement score. Now, I think those errors are very few. Dr. Gardner Murphy also made a similar comparison of errors, and he found recording errors at the rate of 1 error in 1000, or something like that.

Parkes: I don't think Dr. Perry was suggesting that recording errors had often happened. He was instancing a possible way in which a small error could apparently have magnified your effect.

Soal: With regard to the question of ESP being a psychical phenomenon, I mean, ESP contradicting materialistic philosophy, I think that is a question which will elucidate itself in the long run, for philosophy changes. For instance, we may say that ESP is due to some unknown form of radiation, but do we know exactly what is meant by radiation ? Is it anything that we can define? The latest theory is, as far as I can understand it, that electro-magnetic waves are just waves of probability. Are they really physical things at all, or are they more like mental concepts ? You find all these difficulties, I think, when you go into modern physics. What we call 'physical' things may be essentially of the nature of mental concepts. I should welcome a physical theory of ESP, but I should want a theory of not exactly the kind that Dr. Wassermann has produced. It may be an excellent theory in its way, but what I want is some simple theory that would enable us to predict future results and tell us that, if we do a certain experiment, we ought to expect so-and-so.

Brown: I have been saving up one or two things! First of all, I should apologize to Dr. Soal for not mentioning how atypical his work was. This is perhaps unfortunate. If more of us could get results like Dr. Soal, there would be no difficulty at all in accepting a communication hypothesis.

Next I come to Dr. Pratt's gross but good-humoured misrepresentation of what I have been saying. At least I hope I never implied that we look at all these experiments and say that there are not really any results. Of course there are results, and of course they are interesting. The only thing I have said is that I am not sure that all of them, or even most of them, are evidence of telepathy and what not. I have not tried to explain the results away. I have merely tried to explain them. If parapsychology is really a science, it will come to no harm by honest attempts to explain the phenomena it studies.

My quarrel with most parapsychologists is over this lack of imagination. They always assume that what they are looking for is communication and design their experiments accordingly. I think that is why the experiments have been so unfruitful. If we always design experiments to look for one thing, and always get in them results which demonstrate something else, we shall never find out much more about the something else which they demonstrate. This sort of thing might well be in evidence in the difference in scoring between card-guessing experiments and dice experiments. For instance, it is well known that card-guessing experiments, when they have worked, have given bigger deviations than dice-throwing experiments. Now this might be due to the fact that shuffling cards is a more rigidly analysible transformation procedure than throwing dice. If I have a pack of cards and shuffle it in any normal way, there are millions of times fewer orders in which it could be after you had shuffled it, than in which it could be after a purely "random" operation had taken place. With a normal shuffling procedure, we cannot, for example, produce a pack of cards which is in the same order as it was when we started. That shows that our shuffling procedure is an analysible transformation procedure. Suppose that the guessing transformation of a subject happened to be similar to the shuffling transformation of the cards. Then if the subject started off well, he might build up a quite significant score before his guessing got out of step with the shuffle. Now, this sort of result would be disturbed by anything like telling the subject he was doing well, which would throw him off his balance and probably change his guessing transformation. And this, of course, does happen in the psychical research situation. If you tell the subject he is doing well, or disturb the experiment in any way, high scoring often stops.

Wassermann has taken me up again on the question of controls and says that all we are looking for is differential response. He mentioned the smoking and cancer correlations, and said that the Richmond *Paramecium* results were just as valid because they contained a differential response. Now, the difference between the Richmond experiment and the smoking and cancer observations is that the Richmond experiment is unique, whereas the smoking and cancer observations have been repeated. The latter possess, therefore, an inductive validity which the former lack.

Finally, Mr. Langdon-Davies referred to the occurrences in card guessing, where, although we do not get statistically significant results in general, we find very peculiar things happening somewhere in the middle of the experiment. Well, of course, all of us who have done card-guessing experiments are familiar with this; and we have all at one time or another been impressed by it. But this case is exactly similar to the spontaneous case. It is something which we cannot assess statistically.

PSYCHICAL PHENOMENA AMONG PRIMITIVE PEOPLES

M. POBERS

Dept. of Psychological Research, Rijks University, Utrecht

THE myth of the good savage played an important part in the history of European and American Literature. In psychical research, the "myth of the psychic savage" inspired an impressive number of writers. The belief that primitive men possess a profound knowledge of nature and its secrets, denied to members of a civilized society goes back to the earliest stages of our thinking. Pliny and Seneca rejected certain magical beliefs and practices, but did not doubt that natural forces were of a divine character and that men living in direct and constant contact with nature could acquire superhuman powers. Reports of psychical phenomena in unknown Africa or Asia have always been popular: there is little difference between Pliny discussing "dematerialization phenomena" in Persia and the recent writings of W. Searbrook or Ernest Bozzano (Pliny being, of course, the most critical of the three).

A survey of literature dealing with psychical phenomena among primitive peoples is a diverting but disappointing experience. Most of the "eye witness reports" omit to mention names of places and dates. Most of the travel diaries offer second-hand reports, attributed to other explorers or to "reputable sources". The best material is usually found in the papers by missionaries, medical officers or ethnologists who are not interested in psychical research, ignore its problems and methods and, very often, are hostile to its possible implications. There is, for instance, an excellent description of mediumistic séances in the Kasai region of Belgian Congo, in a report published by the Royal Colonial Institute of

Belgium (Fourche and Morlighem, 1939); its authors, two medical officers, are interested in the rôle assigned to the dead in a Kasai community, but are not in the least inclined to discuss the authenticity of the phenomena they observed. The problem is dismissed in one sentence: the effects were similar to those observed at spiritualistic séances in Europe.

The same attitude is noted in Dorsainvil's (1931, 1937) excellent studies of the Voodoo, in Eliade's (1951) outstanding study of archaic techniques of ecstasy, etc. There are a few exceptions, such as Mr. R. Rose's observations of Australian Aborigenes, reported in the *Journal of Parapsychology* or Laubscher's (1937) study of South African pagan diviners and witch-doctors.

It is not easy, dealing with the "myth of the psychic savage" to separate *Dichtung* from *Wahrheit*.

In his book *"Psychic Phenomena in Jamaica"* Williams (1934) described several cases of precognition witnessed in Jamaica before the earthquake of January 14th, 1907.

Waiting for a train for Kingston, he saw a young mulatto girl who "between convulsive sobs kept repeating: something dreadful is going to happen. . . . Half an hour later the ground began to tremble."

Many hours before the earthquake occurred, a number of people heard about a "weird prophet who . . . had passed about the city streets . . . sounding a cry of warning." The author did not see the prophet himself, but "made a point to inquire carefully" before confirming the story.

On January 13, 1921, the London *Times* mentioned the weird prophet:

"a man wearing a red mantle" . . . who "in the forenoon of January 14th, 1907, made his appearance in Kingston warning the people that before evening Kingston would be destroyed.

It is interesting to note that Father Williams, in 1907, did not describe the prophet or quote his exact words ("a cry of warning"), but fourteen years later the *Times* correspondent adds colour to the story ("the red mantle") and makes the prophecy much more specific.

I happened to be in Jamaica in August, 1951, when the worst hurricane in the island's history devastated its South Coast. A number of exciting stories of precognition were circulated; a few were published in the *Daily Gleaner*, Kingston's leading newspaper. There was, among others, the story of a "woman in white" who was seen in the streets of Kingston "warning the people of their day of punishment". With the help of a young reporter, I easily established that the prophetess in white was seen for the first time on August 22nd, five days after the disaster. There were twelve other cases of precognition: people warning their neighbours, mothers refusing to send their children to school, etc. In ten cases "psychical hunches" occurred before the hurricane but after the first broadcast warning by Miami Hurricane Service. In one case a semi-professional diviner did warn his client of "distress and disease about the 16th of the month"—(the hurricane struck on the 17th).

The fact that a prophetess in white was five days late in 1951 does not prove that her confrère in red missed the deadline in 1907. But one is permitted to be doubtful.

However, all my impressions and observations in Jamaica during the fateful month of August, 1951, were not negative. During the first thirty-six hours following the diaster, people were deprived of all the usual means of communication: no radio, no telephones, no newspapers. Many villages were completely isolated, all rail-road, bus and car travel being suspended. At the same time, one felt and knew that news was circulating from family to family, that in some mysterious and "natural" way communications were established. I cannot produce any valid evidence of telepathic communications between the families dispersed by the disaster. No tests or experiments of any kind could be attempted. All I can say is that a very peculiar psychological "climate" was felt by every member of the community, suggesting a form of telepathic communications.

One of the reports received mentioned a mother who appealed to a cotton tree to convey a message to her children, ten miles away: it was alleged that the children did exactly what their mother—via the cotton tree—told them to do. There was, of course, no means of verifying the story. When I tried to question the poor woman why and how she expected the tree to "contact" her children, she said: "Rich people have telephones. I am poor. I have no telephone. I have to try it that way" . . . It does not make the story more credible. But it helps to understand the meaning of the "myth of the psychic savage'', and why some of the less civilized people themselves believe in their psychic powers and in paranormal occurrences.

During my two trips to Haiti in 1952 and 1953 I collected many cases of alleged telepathic communications. No serious verification was possible, the witnesses either refusing to answer, or being too talkative and manifestly unreliable. The significant feature of these reports was the conditions in which the alleged telepathic communications were supposed to have taken place. There were invariably *practical means* to solve critical or conflictual situations, mostly between the members of the same family. One group of cases frequently discussed in Haiti deserves, in my opinion, a careful investigagation: the alleged telephathic contacts between identical twins. The "Marassa" are supposed to possess a wide range of psychical faculties.

To conclude my remarks on Jamaica, I have to mention two cases of "paranormal healers". I do not know whether the prayers and incantations of an old peasant woman "Mother Penny" (a penny being her usual fee) did help her patients, but some of her attempts at "distant diagnosis" were quite impressive. The second healer was a medium, a former school teacher, working in Kingston in co-operation with an M.D. I was told that some of her experiments in "clairvoyant diagnosis" have been submitted to Duke Laboratory for further investigation. The competent investigators at Durham may have reached a different conclusion, but my own observations lead me to believe that the subject had a very extraordinary sensitivity to auditory and olfactory stimuli, so extraordinary that they could be easily mistaken for psychic faculties. Similar cases were described by Villey (1954) in his brilliant essay on the psychology of the blind, by Eller (1941) in his study of body odours, and by Bienfang (1947) who even suggests that certain diseases possess specific olfactory entities.

Some of the observations and experiments described by Dr. Laubscher, a Cape Town psychiatrist, deserve a special mention. His description of faculties and techniques of South African witch-doctors and diviners is exceptionally interesting. He also conducted a number of simple tests, with a diviner Salomon Baba and with a young girl, a gifted hypnotic subject. Let me summarize two of his experiments.

1. The diviner S. B. lives 60 miles from Cape Town. Before visiting him, Dr. L. bought a small purse, wrapped it in brown paper and buried it in the ground. Over the spot he placed a flat brown stone, and on the top a grey stone. From the moment Dr. L. bought the purse, it was not seen by anyone, nor had anyone knowledge of the nature of the article to be used for the test. No one saw Dr. L. burying the purse. Leaving the spot, Dr. L. travelled at an average speed of 35 miles per hour: S. B. cannot be informed by runners before Dr. L's arrival. Shortly after Dr. L's arrival, during a séance-dance, S. B. described in minute detail the article, the spot where it was buried, the wrapping paper, the colour and size of the stones. Dr. L. concluded that the diviner "read his mind telepathically".

2. The subject was a young girl who had "a supernormal ability of time appreciation". Sixty experiments were made over a period of five years. All clocks and watches were removed from the room. The subject was hypnotized behind a screen on a couch. At the other end of the room were two

witnesses who recorded the responses. The time periods the subject was asked by Dr. L. to estimate ranged from thirty seconds to twenty-five minutes, and she was never more than one minute out. In a thirty second period, she was two seconds out. Dr. L. does not conclude that the faculty of time appreciation is of the same nature as telepathy or clairvoyance. It is, in his opinion, a psychic ability for which no adequate explanation can be offered.

In reference to the first experiment, it is obvious that despite all the precautions devised by Dr. Laubscher, he could not match the rigorous laboratory conditions described by Dr. Soal. But can rigorous laboratory conditions be applied in an investigation of psychical faculties of primitive peoples? Is it possible or even desirable to introduce a definite pattern of experiments in testing a group of subjects who shall never accept apparently meaningless and repetitive techniques. There have been a few attempts of cards and dice experiments in Haiti, in French Equatorial Africa, etc. They were bound to fail. Salomon Baba would be interested in finding a lost cow, and he can be made to be interested in finding a hidden object. He is certainly allergic to 500 or 5000 sittings of card guessing. Many sensitives in our civilized society are in this respect not very different from the South African pagan "Igkira".

Dr. Laubscher's experiment in time appreciation is another "borderline case", where an unusual development of known senses comes very close to extrasensory perception. It may not be irrelevant to mention here a curious effect of "time distortion" I observed in Haiti during night-long voodoo ceremonies. After many hours of listening to drums and other percussion instruments, three observers—my wife, a friend and I—noticed the same effect of increasing discrepancy between seeming duration of time and clock time, similar to the effects described by Cooper and Ericson (1954) in their metronome experiment in hypnosis. These phenomena of time appreciation and time distortion should be carefully investigated, both in laboratory conditions and among the primitives.

I cannot discuss here at any length mental and physiological techniques in shamanism. Some of the characteristic problems of psychical research should be re-discovered and re-examined in their original and authentic psycho-physiological context. In shamanistic practices, psychic faculties appear both as spontaneous abilities and as a part of inherited or acquired traditions and skills. Two groups of phenomena seem to me particularly interesting: (1). G. Bogoraz mentions the "double or distant voice technique" of the Chukchee Shamans and states that it seems different from any known form of ventriloquism. (2.) Several works discuss shamanistic insensitivity to heat and fire (Mikhailovski, 1899; Gusinde 1947; Stevenson, 1901–1902; de Martino, 1948, Eliade, 1951) and describe techniques of changes in body temperature and special treatment of the skin which are part of a shar an's initiation and early training. Psychical researchers have been discussing at great length fire-walking in the Fiji Islands and in India, without reaching any definite conclusions.

I have mentioned before the difficulties and limitations of experimental work among primitive peoples. It is important to note that even objective observation can be difficult and often very disappointing. It is admitted that in laboratory conditions the negative attitude of the experimenter can account for negative findings. The same is true in every attempt to observe psychical occurrences among primitive peoples. The danger of becoming "emotionally involved" in the phenomena observed is, however, infinitely greater. I do not believe that "collective hallucinations" or "mass suggestion" can explain away some of the occurrences observed during ritual ceremonies in Haiti or in Africa. But there is little doubt that drums and heavy fumes can result in hallucinations. Only recently, a reliable observer described to me "a distinct impression that a priestess during a dance, resolved herself into a dark, amorphous mass". The same "dematerialization" effect was described by several participants attending Alistair Crawley's incantational ceremonies. In December, 1953, I witnessed an impressive case of abnormal agility:—a possessed woman jumped 5–6 feet high remaining for some time suspended to a beam. The same phenomenon observed from a slightly different angle could have been described as levitation. Finally, even the most experienced investigator can be surprised by the elaborate and inventive technique of simulation and fraud devised by most of the priests, diviners and witch-doctors. "In the west," a native philosopher explained to me, "money leads to power: here power leads to money. A diviner cannot afford in his practice 'hits and misses'. Even if his powers are genuine, he must be a master of simulation and fraud. This is his unemployment insurance. . . ."

In concluding, I would like to stress once more a few essential points:

1. Further investigations of telepathic communications among primitive peoples can lead to very significant findings, provided the investigator remembers that for this group of subjects telepathy cannot be a "game of guessing"; it remains an archaic means of communication in critical and conflictual situations.

2. We need both laboratory experiments and on-the-spot observations of a wide range of "borderline phenomena", and of cases suggesting unusual development of known senses, possibly related to extrasensory perception.

3. We need a serious and systematic study of psycho-physiological techniques in shamanistic practices.

4. There are still a few regions in Africa, South America, Asia, and the West Indies where useful work can be done. But the penetration of technological progress is faster than we think. In a few years time there may be very little left of the phenomena and faculties we are discussing. For the time being, in view of the scarcity of gifted subjects in Europe and in America, investigations in underdeveloped countries offer unusually interesting possibilities.

REFERENCES

BIENFANG, R. (1947). "The subtle sense." University of Oklahoma Press.

BOGORAZ, G., see ELIADE (1951).

COOPER, L. F., and ERICSON, M. H. (1954). "Time distortion in hypnosis." Baltimore: Williams & Wilkins.

DORSAINVIL, J. C. (1931). "Vodou et Névrose." Port-au-Prince: La Presse.

DORSAINVIL, J. C. (1937). "Psychologie haitienne. Vodou et magie." Port-au-Prince: La Presse.

ELIADE, M. (1951). "Le Chamanisme." Paris: Payot.

ELLER, J. J. (1941). *Med. Rec., N.Y.*, 154, 167

FOURCHE, J. A. T., and MORLIGHEM, H. (1939). "Les communications des indigènes du Kasai avec les âmes des morts." Institut Royal Colonial Belge, 9, No. 2.

GUSINDE, M. (1947). *Revue Ciba*, No. 60, p. 2159.

LAUBSCHER, B. J. F. (1937). "Sex, Custom and Psychopathology. A study of South African pagan natives." London: Routledge.

LOOMIS, E. A. (1951). *Personality*, 1, 283.

MARTINO, E. DE (1948). "Il mondo magico." Turin.

MIKHAILOVSKI, V. M. (1899). *J. R. anthrop. Inst.*, 24, 62, 126.

PLINII SECUNDI. Naturalis historiae, XXXVII, 60. "Majorum impudentiae, etc." For SENECA, see THORNDIKE, L. (1905). The place of magic in the intellectual history of Europe." New York: Columbia University Press.

STEVENSON, M. C. (1901–1902). "The Zuni Indians." In 23rd Annual Report of the Bureau of American Ethnology, Washington.

VILLEY, P. (1954). "La suppléance des sens." Le monde des Aveugles, pp. 60–89. Paris: Corti.

WILLIAMS, J. J. (1934). "Psychic Phenomena in Jamaica." New York: Dial Press.

EXTRASENSORY PERCEPTION AMONG PEASANT EUROPEAN POPULATIONS

J. Langdon-Davies

San Felui de Guixols, Spain

Research into ESP is handicapped today by lack of subjects showing any paranormal ability under laboratory conditions. All Dr. S. G. Soal's efforts to find other subjects comparable in performance to Basil Shackleton and Mrs. Stewart have been unsuccessful; and it is believed that at this moment neither in England nor in the U.S.A. is there anyone consistently scoring at their level of statistical significance in any form of card guessing. The evidence which those who are convinced of the reality of some sort of ESP can present to those who are sceptical is sparse. The best may be unimpeachable, but there is not enough of it. The crying need is for more human guinea pigs.

Is the phenomenon of ESP, supposing it to exist, of rare occurrence? Or are the methods used to elicit it wrong? Or is the sample of the human population in which it is usually sought unsuitable? It is hoped that the experience to be described in this paper may throw light on the problem.

On November 27th, 1954, Dr. E. J. Dingwall and I were working together in my study at the bottom of my Spanish garden. My wife (P.L.-D.) came in and asked if I had a pack of Zener cards handy, as she thought it might be interesting to give a trial to A., our cook, and her sister E., who had both been given a month's notice which was about to expire. Her reason for wanting to experiment was the same as our reason for dispensing with their services, namely, that we felt A. to be psychologically unstable and her influence on her sister E. bad. The third member of our staff, M., was quite another

111

story. Aged 15¾ she was healthy, cheerful, reliable, and, incidentally, very fond of us.

The cards were found and ten minutes later P. L.-D. returned to say that A. had guessed sixteen cards correctly out of twenty-five, and that E. and M. had then asked to try, and had made sixteen and fifteen correct guesses out of twenty-five respectively. E. J. D. and I hurried to the kitchen.

A series of runs were made under the eyes of the three of us until E.J.D. left on the 29th, and were continued for the remaining period of A. and E.'s residence, by P. L.-D. and myself. In every case, except a few runs made for control purposes, both subject and agent were Spanish.

The results are recorded in Table I.

Table I

Agent	Subject	No. of runs	Correct	Expected	Average
A.	E.	16	185	80	11·5
A.	M.	7	113	35	16·1
E.	M.	16	159	80	9·9
E.	A.	14	127	70	9·0
M.	E.	14	151	70	10·8
M.	A.	9	120	45	13·3
J.L.-D.	M.	21	196	105	9·3
J.L.-D.	A.	6	27	30	4·5
P.L.-D.	M.	21	157	105	7·5
P.L.-D.	E.	4	24	20	6·0
P.L.-D.	A.	3	11	15	3·7
Spanish only					
	A.	23	247	115	10·7
	E.	30	336	150	11·2
	M.	23	272	115	11·8

From this table it will be seen that for tests when both agent and subject were Spanish:

1. The principal subject of P. L.-D.'s original interest, A., completed 575 guesses with an average of 10·7 correct guesses per run and a critical ratio of 14.

2. E. and M. both exceeded this result by a small margin and had critical ratios of 14–15.

3. Three subjects, the only ones tested, made between them 1,900 guesses with correct guesses in 855 cases, an average of over 11 per pack.

4. The critical ratio for such a result is over 27, giving astronomical odds against chance.

This result is unique in the history of ESP. Not only has the high average seldom been exceeded—even for short periods during a long series—but never have three people consecutively tested all manifested a high degree of ESP. It is noteworthy, too, that the few trials in which P. L.-D. or J. L.-D. acted as agent gave very different results. Here A. in 9 runs, i.e. 225 guesses, scored 7 less than expectation, while the 100 guesses of E. produced an average of only 6. On the other hand, M., whose relations with us were excellent, maintained an average of 8·4, while in her 525 guesses with J. L.-D. as agent the average was 9·3, a c.r. of nearly 10. The results taken in detail gave an accurate picture of the stresses and forces existing between each pair of individuals.

The most remarkable result was the short series with A. as agent and M. as subject, where the score of correct guesses was: 15, 18, 12, 22, 14, 14, 18—giving a c.r. of nearly 13.

It must be emphasized that these preliminary results were made with bare cards, handled by the subjects; on the other hand, E. J. D., J. L.-D. and P. L.-D. all watched with the utmost care for signs of normal sensory leakages and were unable to detect any. Moreover, these were unsophisticated peasant girls scarcely able to understand what they were doing and not likely to be even potentially frauds or conjurors. We were completely unprepared for experimenting and had nothing but two Zener packs to work with, otherwise we would have used rigorous conditions from the beginning. Subsequent statistical analysis, however, does not suggest any serious normal sensory leakage.

After the departure of A. and E., M. became the subject of a large number of tests. The technique used was card matching. After a few trials every card was enclosed in an opaque, doubled, index card; M. never saw what card was in any particular cover, except on the rarest occasions when she might be shown two or three good results to encourage her, and when this happened she did not see the exterior of the covers in any way which might enable her to identify any cover with any card.

Moreover, the covers were removed and shuffled from time to time.

In these conditions the following results were obtained:

Guesses	Expected	Correct	Excess of correct guesses
20,250	4,050	5,848	1,798

This gives a critical ratio of somewhat over 30, with, of course, astronomical odds against chance.

It is obvious that the simple conditions of experiment, due to our unpreparedness for any such discovery, are open to criticism. The most possible source of leakage would be glances or other indications from the agent on seeing the cards. It is important therefore to note that for a substantial series of guesses, 2,000 in all, two methods were alternated. In one (described as T for telepathy) the agent looked at each card, in the other (described as C for clairvoyance) the cards, each covered with an opaque cover, were placed on the table and pushed or moved into place by the subject without the agent having seen them. Clearly the latter method eliminated the possibility of sensory leakages from the agent to the subject. Table II shows the comparison between the two sets of results.

In short, there was no significant difference between the scoring whether the agent saw the cards or not, the results being slightly better if the agent did *not* see the cards.

It is not intended in this brief paper to describe in detail precautions taken to avoid sensory and other normal leakages, but it may be noted that Dr. Soal and Mr. Bateman agreed that, as far as the experiments which they saw were concerned, the method of concealing the cards and handling them ruled

Table II

C runs				T runs		
80				90		
101				96		
110				69		
53				55		
54						
84						
482				310		

	Guesses	Correct	Expectation	Excess	Average correct	c.r.
C runs	1200	482	240	242	10·0	17·7
T runs	800	310	160	150	9·9	13·3

out the possibility of the subject seeing either back or face of the cards.

It will be noted that some of the results in Table II are quite extraordinary, notably the two consecutive sets of 200 guesses in which 110 and 101 correct guesses were scored. The details of these 16 runs are as follows: 8, 12, 16, 15, 11, 9, 17, 13, 14, 15, 14, 16, 16, 11, 13, 11. These were all guessed without the agent seeing the cards and with each card securely hidden back and front by an opaque cover folded with the fold towards the subject. Even these results were once exceeded for a run of 8, when the correct guesses were: 13, 13, 16, 13, 13, 18, 12, 13. In this case each card was seen by the agent, but otherwise the technical details were the same.

During the course of the experiments, minor changes of technique were introduced—for example, opaque envelope corners were substituted for index cards. In each case the scores went down to near chance and rose again according to a very uniform pattern. Thus a change of covers was made on two occasions. On the first, the ensuing 1,400 guesses produced 296 correct guesses, and on the second 290—purely chance results. All these guesses have of course been included in the grand total above.

After some 20,000 guesses, the subject showed unmistakeable signs of becoming tired and bored. The familiar decline set in. It was decided to terminate the experiment, but to wait, if possible, for the sake of morale, until there were signs of improvement. This took 88 runs to achieve, and though the c.r. for these was only 2·8 the last sets of 200 were once more satisfactory, and with 50, 59, 51 correct guesses for the last three sets of 200, M. was allowed to rest. Had this moment for stopping not been selected, previous experience suggests she would once more have reached even higher scores.

Through the interest of Dr. Dingwall and Mrs. Eileen Garrett it was arranged that Dr. Soal and Mr. Bateman should come to Spain in order to form some opinion on M.'s results. She had been at her home for two months while my wife and I were in England. On my return and before the arrival of Dr. Soal and Mr. Bateman, I carried out an experiment on the lines called T above, but with Dr. Soal's animal cards. M. began with purely chance results but gradually built up a significant though comparatively modest critical ratio. Dr. Soal and Mr. Bateman watched the final sets of this and agreed that the only possibility of sensory clues was that the agent unconsciously indicated the right key card after seeing each card to be guessed, although they agreed that there was no noticeable indication whatever that this occurred.

It was decided therefore to carry out a T experiment with Mr. Bateman as agent. P. L.-D. as scorer, and J. L.-D. and Dr. Soal out of the room. The agent was concealed from the subject by a screen, and the cards were covered in opaque covers. If the results were comparable with those of J. L.-D.'s last experiment, natural sensory leakages from an unconcealed agent might be considered as ruled out.

The experiment began, as in all previous experiments, with chance results, and gradually built up a significant critical ratio. This did not reach the heights of previous figures but was sufficient to convince Dr. Soal and Mr. Bateman that the phenomena observed in M. were due to ESP.

But perhaps the most valuable result of this experiment, in which sensory leakage was eliminated, was the added weight it afforded to the belief that sensory leakage was not responsible for earlier results.

Table III shows the remarkable similarity of results throughout between J. L. D.'s previous experiment where the agent was visible, and Mr. Bateman's experiment where the agent was invisible and therefore unable to transmit any sort of information by normal channels.

Table III

Number of runs	Correct (J.L.-D. expt.)	Correct (Bateman expt.)
10	53	60
20	114	112
30	165	176
40	223	225
50	279	281
60	342	339
70	409	396
80	454	449
90	518	512
100	564 (96)	549
140	798	
c.r. (final)	4·1	3·5
c.r. (combined)	5·5	
cross-check, expected	700	480
actual	699	461
Odds against chance	20,000–1	2,150–1
combined odds	26 million–1	

A cross-check of the J. L.-D. experiment with normal expectation of 700 correct guesses gave an actual number of 699 such guesses, and a cross-check of the Bateman experiment with expectation of 480 correct gave 461.

These figures are very strong evidence that whatever the explanation of the excess of correct guesses, it could not be normal sensory leakage, and if the entire series of figures can be regarded as reliable we have in M. a remarkable case of ESP.

But that does not seem to me the most important finding. It must be remembered that M. was one of three girls, all of whom showed precisely the same very remarkable results. To discover one M. is important, but to find three in one kitchen is far more interesting. Indeed, the phenomenon is so singular that it is unlikely to be credited until some sort of repetition can be achieved. For my part there would seem to be justification for a number of working hypotheses upon which further research can be based, and I wish to put them before this meeting as my conclusions from my research into the ESP shown by the three Spanish girls.

1. The type of person most likely to exhibit ESP is the member of an unsophisticated social environment where the functioning of the laws of probability does not enter into everyday thought. A., E., and M. do not know they ought only to guess five cards right. They have not repressed, therefore, an extrasensory faculty which is not governed by such considerations and are able to give it free play.

This does not mean that the most promising subjects will have poor intelligences. On the contrary, M. is bright, but she has not been mechanized. She is prelogical, uneducated, but not unintelligent.

2. Not only must the social Gestalt be correct, but the Gestalt of the personnel of the experiment must be correct. Whatever ESP may be in itself, its exhibition is a function, not of the subject alone, but of the subject, the agent, and perhaps of the scorer and of the other persons present.

3. The successful exhibition of ESP is something that has to be nursed into existence. The mere testing of a person with two or three runs of 200 can tell us nothing at all about the chances of their being potential exhibitors of ESP. The creation of the right Gestalt is essential and this cannot be done by the routine examination of a large number of persons in the atmosphere of a laboratory. A significant warning of what may often have happened in previous examinations was afforded by a brief clairvoyant experiment with Dr. Soal, Mr. Bateman, J. L.-D. and P. L.-D. all present. This led to

completely negative results, as would be expected by anyone who believes that the right psychological environmental Gestalt is an essential factor in the successful exhibiting of ESP.

4. There are many unknown variables involved in an ESP experiment. Some of these are of a type which we associate with motor-automatisms. Any change of technique which throws one of these out of its natural rhythm may be fatal. This must be borne in mind when devising precautions against sensory leakage, etc. The rhythmic motion of a hand and arm may be essential to success in one subject, the rhythmic pointing of a pencil in another. Substitute one motion for the other and failure may result.

5. It is essential to start with rigorous conditions, since changes in the habits first acquired may be fatal. (This was a fault in the present experiment.) But the planning of rigorous methods must be flexible; for example, it must allow of the incorporation of motor-automatisms peculiar to each subject.

6. To fit every subject to a Procrustean bed of technical details designed solely to disarm hostile criticism may be to court an initial failure from which there will be no recovery. For example, the optimum relationship (emotional and spatial) between subject and agent may necessitate close proximity. It would then be foolish to place the agent in a distant room so as to rule out subconscious whispering. Rigorous conditions, yes; but attention to the psychological Gestalt is equally important.

A fuller report is in preparation. It will show many interesting details of the effect of daily and even hourly fluctuations of temper, temperament, fatigue, or anxiety on M.'s results. We can assume that the passing emotions of a rat have little to do with its ability to learn how to get through a maze. This is not so with the human experimental animal and ESP.

My wife and I propose to carry on further experiments with these hypotheses in mind.

DISCUSSION

Parkes: Some of us knew that Mr. Langdon-Davies had some new and very important material to put before this meeting and we have certainly not been disappointed. Maria is obviously going to have a high place in the literature of ESP, and I think we have been fortunate to be the first people to hear about her in any detail.

Dingwall: We have here two very important and very interesting papers and I shall start with Dr. Pobers's paper.

I suppose one of the reasons why I was asked to comment upon Dr. Pobers's paper is that at one time I was a general anthropologist and am now a rather highly specialized one. But as he broadly hinted, it is a very sore point in parapsychology that more has not been done. I remember when I was at University College, in the department of Sir Elliot Smith, that I did my best to persuade my chief to have an addition to the department dealing with magic and religion, which should deal with parapsychology, but although a number of projects were discussed I am sorry to say they all fell through. The result is that a great deal of work which might have been done amongst primitive peoples—we used to call them "food-gatherers"—cannot now be done because of cultural contact which rather destroys the atmosphere that once was there. Phenomena are still reported, as Dr. Pobers remarks, and it is curious that he should have chosen from Dr. Laubscher's book, the case of Salomon Baba, which is exactly the case I should have chosen to illustrate what might be done, and what should be done by skilled parapsychologists. Although I think that Dr. Laubscher was a rather naive and simple person, he did his best to ascertain whether the phenomena he saw were paranormal or not.

One aspect of any investigation of extrasensory perception and other phenomena in primitive peoples is that it may throw some light on the question as to whether ESP, if it is a genuine phenomenon at all, is a dying faculty or a nascent faculty. If it is beginning, we should expect, I suppose, to find it in animals, and that is where experimental work in animals, insects, and so on, is becoming more and more important. On the other hand, if it is dying, it would be very important to catch it while it is still there in so-called primitive peoples, and there are very few really primitive peoples left. I remember that in the old days we used to have a discussion as to whether *any* of these so-called savage peoples could be called primitive, for there were only a few peoples among whom agriculture, the use of the wheel, and so on, were unknown. I often used to meet a great many of our District Commissioners—they were Elliot Smith's old students—and they used to tell me about the things that used to happen to them and about the curious phenomena they encountered. But at the same time, when I suggested publication, they raised their hands—"Oh, we couldn't. We should be thought to share in the superstitions of the natives". So that I suspect that now that ESP is becoming more respectable, some of these people who have notes on it may be prevailed upon to publish some of their observations; maybe we shall then know a bit more.

Certainly Dr. Pobers was very wise in insisting on the great difficulties of investigation. This leads me to say a few words with regard to what Dr. West said yesterday, which I wanted to raise in the discussion, but there was such a mellow atmosphere that I thought I would leave it till today. He seemed to me to imply that it was extremely simple—I think he even used the term "childishly simple"—to devise fool-proof experiments. Surely, the whole history of the subject shows that that is quite untrue. I should have thought that it was *so* difficult to devise fool-proof experiments, that that is one of the main reasons why there are so few. When parapsychologists discuss ESP, we simply hear over and over again the names of Shackleton and Gloria Stewart, Gloria Stewart and Shackleton, because parapsychologists—they would be the first to admit it—can see so many flaws in other investigations. We know that during the early days of mesmeric and hypnotic phenomena, paranormal cognition of various kinds was quite a common event; there are whole books, like Ochorowicz's *Mental Suggestion*, dealing with suggestion at a distance, which quite clearly implies that telepathy was acting, and early hypnotic experiments were designed to show the occurrence of telepathy. Parapsychologists now admit that nearly all those experiments show sources of error. Yet even in 1954 and 1955, we are still having examples published of experiments which undoubtedly show sources of error, which, if it were so childishly simple to avoid, would surely be avoided. I am going to give later, I hope, some reason why that is so, a psychological reason, and it is of great interest because it implies what I call "passive complicity" on the part of the investigators.

Dr. Pobers described some of the events he saw in Haiti. He was extremely lucky. I never saw anything myself in Haiti of that kind. I made a great many efforts to hear about something or see something, either physical phenomena or mental phenomena, but I encountered nothing.

Perhaps I may divert your attention to one of the things that he said, although it does not relate to extrasensory perception, but to what he calls "paranormal agility". For some years now I have been very much interested in paranormal agility, because it is reported in possessed persons, not only in the West Indies but of course in Europe, and is also a feature of the phenomena of the Saints. In my recently published study of the sado-masochist, Mary Magdalene de' Pazzi, I pointed out that even in the accounts in the *Processes*, she was noted as having this abnormal agility, for on one occasion, it is said, she jumped some fifteen feet into the air and hung on to a cornice. Now, what Dr. Pobers said with regard to levitation is exceedingly important, as I think it illustrates that the accounts, which have been left of the phenomena of the Saints, are rather more valuable than they are supposed to be, because, even in the cases of the Saints in which abnormal agility is described, you will not find any mention of levitation. In fact in the case of Mary Magdalene de' Pazzi—who was really a most unpleasant person—I am quite sure that those drawing up the *Processes* would mention anything in her favour, so they had ample opportunity to suggest that she was levitated; yet there was, as far as I know, no suggestion whatever that there was any levitation. Similarly, in the case of St. Joseph of Copertino, the levitation is quite distinct. It has no relation whatever to this jumping, although some of you, who are acquainted with the popular *Lives of the Saints*, will remember that Baring-Gould, in his edition says that there is no doubt that the levitation of St. Joseph of Copertino was really a series of high jumps. Whatever it may have been, it was not simply high jumps, and I think there may have been something more than that. There may have been, of course, some paranormal faculty. But I must insist that this high jumping is quite distinct from, for example, the levitation of St. Teresa, who, when she felt she was going up, said to the nuns, "For Heaven's sake hold me down, I'm going up".

One thing I put in my notes which was in Dr. Pobers's paper but which he did not develop, I think on account of time, was what he said about the element of collective hallucination and suggestion. I am entirely in agreement with what he said. Take the influence of the drums, for example. Now, it is well known that Europeans working in Haiti do get into queer states. There is a good deal of literature about that. I think the last lady who did some investigation had to be escorted from the Island. The Chief of Police of the American Marines, when they were in occupation, was himself bewitched, and I had a long account of the astonishing sensations he experienced when he learnt that his image was being pierced by pins by an old lady down on the waterfront. Again there was a young Scandinavian, who carried out some investigations in Haiti, and he became so attracted by the drums that he began to jig and jig. No doubt Dr. Pobers knows the case. It is said that he was jigging and dancing for some five or six hours till he finally fell exhausted. Haiti is, I suppose, almost.the only place in the world where people interested in these things can still get a thrill. You find curious little images and made-up figures. I remember when I was staying there, someone put a curious image outside the villa where I was living in order to bewitch me, but, alas ! it had no effect. I had no feelings at all. I had no desire to dance; I had no desire even to jig. I was merely, I suppose, observing what was happening around me, and I was interested in the local gendarme, who heard there was a voodoo dance and came to suppress it, and was himself "taken", as they say; his eye-balls rolled up and he began to join in the dance himself.

This leads me on to a discussion of Mr. Langdon-Davies's paper. I was fortunate enough to be in Spain when these girls were first tested; and it was in those very early tests that we got the absolutely spectacular results. To suppose that these peasant girls were able to devise a system of elaborate fraud by which they were able to get these results, seems to me to be out of the question. I cannot believe that they had been preparing for some time; certainly they did not know that I was interested in parapsychology—I think that was out of the question—but it would have meant preparations on a considerable scale and a learning process and so on. The normal clues, when I was there, were certainly ruled out, although I did not see experiments in which the cards were covered. That was the reason why I was so anxious for Dr. Soal and Mr. Bateman to go out to carry on the investigations and to see how far the results could be obtained under conditions which would satisfy them.

Two things, I think, are of great importance to me. Mr. Langdon-Davies referred to what he calls "The Gestalt". Now, at one time, I was one of the most persistent critics of the theory that the surroundings of the experiment had a pronounced effect on the results, that if the surroundings were not made homely and parlour game-like, it was no good trying to get ESP. I thought that there was a grain of truth in it, and secretly I held the opinion that there was more than a grain. But the danger of permitting this sort of thing to gain ground, seemed to me to be great and a warning had to be given to people of what would be likely to happen, namely, that experiments in ESP would degenerate into parlour games in which we should never know at all what the conditions really were. And that is what some of the early and, indeed, later experiments in ESP undoubtedly were.

If I may, I will give you one example of the kind of thing that happens in parapsychology, where the conditions are not standardized. At one time I was engaged in an investigation into what was called spirit photography. The medium was a young man, who got extraordinary markings on plates. I think I had altogether some twenty-five or thirty sittings. Every move was standardized from the beginning. That is to say, everything was exactly the same: the number of plates in the boxes, the kind of box, its position under the darkroom light, who took it out of the darkroom, who handled it and when, and so on and so forth. Sitting after sitting took place, and every plate was blank. One day —I remember to this day what happened—I was developing the plates, and there I saw numbers of curious wavy lines occurring on one plate, a cloudy appearance as if waves of the sea were breaking. I thought to myself, "What is this? Have we at last got something? We will go on for another forty sittings now and see if we get anything more". Next morning, I looked at all my standardized sheets and I saw that on that particular occasion there was one variation. And that variation was that I thoughtlessly used a piece of corrugated cardboard to cover the plates. I remembered, of course, W. J. Russell's classic accounts of the effect of various substances on photographic plates and there was the solution. No more cardboard was used. The thing was standardized again. Nothing. Now, had that not been standardized, had I not been able to consult my records, I should have found that there was something which could not be explained, and probably wasted another two months in going on with the experiments.

Now in a Gestalt, in a situation in which everything is fluid, in which someone goes out of the room to put on potatoes and so on, it is extremely difficult to determine what is happening so that you can describe the experiment in terms which other people can read and gather the necessary information. What we want, and what we are getting gradually in parapsychology, is some form of standardization, of which Dr. Soal has given a classic example in his books, where all the facts are given.

The second thing I want to say with regard to Mr. Langdon-Davies's paper is something, I think, even more important, which struck me at the time. And that is that if we have here a test of genuine extrasensory perception occurring in three peasant girls in a kitchen in Spain, it looks very much as if we are nearing the possibility of the discovery of the kind of mental climate in which ESP may be expected to occur. And that, I think, would be a major discovery in parapsychology. Because here we are testing student after student, man after man, woman after woman, and getting nothing, and yet maybe we shall find in different parts of Europe, people like those three girls, in whom the faculty may not only be investigated but may be developed and may give us a great deal of light. If that is so, if this thing can be substantiated, then obviously the case of Maria and the two others must be followed up. If we are nearing that, then I think Mr. Langdon-Davies will have contributed to this conference what is possibly one of the most important discoveries in modern parapsychology.

Parkes: There is one question I would like to ask immediately. If you had 100 per cent success in your own kitchen, did you try any of your neighbours' kitchens for these sensitives?

L.-Davies: We have not had time to try any more than these three people.

Parkes: But you will do that, no doubt?

L.-Davies: Yes; there is only one very minor case that I can give you. There is a small boy who comes in to play with my son, I think he is aged seven, and I have had my eye on him as what might be called a embryo poltergeist child, the sort of child around whose head plates and everything will begin to roll at the age of puberty, perhaps. And it amused me to try him with cards. He took it extremely seriously, shook his head and said, "It will cost a great deal to divine these cards", and promptly guessed ten right. I let him have another run and he went down to five, and with a third to four, or five, I forget which. And that was the end of the experiment. Next Sunday, when he came in to play, I gave him the cards again. He guessed with equal seriousness and he guessed ten right. I let him do it once more and he went down to four. On the third Sunday, he came again and he guessed nine right. On that occasion I decided that his attention span gave out after one trial and left it at that. Now it is quite possible that if I go on trying this small boy with only one run per week, he will produce spectacular results. And I believe I am right in thinking that if I make that a condition of the experiment beforehand, it will be a perfectly legitimate experiment.

There is another man up the road on whom I am hoping to experiment. His particular paranormal success is, I am told, that he can guess the winning number of the great Spanish Christmas lottery. Unfortunately, he can only guess it at the moment the number is being pulled out of the machine by the choir-boy, which is too late for you to buy a ticket.

I mention these things simply to show that we live in an atmosphere of this kind of thing. There is, therefore, an unlimited field.

Soal: I first heard of this interesting case from Dr. Dingwall and he told me of the marvels he had seen, and he suggested that it would be important for somebody to go to Spain to see these results. But a fortnight or so later, I got a rather devastating letter from him saying, "Maria has collapsed and the phenomena have gone down to chance". However, a week or two later, I got another letter from him and apparently Maria was recovering to some extent. I saw Mr. Langdon-Davies who came to London and took part in some of my own experiments at Birkbeck College and I gave him some packs of cards to take home. He went back to Spain ten days perhaps before I did, and he carried out some experiments similar to what he had been doing; that is to say, there were five cards on the table, each card in one of the folders, with Mr. Davies fully in sight of the girl, and he got an average of about 5·5 or 5·6 hits per run. Mr. Bateman and I arrived in Spain Saturday, January 16, and I think we started experiments that evening or the next day. I had brought with me from England 400 envelopes, each of which contained a card, and these cards were randomized by means of Kendall and Smith's tables, and made up into packs of twenty-five, and we used the packs in the orders in which the numbers came from the table. We had no screen, but just sat at an ordinary table. Maria sat at one side and Mr. Bateman and I sat at the other side. She had five of the target cards face upwards in front of her. The envelopes were quite opaque I tried holding them up to the electric light and could not see any image of the card. She just pointed to the card with a pencil and I laid the card down opposite the indicated target. We did altogether exactly 1200 guesses, and the results were chance results. She got 243 hits, which is only three above chance. That was a great disappointment to us because we had expected to see something spectacular.

If this experiment had succeeded, I should have been absolutely convinced that the case was a genuine one of extrasensory perception without any doubts whatever, because these envelopes had flaps which were turned down and there was no possibility of the girl seeing the contents of any envelope. Mr. Bateman and I were absolutely certain about that. But we were loth to go away without seeing something, and so we suggested to Mr. Langdon-Davies that we should try some more tests under telepathy conditions. I said that perhaps it was my presence which inhibited the clairvoyance experiments, or that I frightened the girl or something. And so I suggested that Mr. Bateman should be the agent and that we should use a screen with a slit an inch high at the bottom, and that the five target cards should be put face upwards underneath the slit. The reason why we did not use an opaque screen in these tests was that we should have to have somebody on the other side of the screen to record Maria's guesses, and she might have been disturbed by a person sitting next to her. I was afraid of that, and so I decided to use the slit. The cards were in the folders used by Mr. Davies; we did not actually randomize these folders, but we just shuffled them; each pack contained twenty-five cards with five cards of each symbol. After shuffling, I gave every pack a random cut at a number taken from a table, such as the twelfth card and so on. That was done and the cards were reshuffled at the end of every experiment.

Mr. Bateman and Mr. Langdon-Davies sat together on the side of the table opposite Maria. They were both hidden by the screen, and Mr. Bateman lifted up the card and made a little bang on the table with each card, just looking at it beneath the folder and putting the card on the table with the curved side of the folder towards Maria, but on his side of the screen, of course, and at some distance from the slit. Well, if she had looked—I watched her for some considerable time and she did not ever look underneath the slit—but if she had looked under the slit, she could not possibly have seen the card. I did check that very carefully.

But there was one thing which I ought to mention and that is, that in these experiments we were using the same folders for the cards that ·Mr. Langdon-Davies had used. We did not change the folders. It is quite true that we sent Maria away at the checking and she never saw, during the experiments that we had done, which card was in which folder. That is quite certain. But the question that I should like to ask is: Is Mr. Langdon-Davies sure that she never in any of his previous experiments saw which card was in which folder?

L.-Davies: The answer to that is that on very rare occasions, amounting perhaps to a dozen altogether, when she got five of one symbol right she was shown the card inside, but at the time she saw the card inside, she could not have seen the outside of the folder, and they were taken up at once. So that as far as I know she never did see the outside of a folder and know what card was in it.

Soal: I think that is a crucial point, because if she had had time to recognize these folders, she might possibly have got some visual clues. But she could only have done that by looking underneath the screen, and as far as we could judge from watching her she did not look underneath the gap. I am quite sure she did not get any clues from Mr. Bateman; Mr. Bateman is a very careful man. But there is one proviso that I must make, and that is that I should not be absolutely satisfied unless I could get Maria to do the experiment in a different room from the cards and the agent. If I could do that I think I should be absolutely satisfied, i.e. with the same conditions of distance as for Shackleton and Mrs. Stewart. I do in my heart think that this is a case of extrasensory perception, but I cannot say with absolute accuracy that the experiment was completely scientific.

Parkes: But it is your firm opinion?

Soal: Yes, it is my opinion, but with that reservation.

I should mention what Mr. Langdon-Davies did not mention, that after we had finished the 2,400 telepathy trials with Mr. Bateman, we carried out another series of 1,800 with Mrs. Langdon-Davies as agent and Mr. Bateman as recorder. These showed the same sort of upward trend, although the score was not quite so significant, and the final result we arrived at, in 4,200 trials, was an excess of $3\cdot86$ standard deviations with odds of 8,000 to 1 against chance. It is not a high rate of scoring. It is only about $5\cdot6$ hits per run of 25 (much lower than Mrs Stewart's rate of success), but it is above the rate that Mr. Langdon-Davies had obtained in the week we left England. One thing I noticed about the scoring was this—it seemed to achieve its effect by a sudden leap of the score into the fifties. It would go 44, 43, 42, hardly ever below 40 on 200 trials, and then suddenly you would get a 53. Then it would fall to just above chance-level—43, 48 perhaps, 46. Then up it would go to 52. And it was due to those leaps into the fifties that we really got the significant results.

On one interesting occasion, it went right up to 58, i.e. 58 in 200 trials, and we thought ESP had really arrived at last. Then the next score was 52 out of 200, and after that it went down again. We carried out the experiments until the last evening before we were due to leave for England, which in a way was rather unlucky; if we had not done that final experiment before we left, we should have had 4·3 standard deviations. But we did the experiment and the significance went down to 3·86; in fact, the last score was a below chance score. I don't know if it was due to the girl getting excited and perhaps a little self-conscious.

There were one or two other things. On some occasions it disturbed Mr. Bateman very much when he was the agent or the experimenter, that Mr. Langdon-Davies would suddenly come into the room to see what the score was; sometimes in the middle of a run Mr. Bateman used to notice that if Maria was scoring 8's or 7's in successive sets of 25, the score would immediately go down to 2 or 3 when he came into the room.

Parkes: Scoring significantly below probability.

Soal: Yes, 3 or 4; I am talking about successive sets of 25, not of 200 trials, and Mr. Langdon-Davies would spoil what seemed to promise a very good score for the 200. Also this girl was taking her task, I think, far too seriously, since her fellow servant on two occasions reported that she was screaming in the night about the cards. So we thought it must be getting on her mind, and we had to give her a complete rest on separate days as a result.

L.-Davies: Perhaps I might just add one thing on that, not that it matters, but on one occasion when I went into the room the score went up to 12!

There is one other point that Dr. Soal has not mentioned: it was rather extraordinary that the 58 score started with a nought. Well, noughts are very uncommon anyhow, and here in her first run though she got no guesses right and then did her biggest aggregate with the other seven. I don't know whether it is significant or not, but it is the sort of thing that makes you think when you see it.

I should also like to say that in every one of the experiments that Dr. Soal has been alluding to, you are looking at the lower end of the curve before it begins to take its upward trend. There is no way of proving this, but I suspect that if each of those experiments had gone on for another 100 sets, we might have got into the upper reaches. In my longer series, exactly the same phenomenon that Dr. Soal has mentioned, happened at least three times; that is, after a long series of just over 40, with none under 40, or perhaps one 39 and one 37 in about a dozen turns, up she went to the fifties, and on two occasions up to the eighties and the hundreds. It was as if done by jerks.

There is one thing that I would like to add, and this is going to be a most dangerous thing to say and I suppose a grossly unscientific one, but the question of repeatability has come up. I would be prepared to say that I would undertake an experiment with Maria, under whatever conditions Dr. Soal lays down, and that there is a good chance, in my opinion from past experience, that she will repeat the same kind of curve that she has already repeated four or five times. I believe that, if, on my return to Spain, the other elements in the Gestalt (which includes looking after children and many other things) are still propitious, we could try as Dr. Soal suggests, a room-to-room experiment, and be entitled to expect that she would repeat the same kind of curve. The similarity between the curves on these five occasions is rather more considerable than one might expect.

Soal: You mean the period in which she got chance results?

L.-Davies: Yes, a period of just about 40 runs with chance results but seldom falling below chance, followed by a definite turning-up of the curve into the fifties, and perhaps further on into higher figures still.

Brown: May I offer a comment on this shape of the curve? It is not very typical of work in psychical research—Mr. Langdon-Davies's example of the boy who began with good results which later got worse is more typical of psychical research. The earlier curve is more typical of a learning process, where the subject begins by not knowing exactly what to do, but gradually finds out as the experiment goes on. Not given any more information, a learning hypothesis seems plausible.

Gaddum: It seems to me that the results in Table III start well and then fall off at the end.

Soal: But I should say this, that this kind of thing was constantly what happened to Mr. Tyrrell's subject, Miss Johnson. Whenever the conditions were changed, for instance when Tyrrell changed from the keys to the mechanical selector, the results immediately fell to chance. They went to chance for several thousand guesses, and then by coaxing the subject or humouring her, Mr. Tyrrell got her to work with the mechanical selector and soon she got just as high scores as she did with the keys. But I do not think that in Tyrrell's case there was any possibility of sensory clues.

Brown: I am not altogether sure about that. I did a series of psycho-kinesis experiments in which I got exactly the same sort of results, and I found eventually how it was done. It was not done by psychokinesis at all. It was done by unconscious dexterity which I was gradually learning during the experiment.

Soal: Yes, but the conditions of Tyrrell's experiment were very different from that, I think, He had a fool-proof electrical machine and recording apparatus.

Nicol: I should like to ask Dr. Dingwall a question. He has spoken about the value of the evidence offered in the case of the Saints, including St. Joseph of Copertino. I think the point arises, what qualities did the witnesses have as observers? How long ago did the incidents take place? And what is the state of the records? I will indicate what I mean by an experience of my own.

A good many years ago I spent considerable time investigating the manifestations said to emerge in the presence of a lady who claimed to be a physical medium. The séances were held mainly in darkness; on the table was a trumpet marked with luminous paint, by which means you could follow—or try to follow—its swift movements about the rather small room. On one occasion in the presence of two men of undoubted scientific competence and, indeed, distinction (they were both Fellows of the Royal Society, one was a Nobel Prize winner and the other was a Professor of Medical Chemistry; both now deceased) various things happened. After it was over, I remember those men making two unsolicited pronouncements: one, spirits had nothing to do with it; and two, it was certainly not due to fraud. They had had only the one sitting, held in a state of very poor illumination at the best, and they had no control over the séance conditions; yet they did not hesitate to utter an opinion that was incautious and unnecessary. Yet these were men who were trained observers. How does such a case compare with that of St. Joseph of Copertino and others of that quality?

Dingwall: Of course, I could talk for half an hour on that. We do have any amount of cases of these important people, who without any real training, go to séances and become convinced. I could tell the most devastating stories of the people I have seen in action, quite incredible things. But in the case of the phenomena of the Saints, I think it is essential, first of all, to immerse yourself in the kind of evidence that is given and the kind of people who give it to you and the reason why they give it. You get a feeling at the end, that they are not the poor observers that so many people consider them to be, that they do know a good deal about the kind of evidence that is wanted, and on some occasions it is very difficult indeed to say that they must have been either completely deceived, or are liars, or so on and so forth. And one important point, if I may add it, is that in the phenomena of the Saints, I think it is rather noticeable that those parapsychological phenomena, which nearly all parapsychologists today regard as 100 per cent fraudulent, are practically never found in the records of the phenomena of the Saints. I think that is interesting.

Wassermann: I have already informed Dr. Perry and Dr. Pobers of a number of things privately, but I cannot present all my arguments and so I am going to deal with something said by Dr. Soal. Dr. Soal maintained in all seriousness that a suitable theory has to be simple. If this is correct, then we shall have to dismiss theoretical physics altogether, because theoretical physics is not simple in the sense implied by Dr. Soal, but has very complicated constructs. My theory tries to establish an Ockham's Razor, in other words it is attempting to reduce parapsychological phenomena and other phenomena in biology and psychology to the same type of laws that we have in physics. Now as the laws of physics are not derivable from simple relations, as far as we know, there is no reason why biological laws should be derived from simpler ones. Another point raised is the idea that a theory should make predictions. First of all, my theory is not a predictive calculus; it is an interpretive theory. Secondly, quantum mechanics, when it was first introduced, did not make any predictions at all, and as far as I know, it has made relatively few predictions. In 1926, a host of already known data had to be interpreted and since then quantum mechanics has been trying to do so, and is still trying to do so. Much of theoretical physics is built up in order to interpret and correlate things, rather than to predict new ones. It is very nice if a theory predicts something, but a theory has also another function, namely, to correlate large number of independent data in terms of a few hypotheses. And I think that is the point which my theory is mainly trying to do. I don't know how far I have convinced Dr. Perry on this point.

Perry: I am sorry; for me it is a difference between conviction and explanation.

Parkes: In any case, I can assure you, Dr. Wasserman, that Dr. Perry is easier to convince in private than in public!

A CASE OF PSEUDO-ESP

S. G. SOAL
London

JOSEF KRAUS (known as Fred Marion) was born at Prague in 1892 and was educated there at the Commercial Academy. Two years after leaving school he attracted public attention in Prague by undertaking to discover the whereabouts of an object that had been hidden somewhere in the town by a committee of journalists and police. Marion succeeded in finding the object, and on the strength of this success was offered an engagement at a concert hall, where he mystified his audiences by finding articles hidden by them in various parts of the room, or by guessing numbers and colours chosen by members of the audience. Marion in the years that preceded the First World War appeared in numerous Continental capitals, but paid his first visit to this country in January, 1934. Between January and July of that year I made the first scientific investigation of his alleged powers.

Though Marion's most spectacular feat is the location of hidden objects (which he himself attributed to telepathy), he also claims to be able to describe events in a person's life by scrutinizing a specimen of his handwriting. Personally I was unable to find any confirmation of this claim and my own experiences convinced me that he was not even a moderately good graphologist. Nor did I discover any good evidence that Marion employs telepathy or any form of extrasensory perception in his performances, though he was certainly able to pick out a playing-card which he had previously handled after it had been mixed with several others in the dark. This was, however, to be accounted for by his possessing a good tactile memory. With playing-cards he often succeeded in

131

recognizing a card by means of a slight flex which he had imparted to it while it was in his hands.

Marion failed invariably in guessing Zener cards which were screened from his sight, and obtained no more hits than were to be expected from chance. Judging from an introduction written to Marion's autobiography, two English experimenters appear to have reached the conclusion that he possesses genuine extrasensory abilities, though they have not published any report. My own experiments certainly did not lend any confirmation to this finding. In the investigation of a professional mystifier such as Marion special precautions have to be taken to guard against his general trickiness. It is possible that the experimenters preferred to treated him as a collaborator as anxious to discover the truth about his gifts as they themselves. Unfortunately, it has been proved up to the hilt that Marion will take instant advantage of every loophole left open to him for securing his effects by illegitimate means. Precautions, therefore, have to be absolutely fraud-proof.

The 1934 experiments with Marion were carried out in the rooms of the University of London Council for Psychical Investigation at 14D Roland Gardens, S.W.7.

For his demonstration of the hide-and-seek game before a large audience Marion asks that some lady or gentleman in the audience should hand him a small object such as a cigarette-lighter or a fountain-pen. He holds the article in his hands for half a minute or so, in order, as he explains, to "sense" it, and then returns it to the owner with instructions to hide it while he, Marion, is out of the room. Before leaving the room Marion tells the audience that everyone is to think hard of the place where the object is hidden and to image the movements which Marion must make in order to reach this spot. Marion then leaves the room with a guardian, who accompanies him in order to testify that he does not listen at the door or spy through the keyhole. When he is out of the room the owner of the article hides it in some place where it is invisible, e.g. in a lady's handbag or a gentleman's pocket or behind the radiator, etc. Marion is then recalled to the room. He enters with his eyes half-closed, with his left hand on his forehead, his right hand held out in front of his head, and appears to be oblivious of his audience. He first walks rapidly round the room, stops suddenly and walks straight towards some object in the room or some particular person. Then he silently catches someone by the sleeve, makes him stand up, and produces the object from a pocket or a handbag. Sometimes, however, he will exclaim: "It is no use my going on, I am certain it is on this gentleman, perhaps in his boot", whereupon the man will unlace his boot and reveal the object. When the audience is a large one Marion will frequently discover the whereabouts of the hidden article within a minute or even half a minute after entering the room.

After a few successful experiments of this type I put the experiment on a statistical basis. At first sight it would seem that Marion's performance has much in common with that of Stuart Cumberland and is a variation of the "willing game". Marion, however, is a step in advance of Cumberland, who required to take his victim by the hand, whereas with Marion there is no physical contact between him and any member of the audience.

Briefly the method we adopted was as follows.

Six rectangular tin boxes provided with lids were placed around the room in six chosen positions, e.g. one on the floor, one on a small table, one on the edge of a bookcase and so on. These positions were numbered 1 to 6 in clockwise order. The object to be hidden was a small unscented white handkerchief. The handkerchief was given to Marion to hold for a few seconds and he then handed it back to me. Meanwhile the observers (about half a dozen in number) had seated themselves around a large table in the centre of the room. Marion then left the room accompanied by one of the audience, and the door, which had no keyhole, was carefully closed. I then took from my pocket a die which I shook in one of the tin boxes. I did not speak about the number which turned up but showed it to Miss Beenham, the recorder, who entered it in her notebook. This number decided in which of the six boxes the handkerchief was to be hidden. I then walked round the room with the handkerchief in my hand, now and then stopping at a tin, taking off the lid and putting it on again. When I came to the tin in which the handkerchief was to be hidden, I carried it to the middle of the floor put the handkerchief inside and closed the lid carefully. I then carried the tin back and put it gently in its position. I then gave every tin a random push and put the die in my waistcoat pocket. Miss Beenham then covered the record of the die number in her book. All took their seats round the table and I shouted for Marion to come in. It was understood that the audience were to follow Marion with their eyes in all his movements round the room, willing him to go to the right tin, but that they were not to give him any obvious indications such as a nod of the head or other sign. Complete silence was preserved while Marion was in the room.

As regards Marion himself, he was told that he was not to touch any tin unless he meant to lift it and open it. If the tin he opened contained the handkerchief the experiment was finished, but if the tin did not contain the handkerchief he was to open one of the remaining five tins. After he had opened the second tin the experiment was finished whether this tin contained the handkerchief or not. The lids of the tins that had been opened by Marion were not replaced until Marion had left the room again for the next experiment. The tins were always replaced in their original positions. The tins whose lids had been removed, as well as the one in which the handkerchief was to be hidden afresh, were carried to the centre of the room and the lids then replaced. When the handkerchief had been concealed and the tins returned to their original positions each was given a random push of a few inches.

When Marion entered the room his eyes would seem half-closed, his left hand would be usually on his forehead and his right hand extended at the level of his head. He would then begin to walk rapidly round the room, usually in a counter-clockwise direction. As he came to each tin, he would pause slightly and wave his right hand once or twice above the tin, bringing it as a rule to within two inches of the lid, but without touching the tin. He would pass on, doing the same thing at each tin. When he had completed the circuit of the tins, he would stride across to one particular part of the room, say towards the bookcase, hesitate a moment, and then cross, for example, to the tin on the gramophone. Then suddenly he would return to the bookcase and, without any hesitation, open the tin on its ledge, and pull out the handkerchief. The chance of his opening the correct tin at first try is of course 1/6, and in ninety-one trials under these conditions we should expect him to find the handkerchief at first try fifteen times. He actually scored thirty-eight successes at first try, and the odds against as good a result or better than this being due to chance are nearly 71 millions to 1 worked out directly from the expansion of $(\frac{5}{6} + \frac{1}{6})^{91}$. There was then no question that Marion could locate the handkerchief under these conditions.

We next did a series of experiments in which no one in the room knew in which of the six tins the handkerchief was hidden. The result was a complete contrast to the first series and Marion succeeded no more often than chance would predict.

During these new tests Marion appeared to have lost his confidence completely and kept repeating: "I am only guessing; I can get no real feeling at all."

We also showed that Marion's holding the handkerchief had nothing to do with his success or failure. He also succeeded in discovering an imaginary hiding place concentrated upon by the audience when no actual object was hidden.

We next studied the part played by the audience in Marion's success.

In the first series I accompanied Marion outside the room and led him into the outer office. During our absence the sitters completely covered their heads and shoulders with thick blankets (after the handkerchief had been hidden), and pressed their fingers into their ears. I remained uncovered while Marion perambulated the room, moving about so that he could never get his back between me and a tin. Under these circumstances Marion did not succeed in locating the handkerchief more times than chance would predict.

Our next plan was to have an opaque white curtain rigged across a corner of the room. At intervals in the curtain were tiny peep-holes a quarter of an inch in diameter, so that the people behind the curtain could watch Marion's movements inside the room without Marion being able to see any of their bodies or of their movements.

In these experiments I accompanied Marion outside the room and the other sitters threw the die and concealed the handkerchief. They then went behind the curtain and watched Marion through the chink-holes, willing him to go to the correct tin but being very careful not to disturb the curtain in any way. I, who did not know where the handkerchief was hidden, acted as umpire. In a total of sixty-four trials of this kind Marion found the handkerchief only thirteen times at first try, which is just a chance result.

These tests showed that for Marion to succeed it was essential for him to see some part of the body of a person who knew the hiding-place.

In another series of tests Marion was followed round the room at a distance of one yard by a single person who knew the hiding place, the other sitters (except myself, who was ignorant of the hiding place) being behind the curtain. He was brilliantly successful in these conditions.

In certain tests the follower wore over his head a tea-cosy of thin coarse linen and over this a black stockinette hood which covered his face, neck and shoulders. He was able to see Marion through the mesh but his features were quite invisible to Marion, who succeeded five times in five times (odds 7,775 to 1 against chance).

These experiments showed that Marion did not rely entirely on changes in facial expression for his cues.

We next had constructed a light rigid plywood box fifty inches high. The box was open at one end and in the bottom a circular hole was cut. The box was put over the follower's head so that his neck passed through the circular hole and the very light weight of the box was supported by his shoulders. The arms, trunk, and legs down to the ankles were enclosed in the body of the box. The follower's head was then covered by a rectangular cardboard hood which rested on top of the box, and an oval hole in a vertical face of the hood was covered with stockinette through which objects in the room could be seen. As the man who wore this contraption followed Marion in his circuit of the room, only his feet and one and a half inches of his legs were visible. The man's head made no contact with the interior of the hood, and movements of his head *relative* to the trunk, i.e. noddings or rotatory movements, were absolutely invisible to the onlooker. Trunk movements from the hips could be observed by the rotation of the box and hood. The man gave the impression of a weird sort of walking robot and we nicknamed this contrivance the "robot-box". I left the room with Marion, taking him as usual into the office. The robot-box and hood were placed upon Mr. H. S. Collins, and he stood near the door ready to follow as soon as Marion entered. The die was thrown and a small fur toy cat put into the corresponding tin. The throw was recorded by Miss Beenham and the die concealed. The tins were manipulated as usual, and the sitters, including Miss Beenham, all went behind the curtain and watched through the chink-holes. Marion and I were recalled to the room and I acted as umpire, watching Marion and the tins. Mr. Collins followed Marion round the room at the distance of about a yard, stopping when he stopped, and willed him to open the correct tin.

We did six experiments under these precise conditions. The first was a complete failure, but the remaining five were all successful at first try. (The odds against five or more successes in a series of six trials are 1,504 to 1.) Later in 1939 we confirmed these results by further experiments with the box.

This success makes it probable that when Marion is followed he gains his principal clues from the movements of walking, e.g. hesitations in footsteps, sudden stoppings, turnings, startings, accelerations and retardations on the part of the follower. When we remember that the constantly swaying box is not altogether under the control of the wearer, it does not appear likely that much reliable information could be gained from slight movements of the trunk.

We next had constructed a kind of sentry-box on wheels. This box was 6 feet 7 inches high and closed on three of its vertical sides and at the top and bottom. The front of the box was left open so that a man could enter and stand comfortably in it. The open front of the box could be covered by five rectangular panels of plywood each about $14\frac{1}{2}$ inches high, so that by the removal of a panel any part of the occupant's body could be exposed to Marion's gaze. For instance, if the four lower panels were in position and the uppermost panel was removed, his head and neck alone would be visible. He himself was able to watch Marion through a tiny crevice which separated the top panel from the one immediately below it. When all five panels were in position the man was completely invisible.

This wheeled box was provided with a pair of handles fixed to its base so that the box could be pushed round the room from behind in such a way that the panelled front of the box always faced Marion. The small wheels beneath the box were so arranged as to allow the box to be turned rapidly so as to face in any direction, and to allow free movement both backwards and forwards. In order to gain space for these evolutions, we removed the central table from the room.

By wheeling the man round in the box we hoped to eliminate all clues that Marion might obtain from the movements of walking. Needless to say, the person who pushed the box round went outside the room with Marion and myself, while the rest retired behind the curtain. In the first series with this sentry-box Mr. Collins was wheeled round behind Marion with all the panels removed so that his whole body was exposed to Marion's gaze. Marion was very successful under these conditions.

A number of tests were then made with all the panels closed, so that no part of Mr. Collins was visible. Under these conditions Marion failed to find the object more often than chance would precict.

In a final series all the panels were in position except the top one so that Mr. Collins' stockinette-covered head alone was visible. It was during this series that we observed on several occasions how Marion would glance repeatedly at the hooded head while he was hesitating with his hand over a tin, apparently waiting for a tell-tale movement that would inform him whether or not he was at the right tin.

Marion succeeded in these tests, the odds against his result being due to chance working out at 2,408 to 1 in twenty-five trials. It is certain that involuntary head-movements furnished the cues by which Marion located the hidden object.

It is probably persons of the emotive type who, in their anxiety to see Marion succeed, unconsciously give away hints; apparently he does not succeed with those who are perpetually on their guard and who keep their muscles well under control. But persons of the "motor" type are to be found in any considerable audience and they serve as living sign-posts to warn him when he is approaching his object or receding from it.

When we asked Marion why it was, if he was succeeding by telepathy, that he failed when the agent was completely invisible inside the box, he replied that this only proved that thought could not penetrate wood—a view to which many university teachers would subscribe.

It should be added that while we have no reason to believe that Marion possesses real powers of telepathy or clairvoyance, he is able to give a very interesting demonstration of pseudo-telepathy. For instance, on February 1st, 1934, the experimenter produced a pack of twenty-five white cards blank on one side and printed on the other with numbers 1 to 25. Marion left the room and in his absence one of the sitters chose card No. 18. The cards were shuffled and put in a pile on the table. Marion was recalled to the room and he asked us to think hard of the number chosen. Marion took up the pack and facing the audience showed them the first card and then dropped it on the table. He went through the cards one after another, always showing the cards to the audience. He then collected them in a pile and repeated the operation. This time he put four cards aside from the rest. They were Nos. 3, 13, 18, 22. These he showed separately to the audience. Finally he chose No. 18 without hesitation.

Marion is no conjuror and all his movements are slow and deliberate. His performance has little or nothing in common with those of the numerous couples who simulate telepathy by means of codes, concealed microphones, misdirection of attention, or careful pre-arrangement. He works alone and employs no confederates in the audience. He possesses a flair for the interpretation of small *indicia* given away unwittingly by certain members of his audience. There is no reason to believe that he possesses any kind of sensory hyperaesthesia, though undoubtedly his sense of touch is delicate.

The case of Marion has obvious lessons for experimenters in telepathy and clairvoyance. It emphasizes the vital importance of screening the agent in telepathy tests and of screening the cards in all ESP experiments. There seems little doubt that in much of Dr. Rhine's early work the precautions taken were not very satisfactory, though of course this remark does not apply to such experiments as the Pearce-Pratt experiment or the Pratt-Woodruff series. It seems highly probable, however, that some of the subjects for whom Rhine claimed extrasensory powers were simply people who learned the cards from their backs or glimpsed the impressions which showed through the backs when the cards were held at a certain angle to the light.

Acknowledgement

Details of this experiment were first published in the volume entitled " Modern Experiments in Telepathy " by S. G. Soal and F. Bateman, published by Faber and Faber Ltd. and in the U.S.A. by Yale University Press.

THE SIMULATION OF TELEPATHY

E. J. DINGWALL
London

FROM very early times the power to divine the thoughts of others has been sought but, so it is claimed, this gift has only been bestowed upon certain privileged mortals both in the Western and Oriental worlds.

Such a power enhanced the prestige of its possessor and made him an object of respect, veneration and even awe. Many examples of persons alleged to possess this gift are found in the records of the Saints of the Christian Church and among the holy men of the East just as they have been recorded in the literature relating to less civilized peoples in various parts of the world.

Demonstrations of such phenomena sometimes formed part of the performances of famous wonder-workers; and the séances of Alexander of Paphlagonia are familiar to readers of Lucian. There is little doubt that Alexander, who flourished at the beginning of the second century, was one of the greatest mediums in the ancient world, and his performances in reading the contents of sealed billets were almost identical with those which used to be quite common in England and the United States. By simulating telepathic powers he was thought to obtain knowledge of what people had secretly written on folded pieces of paper, whereas in reality he used simple methods of obtaining the information through purely normal means.

Among less civilized, or, as they are sometimes called, primitive peoples, cases of apparent telepathy have often been recorded, but how far these phenomena are due to normal causes it is hard to say. It must be remembered that one of the most fundamental features of magic is the belief in the sympathetic influence exerted at a distance, and this not only

141

on persons but on things as well. The hunter's success may be jeopardized by what goes on at home when he is away; the fisherman's catch may be poor unless his kinsmen take certain precautions while he is out at sea. Actual information is sometimes conveyed to a distance by what some have thought to be a telepathic process. A good deal has been written on the so-called "bush-telegraph", a means of communication by means of drums. There is good reason to suppose that simple items of information can be conveyed by means of the drums over short distances, but I am very doubtful if the more striking instances of information being conveyed over an area of some 2,000 square miles can be due to such means. It may well be that the records are inaccurate and that the incidents were not actually so impressive as they sound. Generally speaking, the language of the drums will travel up to about ten miles in calm weather and would then have to be relayed. It would, therefore, be hardly fair to maintain that the African people, who use the veld-telegraph, are simulating telepathy. Even if the information is actually conveyed by the sounds, it may well be that their secrecy about it is due to the difficulty of explaining exactly how it works. If there is any telepathy in the process, it is probable that they know as little about it as we do, and possibly a good deal less.

Among Western peoples public demonstrations of simulated thought transmission were stimulated by two facts, both of which are of importance in the history of alleged telepathic displays. Of these the first is the claim that examples of what were taken as cases of genuine telepathy were observed in mesmeric and hypnotic performances. Indeed, at one time it was thought that proof of telepathy was to be sought through hypnotism; and as late as 1925 the French writer, Paul C. Jagot, wrote a book on it. The early literature is full of examples of mental suggestion at a distance which are nowadays considered to be mainly of academic interest.

When we read some of these accounts it is remarkable that more has not been done within recent years to try to repeat some of them. It seems that many of these experiments were carried out with some care, but the observers, judged by modern standards, seem to have been unable so to control the procedure that simulation of telepathy was excluded, Since, in many instances, the subjects were hypnotized, it cannot fairly be said that they were playing conscious tricks on the observers. Rather, the conditions made possible results which the experimenters, quite wrongly as it appears, attributed to telepathy acting between operator and subject or even between the subject and others. The tests formerly carried out for demonstrating telepathy belong to a different class of experiment altogether. Here, if the more simple sources be excluded, we have either telepathy in action or, what is more likely, simulation of telepathic effects by adroit persons who were both willing and able to deceive experimenters engaged in serious study, all unsuspecting that they were being made the victims of conscious and well-designed trickery. What is abundantly clear is that in very many of the investigations the experimenters were not in any way competent to detect simulation, and thus a great many of their conclusions can no longer be considered as valid.

The second fact to be taken into account is the rise of what was called muscle-reading. In demonstrations of this kind by such performers as Randall Brown, Stuart Cumberland, Washington Irving Bishop and Alfred Capper, many simple people found it difficult to believe that the successes of the performers were due solely to the unconscious indications given by the voluntary assistant and by the spectators, or at least by some of them. They thought that some kind of thought transmission must be taking place, and the performers did not attempt to restrain them from such opinions. As a matter of fact, the theory of telepathy was strengthened when similar performances began to be given with one striking difference, namely that no contact was made between the performer and any member of the audience.

One of the earliest of these, if not the earliest, was the English woman, Maud Lancaster, who, towards 1893, gave a beautiful performance extending even to the reading of the numbers on banknotes. She was followed by others, but few have equalled the skill of Eugène Rubini and Fred Marion. In the case of Rubini, whom I think I saw only once, the method was as follows. When the performer left the room the company decided on some object to be hidden or some task to be performed by the sensitive when he returned. This having been done, the medium was told that he could come back, and the person chosen to act as conductor was given his instructions. In Rubini's case the assistant was told to hold his hands close on his own chest and then to follow the performer step by step at a distance of anything up to about five feet. As the assistant follows the sensitive, the former is asked to will him to do what had been decided on before the test commenced and when the medium was out of the room.

To some persons, as I have said, these non-contact performances indicated the exercise of a telepathic gift, but the facts seem to be that they are quite clearly mere simulations of telepathy. For example, they usually fail when the feats demanded are not founded on some action basis. These performers have to do something or carry out some task known to one or more persons. They cannot tell you what card you are thinking of or what is written on some piece of paper now resting in your vest pocket. At least non-contact mind-readers like Rubini did not, as far as I know, ever attempt such feats in the course of their demonstrations. Other methods have to be used to simulate telepathy in this way and to these I will now turn.

As interest in mind-reading increased under the influence of experiments in mesmerism, so did professional conjurers begin to see the advantage of making use of it for their own benefit. They were, however, merely improving and developing feats of simulated telepathy which go back at least as far as 1570, as Mr. Trevor Hall pointed out in his Hoffmann Memorial Lecture in 1951. In the early cases, cards mentally selected were named by the performer; later, the revelation of the thoughts of the audience became an act in itself, but the methods utilized were, generally speaking, quite different from the early feats of performers working alone and as described in Reginald Scot's *Discovery of Witchcraft* (1584). At the end of the eighteenth century, the famous magician Pinetti and his wife were giving a second-sight act, and by the middle of the nineteenth century books began to be issued explaining the codes used by the thought-readers in their performances. At first, audible codes were used, and such performers as Robert-Houdin and Heller were famous in their day, to be followed by mind-readers like Donato and his pupil Pickman, who combined a thought-reading show with a hypnotic demonstration, which gave an air of pseudo-science to their performances.

As the development of new and subtle codes proceeded, so did these simulations of telepathy become more puzzling. The Zancigs, the Zomahs and the Piddingtons will long be remembered for their performances, but the demand for even more convincing tests had to be met and thus the development of silent acts showed marked improvement. Such examples as that of Mr. David Devant's Translucidation and Mental Magnetism or of Mr. and Mrs. Salvin's act, which gained them a prize at the Paris Magical Congress, indicated how far conjurers had gone since the days of the eighteenth-century performers.

Apart from the simulation of telepathy as an act in itself, a word should be said in conclusion on the growing interest in mental effects among conjurers generally. This arose partly on account of the wish to develop the various methods of card divination, which I have already noticed, but also through the natural desire not to allow the fraudulent medium to monopolize the field of psychological misdirection and trickery generally. The brilliant performances of such mind-readers as Bert Reese and Ludwig Kahn showed that their methods could well be incorporated into shows devised not for fake mediumship but for legitimate entertainment. Gradually, a whole system of such effects was built up containing some of the most brilliant deceptions ever devised. For simulation of telepathy some of these effects are unequalled, and the methods by which they are worked are some of the most jealously guarded secrets in the magician's armoury.

I remember many years ago being rung up by a distinguished literary man who had for long been very sceptical on the subject of telepathy. He told me to my surprise that he had at last become convinced and then proceeded to tell me the following story. He said that he had recently acted as host to a man whom he did not know well, and during the course of conversation the subject of telepathy cropped up. He told his guest that he did not believe in it, whereupon he was told that he could have the proof for the asking. On demanding an explanation, his visitor told him that he was a powerful telepathic agent and that he was able to transmit thoughts to a friend of his at a distance. My friend thereupon suggested a test, to which his visitor willingly complied. Asking his host to name any card in the pack, he then told him to ring up the lady to whom the information was to be transmitted, to tell her what was happening and then ask her to tell him what was the card that he had chosen and on which her friend was concentrating. After a few moments she named the chosen card. This incident convinced my friend that telepathy was a fact, but when I told him that he had been deceived and that it was only a trick he became so disgusted that he has, as far as I know, taken not the slightest interest in telepathy since that day. I often wonder what he would say today if he knew the number of complicated methods for performing the telephone effect since it was first invented at the beginning of the present century.

All feats of simulated telepathy should be carried out under conditions which seem as natural as possible. Apparatus should be rigidly excluded from sight, and any suggestion of ordinary conjuring avoided unless the feat is part of a show devised purely for entertainment. If manipulations have to be carried out, then these should be concealed under movements which apparently have no conceivable connexion with the experiment on hand, and so are promptly forgotten by the observers. Indeed, it is sometimes possible to get the observers to perform some of the necessary moves themselves without knowing it. Two clever performers, whom I saw some thirty years ago in Poland, used this method and completely deceived the many parapsychologists who were present.

The secrets of many of these effects have never been published, but the general principles are well known to those who have made a special study of what today is called *mentalism*. Hence, it is not really very difficult to distinguish the genuine from the spurious if you are once allowed to investigate. It is, I think, true to say that so far no stage demonstration of thought-transmission has ever been mistaken for genuine telepathy by anyone even moderately acquainted with the facts as magicians know them. What would be of great interest would be the presentation of some example of mentalism which, although based on purely normal means, would stand up under the kind of investigation to which all such phenomena are submitted by competent parapsychologists today. I would not go so far as to deny that such a thing might be possible, but I do not think that it would be very likely. Were it to take place, it would go some way, I think, towards supporting the opinion, still held by some, that there is no such thing as telepathy and that its demonstration is always mere simulation. Time alone will show, and all that we can do is to hope that such an effect may be devised. I conclude by saying that I do not think that we should be too optimistic.

DISCUSSION

Pobers: These two papers we have been listening to were fascinating; there is very little one can say in introducing this discussion.

I happened to be in Stockholm one day with Dr. Dingwall, discussing with a well-known scientist, a Professor of the High Technical Institute in Stockholm, the question of simulation or fraud in clairvoyance and telepathy. This very prominent scholar told us a story about his own daughter: "I tried to make an experiment in clairvoyance with my daughter, who was quite gifted; I removed a card from an ordinary pack of playing cards, and concealed it in my pocket. I then asked my daughter to guess what card was in my pocket. She asked me for an hour to concentrate: and indeed an hour later correctly guessed the card. Of course, some of the people, who are opposed to parapsychology, might get the idea that my daughter used this hour to go through the pack of cards to find out which card was missing. To prevent this type of criticism, another time I removed the card and put the remains of the pack in the drawer of my desk. A very curious thing happened. My daughter once more went away and came back an hour later, and she simply could not guess the card. What disturbed her was the lack of confidence. This is " (and Dr. Dingwall can correct me if I do not recall it exactly). "This is a very peculiar thing," he said, "in the personality structure of most of the sensitives."

Another story was told to me recently by the French poet, Jean Cocteau, who is very interested in parapsychology. An Italian peasant woman rushed into a lottery office, and asked for a ticket No. 23 a few hours before the draw was to take place. The ticket was not available, but she insisted and they got her ticket No. 23. She won the first prize in the lottery with this No. 23. She was later interviewed by a newspaper man who asked how she had guessed this No. 23, and she described a precognitive dream. "I saw myself, rich and happy, and there were two figures, 15 and 6. Now, adding up 15 plus 6, you get 23!"

The case of the Swedish Professor suggests that there is, in many cases of simulation, an element of complicity by the incompetent observer. In many cases one is really at a loss: was it conscious or unconscious fraud? Who is fraudulent, the alleged sensitive or the incompetent observer? My second point, the lottery story, is that in this type of investigation, in addition to conscious or unconscious simulation, one meets very extraordinary, singular effects. Very little is said about these strange effects and strange coincidences, which sometimes lead to fantastic conclusions.

The question of conscious or unconscious simulation is very important. During the last three or four weeks, a young Swiss mentalist was holding very impressive sittings in France, in which he demonstrated that the audience, unconsciously but very actively, collaborated with him in order to produce spectacular effects with table-tilting, ouija board etc. At the end of the sitting, he explained to the audience how they themselves have produced the results they have been admiring. His technique consisted in explaining to a selected group in the audience that he will be fraudulent in certain cases: "I will push the table, or operate the planchette for such a length of time on so many occasions, but later, I will not do anything, and please *you* be careful not to move." But if he did not push the table, from the very start the audience replaced him; they did exactly what he described as a fraud. A Dutch Professor of Psychology and I observed similar effects last summer in experiments with table-tilting. Unconscious fraud plays a very important rôle.

Finally, in reference to the Marion case and a good many similar cases, we know too little about the astounding development of known senses. Muscle-reading or an exceptionally acute sense of hearing explain some of the startling effects in Dr. Faller's hypnotic experiments in Finland. In unconscious simulation, a strange activation of normal senses sometimes takes place, which can induce both the subject and the experimenter to conclude that genuine telepathy or genuine clairvoyance were present. I understand that Dr. Soal admits, for instance, that with Marion there was an element of unconscious simulation; that he was not always conscious of how he was getting results. I just wonder whether it might not be profitable to discuss further this factor of unconscious fraud and simulation and of active complicity by credulous or incompetent observers.

Wassermann: I should like to ask Dr. Soal one question He mentioned the earlier experiments of Rhine in which he pointed out that the subjects could see the backs of the cards. If they had been learning clues slowly, one could expect that there would be a learning curve, something of the type that Mr. Spencer Brown mentioned. Was anything of that sort every observed?

Soal: No, I do not know of any, but I was told that in some of the earlier experiments, Dr. Rhine just sat with a pack of cards at a table with the subject on the other side; Rhine lifted up the cards and said "What's this?" The subject would call a symbol and Rhine would write it down, and then the next and so on. There was a certain possibility there, I think, of learning the cards, if the subject helped in the checking up and had some opportunity of associating the faces with specks on the backs. And if he only learned one in 25, that would soon make a significant score.

Pratt: I assume that it is not within the scope or purpose of this Symposium to attempt to divide or assign the personal credit or blame, depending on the point of view, for the developments in the experimental study of ESP. In the interests of not diverting our attention from our stated objectives, I do not want to take time to say more than that my silence—or further silence—on remarks made regarding the purpose or significance of some of the earlier Duke ESP experiments is not to be interpreted as agreement with the views expressed.

McConnell: In 1947 I visited Duke University to find out if just possibly there was not more to the story than I had been able to discover from the printed papers. As a physicist I found it very difficult to accept ESP and so I spent a month at Duke going around interviewing all the members of the Faculty of the University, beginning with the President and working on down, in so far as they were willing to tell me, quietly in a corner, what was their opinion about the work at Dr. Rhine's laboratory.

The only thing that I am going to tell now, although it makes a very interesting story in its entirety, is that one of the Professors, who was not favourable to the ESP hypothesis—in fact said that he could not accept it himself—did say that he felt that there was one criticism, which was frequently made and which, in his opinion, was not justified. And that this was criticism of working initially under poor conditions. This psychologist did give Rhine credit and acknowledged that his purpose in conducting these experiments under very informal and admittedly inadequate conditions initially, was to try to make a transition slowly from poor conditions to good, so as not to disturb or destroy any phenomenon that may have been there. And I think we must judge all of this early work, not by the poorest examples, but by the best examples.

Now, there is an objection to this, however. The critic will say: "Well, why in his first book, did Dr. Rhine publish all of these poorly done experiments?" I think there is an answer to that objection. Dr. Rhine's purpose, I presume, was to give as much of the psychological picture as possible, to try to convey to people an idea of how he had proceeded in order to get finally some experiments under good conditions. And this psychologist at Duke, who did not accept ESP, said that he felt that, in all honesty, it was necessary to recognise that Dr. Rhine had a good point in proceeding as he did.

Parkes: I have some sympathy with the view that you have expressed, because, if this is some very delicate mechanism which we do not understand, it is easy to conceive that it might be upset by the weary monotony of making 50,000 guesses of cards which you do not see. And I can understand an attitude of mind which accepts, to start with, conditions less rigid than would be required for a laboratory experiment.

Nicol: It is with regret that I must refer back to Dr. Pratt's statement. Unlike Dr. McConnell, whose visit to Duke was extremely brief, I spent a year there. The subject under dispute is too large to be effectively examined at this conference, and I have no doubt it was with the best intention in the world that Dr. Pratt gave his broad assurances. I will be equally brief and say I do not consider that the assurances are appropriate to the facts, nor do they deal with the true nature of the criticisms that have been made by many psychical researchers from 1935 until the present day.

West: I feel that we have wandered a very long way away from controlled experiments in extrasensory perception and, in wandering away, we have come upon a different sort of field. The anecdotes that travellers bring back from their excursions among primitive people take us into a field where one is particularly dependent on human testimony and the judgement of human testimony. I feel that is quite different from the work that we have hitherto been discussing, and the distinction between the two should be drawn very clearly. As regards the study of the anecdotes about primitive peoples, I am all for such studies, but I am also for the study of the similar phenomena which are supposed to be happening all about us. Anybody who cares can read a paper called *The Psychic News*, which is a spiritualist periodical, and in this periodical he will find stories much more remarkable even than those we have heard from Dr. Laubscher and others who have come back with reports of the psychic powers of primitive peoples. If we cannot establish what happens or does not happen immediately about us by way of spiritualistic phenomena in our own community, we have less chance of understanding and coming to a conclusion about what happens in distant lands.

I should like to refer to a point which has been raised about the difficulty of conducting experiments. I think Dr. Dingwall drew attention at one stage to a remark that I made that these experiments were childishly simple to carry out. Well, I still maintain that they are childishly simple to carry out, provided that one is conforming to a formal standard technique such as that given to us by Dr. Soal. It becomes immensely difficult to carry out researches of this kind once one deviates from that, and starts to say, "Maybe we must try informal conditions for the benefit of the subject's sensitive mentality. Maybe the effect will not occur unless we try it in the kitchen with so-and-so there or so-and-so not there." I agree that there is something in that point of view, but I feel that these hypotheses can best be tested by using a formal and rigid and standard technique, and applying that technique in different circumstances, and not by abandoning the technique altogether and conducting the experiment in informal conditions, because, if you do, whatever result you get, it can never be conclusive. I fully appreciate what Dr. McConnell has said about Dr. Rhine's motives in his early informal experiments, but it is a point of view with which I would very strongly disagree.

Parkes: I think that is a very real difficulty. Either you have the conditions so rigid that the subject, whom you agree in calling a sensitive, is subjected to a routine which would put a calculating machine in need of overhaul, or else you make the conditions sufficiently informal and loose as to invite future criticism.

Pobers: I cannot agree with Dr. West's comparison between the paranormal phenomena among primitive peoples, and the cases reported in *The Psychic News.* Careful observation, detailed description and a few simple experiments are possible among primitive peoples; it is important to study first of all the nature of extrasensory perception, and secondly, to investigate the curious and disturbing development of known senses to such an extent that there is a suspicion that they develop into something extrasensory. We discussed, for instance, "paranormal agility". Paranormal agility was not observed only among primitive peoples. As you know, Janet described very carefully the case of Madeleine who had this strange faculty. We have detailed reports about the convulsionaries of St. Médard. There are many striking cases in the lives of the Saints, etc., but it is obvious that a serious study of this type of phenomena in the right physiological and psychological context can only be carried out among primitive peoples.

Ethnographers who have observed these and other phenomena, believe that they correspond to faculties intimately connected with an archaic structure of society and an archaic means of communication. It is significant that most of the reliable reports about paranormal come either from Haiti, or from Dahomey, or from the delta of the Kasai river in the Belgian Congo; these are regions where communications are difficult and where small closed communities communicate very little with each other or with the outside world. The inhabitants of the Turtle Island or of the Cayman do not write letters to the editors of psychic papers. I do not believe that one can compare their living experience with the phenomena described in the spiritualist press.

It is essential to place extrasensory perception in a wider context of interpersonal relations; how it works in the relations of man to man, not only in laboratory conditions. A statistical evaluation, indispensable to prove that extrasensory perception exists and is measurable, empties a human faculty of its essential human content. I think that an ethnological approach can replace this phenomenon in the context of human inter-relationships.

I will give you just another instance; the problem of identical twins. I do not believe you can learn much by reading reports in *The Psychic News*, but you can investigate it to-day in Dahomey in the Kasai area, and probably in Haiti. It is a fascinating problem for I believe that there is definite evidence of telepathy and unusual physiological interrelation between identical twins.

West: I am very sorry, I obviously expressed myself badly. I did not mean that the interesting things that happen among primitive peoples should not be studied, but rather that we should try to export our experimental methods. I think if Dr. Soal were to go to these places it would be an interesting project.

Pobers: Totally different methods would have to be used.

West: I think Dr. Soal might be adaptable; he changed his methods to cope with Marion and so he might be able to adapt his experiments to other situations.

Wassermann: It strikes me that these studies are certainly required, but I have been feeling for a long time that the word parapsychology has the root psychology in it, and there are certain psychological features occurring in experiments, for instance, increased interest. It was shown in the Pratt-Woodruff experiments that if you increased the stimulus size the scoring went up very significantly. Again, the important experiments by Dr. Schmeidler and Dr. Humphrey and Mr. Fraser Nicol have also shown very significant psychological factors, such as attitude. Therefore, I feel that by being somewhat more lenient at the beginning of an experiment, provided one does not take it too seriously and states the facts, it may encourage a weak subject sufficiently to enable him to score at a better level than he would do otherwise. There is much evidence for that. Now I cannot say that everything Dr. Rhine has done is perfect, but I think he is nevertheless one of the greatest experimenters and pioneers in the field. There may be initial weaknesses, and I think one ought to use a certain amount of common sense in assessing them. One should not lay down a rigid law and say we must dismiss all this once and for all because those experiments do not come up to the standards which we demand now.

Perry: May I make a short plea for a revision of thought about statistical method? We seem to be accepting that it must invariably be extraordinarily dull. I don't see that it follows that the only adequate controlled method that has been used so far, namely that used by Dr. Soal, is necessarily unique. There appears to be no reason why an equally well-controlled statistical method should not be more interesting both to the operator and to the subject.

L.-Davies: May I supplement that remark? It seems to me that the important point is that whatever the rigidity of control should be, the matter should remain a game rather than a trial in the witness box. For example, chess has got some extremely rigid rules, and nobody pretends that they object to that fact when they are enjoying a game of chess. On the other hand, if you get your subject imagining that they are suspected of all sorts of underhand dodges, and that the only way to control them is to have a machine to shuffle the cards and another one to switch on a light at the wrong time in the wrong box and things of that sort, you are bound sooner or later to turn a game, in the best sense of the word, into a trial of common decency. I would like to suggest that Dr. Soal could give us very easily what might be called a minimum code of rigidity. I should suppose that that would include such items as a method to prevent the subject seeing the agent, a method to prevent the subject seeing the back or front of the cards and perhaps one or two other items. I think any experimenter who used such a minimum code could nevertheless maintain the informal social atmosphere which is most certainly necessary for a successful treatment of a really sensitive "sensitive". For myself, returning to the rather emotional aspect that Dr. Wasserman brought up, I found it of the greatest assistance at the beginning of each set of eight runs of twenty-five cards, to put a one peseta note and a five peseta note on the table, and to tell Maria that directly she scored ten or more she got the one peseta note, and if the total for 8 runs was more than fifty, she got the five peseta note. I don't know what would have happened if I had not done that: perhaps she would still have got the tens and fifties required. But it pleased her, she felt that this was rather fun, and whether it affected her or not, it was at least pleasanter for her to know that if things went right, she had money to take her to the cinema on Sunday. But that does not involve lowering a minimum code of rigidity, and I do want once more to emphasize that any lack of rigidity in my earlier methods was not something that I desired, but something which was forced upon me by a complete lack of any kind of material for carrying out any kind of experiment. Yes, let us have Dr. Soal's minimum code of rigidity, which he will make out with his extremely human attitude: he will not turn the human subject into an experimental animal, but at the same time it will be a code which everybody will accept, because it comes from Dr. Soal.

Parkes: It seems to me that there is a feeling in some quarters that every experiment of this kind must start out with the idea that either the subject or the experimenter will try to cheat in some fashion. Whether or not that is correct, I don't know, but it is a very different attitude from that which we find in other branches of research. One takes the good faith of the investigator more or less for granted in ordinary laboratory work, and it is a very different matter if one has to assume that fraud will be practised as much as possible.

Soal: I don't think that is the object of the precautions. The object is not so much to prevent the subject from cheating as to ensure that there are no sensory clues.

Parkes: But surely putting two people in two different rooms is enough to settle that?

Soal: Yes. But it never entered my mind that Mrs. Stewart or

Shackleton would try consciously to cheat, they are not the sort of people who would cheat.

Wassermann: It is most vital that sensory clues should be cut out. But there are certain psychological situations where one must be careful not to put the subject off at the start with the rigidity of the experimental technique.

Soal: I feel that if one starts a subject under slack conditions and gets him to score high under those conditions, it is very much harder to accustom him to score in a different room, whereas if you start at once with no fuss at all, and "Well, you go in here and we'll sit here," he takes it for granted and you don't have the trouble of conditioning him afresh.

Parkes: Yes, I agree.

Brown: I cannot support this idea of starting with minimum rigid conditions. It is absolutely alien to the concept of scientific investigation. There is no question, for example, when Faraday discovered electromagnetic induction, of applying minimum rigid conditions to his first experiments: it would be absurd. Our first results we get from an extempore experiment, or even by accident. Life is too short to begin with refinements. In any case, until we have some results we don't know what to refine. It is the same in this work: we cannot specify any conditions to begin with, but once we have a result, then we must look for the recipe to find it again, and remove from our experiment what turns out to be irrelevant to this end.

Dingwall: I think I ought to add one thing to what Dr. Pobers mentioned in his paper, and that is the question of what I call passive complicity by the experimenter, involving an emotional situation. In a paper I wrote some years ago describing a haunted friary in 1509 (which brought out partially the Swiss reformation), I described some of the investigations in modern terms and showed how even in those days there was this strange passive complicity on the part of the investigators, due of course to this emotional involvement in which parapsychologists always seem to get entangled (it is also true in archaeology and even in bibliography). The investigator is apt to gloss over—"After all, you had a pain after breakfast, we will forget that series". So long as that attitude is present in investigators, I think our red light ought always to be burning. The history of parapsychology does show that the most eminent parapsychologists in the past have been involved in what is quite clearly passive complicity in frauds, in the sense that "We will not say anything about it this time," or "We will forget what she did last year." That I think is what Dr. Soal means, and certainly what Dr. Pobers means. It does exist, and it exists, I think, more than the public have any idea of. It is not only in parapsychology, because my archaeological experiences are also very unpleasant.

McConnell: From a broad methodological point of view there are two things which stand out. Parapsychologists as a group have shown a narcissistic tendency which I don't think is apparent in most of the rest of science. I am not sure it is entirely a healthy thing. Secondly, I don't believe we should try to tell experimentalists how rigidly they should go about the discovering of scientific facts. The methods which have been used in different fields of science are quite different in different cases, and what counts is what works in the long run. Our objective in science is to find a consistent picture. I think it is quite out of place for us, as individuals, to try to tell someone else how they should go about approaching the problem.

Parkes: Dr. Soal, would you like to wind up the discussion?

Soal: I should like to say that I agree with Mr. Langdon-Davies, that you should keep the conditions as far as possible informal and friendly, and there is no objection to offering small rewards to a subject, or to having a social background. When we did the experiments with Mrs. Stewart, we always spent half an hour in a social talk, and I think that fitted her for the experiment. I am all for that sort of thing, but I am not for relaxing any of the conditions. It is quite wrong to begin an experiment under slack conditions.

Dingwall: I think Dr. Soal and I hold identical views with regard to this matter of how conditions should be set up.

THE SENSORY NATURE OF BIRD NAVIGATION

G. V. T. MATTHEWS

The Wildfowl Trust, Slimbridge

THE excuse for my presence at this Symposium is not that I have shown an interest in ESP, but that the parapsychologists have shown an embarrassing interest in my work. In the biological Gestalt in which I was reared, a sympathetic interest in ESP is equated with dalliance with Lamarckism—regrettable but transient stages through which most young biologists pass, intellectual pimples, if I may use the term. I was apprehensive, therefore, when I found my earlier work quoted with approval by parapsychologists in their papers and books until laymen could be forgiven for thinking that I had been conducting some "Modern Experiments in Telepathy". It was a considerable relief to find my ideas, as they developed on sensory lines, were such that Dr. Pratt demanded that they be "rooted out", before their corruption spread.

To my mind the parapsychologists have yet to convince the great body of sceptics that there is any asensory form of cognition in human beings. It would appear premature, to put it no more strongly, for parapsychologists to attempt to demonstrate ESP in any and every natural phenomenon that has not yet received an adequate sensory explanation. One can sympathize with their desire to escape from the weary routine of card turning, and welcome them as investigators in one's own field. But there must be insistence on rigorous research into all the sensory possibilities, and no hasty retreat to paranormal explanations.

Bird navigation is one of the subjects that has attracted the attention of parapsychologists recently, quite unnecessarily as we shall see. Until a few years ago it was not clear whether any navigational ability, by which we mean directed flight in unknown territory, did exist in birds, for random wandering could be made to account for most of the homing achievements. But two grades of navigational ability have now been demonstrated beyond reasonable doubt. First, and more simply, there is the ability to choose and determine one fixed direction. This suffices as long as the point of release (A) always lies in one direction from the goal (B). Thus if A is north of B and the bird flies south, all is well. But if displaced in a novel direction such that A is, say, west of B, the bird still flies south, no longer in the home direction. Experiments with this result have been carried out with a number of species. The selection of one direction may be induced by learning, as when a homing pigeon is always released in that direction from its loft. Or the selection may be part of the bird's innate equipment, as when young migrants fly for the first time to an unknown goal, the wintering area. They choose the right direction without guidance from old birds, and fly for approximately the right distance owing to the operation of another innate factor, the duration of the migration impulse. Direction tendencies, learnt and innate, have been clearly demonstrated by birds confined in small circular cages, providing a useful means of investigating the phenomenon experimentally.

There is no need for any recourse to ESP here. The orientation depends intimately on the sun. When the bird is placed in the cage with an overcast sky it is unable to pick up its direction; when the sun's apparent direction is changed by a system of mirrors, the bird's orientation is changed in a like sense. Even more convincing, when a bird has been trained to react to a fixed artificial sun, it will change the angle it makes to the "sun" throughout the day, as if the "sun" moved across the sky. Migration does occur with overcast skies, but the evidence suggests that this is merely the continuing of a directional flight determined earlier when the sun was visible. A similar situation would appear to exist with night migrants. These possess a well-developed sun-compass mechanism and presumably get their bearings around sunset, maintaining the chosen direction as best they can through the hours of darkness. The severe drifting effect of beam winds on such night migrants is additional evidence for this interpretation.

The second, more advanced grade of navigation enables birds to orientate towards home and fly straight back from unknown territory, no matter in what direction they have been displaced. If A is north of B, the bird flies south; if A is west of B, the bird flies east. Such homeward orientation of the fan of departure bearings (at which the birds are lost from sight in binoculars) has now been demonstrated in pigeons, gulls and shearwaters. As clinching evidence a good proportion of the birds reach home in such a short time that there could have been little deviation from the straight line from the release point. And of course one can cite remarkable homing flights such as that of a Manx Shearwater which returned from Boston, Mass., to its burrow on Skokholm Island off Wales, a distance of over three thousand miles, in twelve and a half days.

It was in homing flights of this kind that the parapsychologists appeared to have their most promising field. But so far I have been unable to extract from them any statement of the way in which ESP could be used in bird orientation. I contend that until some tentative hypothesis has been formulated there is no more justification for saying that unexplained features of animal behaviour are due to ESP than there is for invoking FTQ or what you will. There would appear to be considerable logical difficulties in the way of such formulation. Even if the evidence for telepathy, clairvoyance and psychokinesis in human subjects was quite indisputable, how could such phenomena form the basis for navigation? The claims of the parapsychologists have emphasized the apparent independence of such occurrences from ordinary considerations of space, even of time. They could therefore hardly provide a basis for two-dimensional orientation. At best we might postulate a much-travelled pigeon in the home loft clairvoyantly perceiving the release of inexperienced pigeons at a point it had previously homed from, and directing their flight by telepathy or psychokinesis. The elastic thread of credulity could hardly stand the strain of such assertions even if we were dealing with a basis of established fact. In any case, homeward orientation has been observed from places in which no member of the loft community had ever been; in the case of shearwaters, from places unknown to the species. A more reasonable suggestion would be some form of extra-sensory "beacon" radiated by the birds left behind or by the home itself. This would be an entirely new "type" of ESP, rigidly tied to spatial dimensions, and the parapsychologists would seem to be seriously weakening their theoretical position in making such a suggestion. Moreover, there is a serious experimental objection to theories involving "beacon" effects, be they of a sensory or extrasensory nature. With such a "beacon" orientation should become more and more precise the closer the release point is to home. Instead, it has been shown with pigeons that navigation breaks down at distances below about thirty-five miles, being replaced at shorter distances by pilotage on visual landmarks. The distance at which the latter occurs will naturally depend on the local topography and the experience of the birds con-cerned, but in some cases has been found to be about twenty miles from home. In between there appears to be a zone in which both orientation by true navigation and by means of landmarks is lacking, and the birds depart at random. We would expect this state of affairs if the orientation was by means of a navigational "grid"—by the detection of *differ-ences* between values of physical factors. A certain minimum displacement would then be required if the value at the release point was to be sufficiently different from the value at home for the discrepancy to be detected and acted upon.

But the most cogent argument against ESP being concerned with this second grade of navigational ability is the latter's dependence on a physical phenomenon, and hence on sensory processes. When birds are released in unknown territory with overcast skies, they depart at random or drift downwind, and their returns are slow and of an order that could be expected from random search for known landmarks. This disorientation in the absence of the sun, as opposed to strong orientation with sunny skies, has been demonstrated repeatedly in pigeons, gulls and shearwaters. The evidence also suggests that at night birds are likewise unable to orientate when released at an unknown point, even when it is their habit to fly at night. As in the case of one-direction navigation, there appears to be no reason to doubt that a view of the sun is an essential factor. The only way in which the effect of overcast could be fitted into an ESP hypothesis would be to suggest that the birds were grossly disturbed by the gloomy sky and that their delicate extrasensory processes were thrown out, in the same way as it is claimed that human subjects fail to demonstrate ESP when emotionally disturbed. While it would seem unlikely that English pigeons would be much upset by the sight of a cloudy sky, the proposition has been tested experimentally. Pigeons released close to home, or at a distant point with which they had become very familiar through repeated releases there, showed excellent orientation and swift homing *despite* heavily overcast skies. When the birds had an alternative means of orientation, known landmarks, their behaviour showed no signs of disturbance. The effect on orientation at an unknown distant point of overcast skies is therefore a direct one, acting by the removal of an essential navigational feature.

We have seen that the apparent existence of a zone of disorientation at moderate distances from home favours a form of "grid" navigation, and this may now be discussed more fully. If some factor X varies in a regular way over the earth's surface, the isolines joining places having the same value of X will form a parallel series. If another factor Y varies regularly but at an angle, the isolines marking its gradient will form a meshwork or "grid" crossing those of the X factor. The "grid" formed by the lines of latitude and longitude is a familiar example. If X and Y can be measured and compared with the remembered co-ordinates of home, the relation of the release point and home in terms of the "grid" will be established. The orientation of the "grid" in relation to the unknown surroundings must also be determined if the bird is to fly straightway in the home direction. In the same way it is no good knowing one's relative position on a map unless we have a compass by which we can coincide the latter's northing line with geographical north.

We have seen that birds showing simple one-direction navigation were clearly using the sun as a compass to determine which was their chosen direction. If this is the sun's rôle in complete navigation, it is logical that the primary navigational system must be a "grid"; for only thus would the information be "given" in terms of compass points. The question now is whether the sun's rôle is only to act as a compass, or whether it can itself provide the "grid". This is biologically more acceptable since it does not involve symbolic transference from one sense to another. We may first discuss any possible alternative co-ordinate systems. Even the most ardent parapsychologist would hesitate to suggest that there could be an extrasensory "grid" over the earth's surface, unless, perhaps, he would postulate three or more super-animals spaced hundreds of miles apart and sending out transmissions to set up the equivalent of a "Gee" radar meshwork. We need not labour such absurdity, but again note in passing that there would be a necessity for ESP to have rigid spatial relations. Latitudinal isolines could theoretically be provided by various dynamic consequences of the earth's rotation. But the effects on a bird would be so slight that their detection and measurement to the necessary precision would be beyond the power of the sense organs concerned. There are similar theoretical objections to the detection and measurement of the earth's magnetic field, whose intensity isolines could give another set of co-ordinates. In addition, interference with the magnetic field, by the attachment of magnets to the wings, has no effect on navigation. Also, massive field experiments failed to show homing to a point far from home but having the same magnetic and latitudinal characteristics.

No other suitable form of geophysical "grid", other than that provided by the sun, is known to the geophysicists, who should certainly be aware of all the possibilities. But even if we could accept the existence of a completely unknown, XY "grid", set by using the sun simply as a compass, there would still be considerable objections. A compass is needed to ensure orientation soon after release, while still in sight of the observer, but the bird could, by making exploratory flights, determine the direction of the factor gradients making up the "grid". It could then "feel" its way home over the "grid", and although the initial departure would appear random, it should reach home with a relatively short delay. But, in fact, when pigeons were released in overcast conditions which lasted for many days, not only were their departures random, but their returns were very slow, at irregular intervals over the whole period. A second objection is to the assumption that the bird uses the sun's azimuth position, its displacement round the horizon, as the clue to obtain its compass direction. The relation of the azimuth position to a given compass point is changing throughout the day, at a rate which varies markedly according to the time of day, to the season of the year, and to the latitude and longitude of the observation. Far from being a simple matter, determination of compass direction in this way is a highly complicated procedure, calling for the equivalent of a nautical almanac. But the sun does provide one fixed reference point. The highest point on its daily arch across the sky is always due south in the northern hemisphere.

This highest point of the sun arch is always reached at local noon, and so provides a reference point in time. Changes in longitude can then be determined by comparing local time with a record of home time as kept by some form of internal chronometer. With displacement east the local time is in advance of home time—the sun has moved further round its arch. With displacement west local time is behind home time —the sun has not moved so far round. The existence of such time-keeping mechanisms in animals is not disputed, nor is their accuracy, though much more work needs to be done on this score. It appears clear that whatever the internal rhythmic processes may be, they are kept in step by external pacemakers, particularly by the diurnal light/dark rhythm. Indeed, by artificial manipulation of this rhythm, changes in orientation have been produced. Thus starlings trained to take up one direction in a cage, altered their choice through 90° after treatment with an artificial day six hours behind the normal time. Pigeons subjected to a sequence of irregular light/dark periods, scattered at random when released at a distant point. When such treatment was directly followed by a regular artificial day three hours in advance of or behind home time, they showed strong tendencies to orientate in directions opposite to home when released, respectively to the east and west.

The highest point of the sun arch also provides a means of displacement determination in latitude. It is raised by a southward displacement, lowered by a northward one. The point also rises and falls with the changing seasons. There is some evidence that if pigeons are prevented from observing this change at a time (the equinoxes) when it is most marked, they may subsequently show a false orientation when subjected to latitudinal displacement. However, the inclination of the sun arch to the horizontal remains constant for any given latitude throughout the year and would be the most suitable measurement of north/south displacement.

The sun arch is thus capable of providing both co-ordinates of a navigational grid, as well as a compass. Moreover, the accuracy of navigation so far demonstrated only calls for the detection of angular differences some hundreds of times larger than the minimum of which the bird's eye is theoretically capable. It should be noted that the present hypothesis invokes the use of that sense organ which is the most highly developed in birds, the eye. This avoids any difficulty over the evolution of early stages of the organ concerned with navigation when it could have no selective value for that purpose. An extremely fine compensating mechanism based on the semicircular canals gives a rock-like constancy to the bird's head in flight, providing both a stable "instrument bed" as well as an "artificial horizon". Since orientation is by no means confined to local noon, determination of the sun arch by some process of extrapolation would seem to be necessary. This does not appear to be beyond a bird's sensory capacity, though more experimental investigation of this point is necessary. In this connection it is particularly interesting to note that a period of apparently unorientated flight follows release, before the bird settles on a more or less straight course. During this period the movement of the sun along its arch greatly exceeds the theoretical lower limit of detection.

While the particular hypothesis of sun navigation requires much more testing, such evidence as has been forthcoming tends to support it. Even if it should be found wanting in some respects, it is clear that the answer will lie in a better appreciation of the precise way in which the bird interprets and acts upon the information provided by the sun. And this will be a sensory process.

REFERENCE

A full review of the situation in this field and a lengthy bibliography is given in MATTHEWS, G. V. T. (1955). Bird Navigation. Cambridge University Press.

TESTING FOR AN ESP FACTOR IN PIGEON HOMING

Requirements, Attempts, and Difficulties*

J. G. PRATT

Parapsychology Laboratory, Duke University

Introduction

Two years ago I published a general review of the homing problem, with special reference to work with the pigeon (Pratt, 1953). It seemed that most of the sensory hypotheses advanced thus far had been largely discredited experimentally, and that none had been established. I felt justified, therefore, in raising the question whether something in the nature of an ESP factor might be involved.

During the past two years much work has been done on the homing problem. The Max-Planck-Institut in Wilhelmshaven, Cambridge University, and Duke University have had research programmes operating on a full-time basis. It seemed to me that the members of this Ciba Symposium on Extrasensory Perception would like to hear about some of the developments in this area that might bear directly or indirectly upon the question of an ESP factor in pigeon homing. Is the problem still open to the ESP interpretation? If so, what has been done toward developing a method for answering this question? What more is needed before the parapsychologist can say definitely whether pigeon homing really belongs within his research area?

In the review mentioned above, the opinion was ventured that the homing problem is one upon which biologists and

* The research covered by this report was conducted under a contract between the Office of Naval Research and Duke University, NR 160–244. The research was supported in part by a grant from the Rockefeller Foundation.

parapsychologists might collaborate at the present stage.
This hope has since been realized. It has been our privilege
at Duke University to have Dr. Gustav Kramer and Dr.
Ursula von St. Paul as part-time collaborators in the homing
research. Dr. Kramer was informed regarding our approach
to this problem when he first visited the Parapsychology
Laboratory, and after he came he was the first to suggest an
active collaboration between the Max-Planck-Institut and
the Duke investigators. This does not mean that he and Dr.
St. Paul think that pigeon homing must be explained in
extrasensory terms. Indeed, I know that their opinions lean
quite the other way: they think, in agreement with most
biologists, that the solution will ultimately be found within
the framework of sensory physiology. At the same time, Dr.
Kramer readily agrees with me that the possibility of an extrasensory basis cannot be excluded as long as no adequate
explanation on a physical basis is available.

On two essential points my biological colleagues and myself
are in full agreement. First, the homing results as they now
stand do not lend strong support to any particular hypothesis.
The question is open not only to the ESP type of explanation;
it is also open to the possibility of explanation in sensory
terms, even though the correct physical hypothesis may not
yet have been formulated. Secondly, the methodological
approach followed so far may be shared in common by people
of both the sensory and ESP opinions.

Dr. Matthews contends that since we cannot now conceive
of how an extrasensory factor in homing orientation could
work, we need not consider it as a possibility. But the history
of science is full of examples which show that human conceptions of the nature of the universe are not dependable guides
for setting the outer boundaries of scientific discoveries. Why
should we suppose that the prevailing scientific conceptions
of today give any better basis for laying down the limits for
further research progress than were those of the past? I think
that we may first consider the question of whether there is
an ESP factor in homing and then concern ourselves with

advanced questions about the nature of such a factor if the evidence is sufficient to establish it.

Dr. Matthews also claims that the absence of any other full-fledged sensory hypothesis is an argument in favour of homing by sun navigation. But the absence of a rival sensory hypothesis at this time does not mean that no alternative physiological explanation is possible. We may simply not yet know enough about the basic characteristics of homing to conceive of the correct sensory basis. Dr. Matthews offers the evidence of his "waiting" experiment (in which birds are prevented from seeing the sun at home for several days near, say, the fall equinox and are then displaced south, but not far enough to compensate for the decrease in the sun's altitude) to support the sun-navigation hypothesis (Matthews, 1953). But Kramer (1955) and K. and A. Rawson (1955) have also performed the waiting experiment and have obtained results contrary to those of Matthews. Furthermore, there are serious theoretical difficulties facing the sun-navigation hypothesis, particularly as regards questions of the higher complexity of the shape of the curve traced by the apparent motion of the sun than that considered by Matthews. Also, many observations made at the Max-Planck-Institut and at Duke University show such quick orientation after the bird first sees the sun that a serious doubt is raised whether opportunity to observe the sun's motion is a factor in homing (Kramer, 1953; Pratt and Thouless, 1955).

And so, while I want to keep the question open to the ESP explanation, I recognize that it is open as well to the possibility of a yet-to-be-discovered sensory explanation. As matters now stand, we simply do not have the answer. The present position of the homing research is one in which the primary need is for more facts. When new hypotheses are advanced, we may hope that they will emerge from the facts rather than from purely theoretical considerations.

At this stage of the conference we have already reviewed the evidence for extrasensory perception, and I take as my starting point the fact that the existence of an ESP capacity in humans has been established. After the investigators were sure on this point, it was inevitable that the question should be asked whether a comparable capacity exists in any of the other species. It is essential to our understanding of ESP to know how the capacity is distributed within the animal kingdom, whether its development in the process of evolution came early or relatively recently.

In addition to the theoretical grounds for asking about ESP in animals, there are compelling reasons for raising the question because of unexplained behaviour, especially the remarkable way-finding abilities of many species for which no adequate sensory basis has yet been found. Rhine (1951), in reviewing this behaviour, pointed not only to the unexplained migration and homing of birds and other species, but also to the surprising number of reports of both long-distance homing and trailing into strange territory by mammals, especially pet cats and dogs.

These cases of animal behaviour which suggest the operation of ESP ability are, like any anecdotal material, only a starting point for experiments. And we would all agree that the experiments should be conducted under laboratory conditions provided the controls imposed do not inhibit the kind of behaviour we wish to study. A few efforts to make controlled studies of ESP in animals have yielded encouraging positive results. The first of these were the testing of circus dogs (Bechterev, 1924) and of a horse (Rhine and Rhine, 1929) for carrying out unspoken commands. More recently cats were tested for ability to respond in a simple choice situation when the experimenter willed the animal to go to one of two food cups (Osis, 1952) and, in a second study, when the animal had to choose between a cup with food and one without, with the experimenter not knowing which was which (Osis and Foster, 1953). All of these investigations gave results which the experimenters were only able to interpret as supporting the ESP hypothesis.

The Duke pigeon homing research is another consequence of raising the question whether animals have an ESP capacity.

The question in this instance happens to be the one with which my own research is concerned and is therefore the one with which the present discussion will deal in more detail.

The first question is: Does the pigeon show homing orientation which cannot now be explained in sensory terms? Or putting the issue more specifically in terms of pigeon performance: Does the bird show orientation toward the loft and success in returning home when released in strange territory in a new direction and at a distance that excludes familiar landmarks? The evidence for this kind of homing is strong and is rapidly increasing, though it is not as strong as the evidence for an ESP capacity in humans. Dr. Matthews has referred to some of the evidence for this mysterious type of homing. Without attempting to summarize all the unreported results of this kind from the Duke work, I will describe in detail one experiment which incorporated a number of desirable controls.

A pigeon homing experiment

If a pigeon homing test is planned for a single release point, the use of birds from two lofts with the two homes lying in nearly opposite directions is a procedure that offers distinct advantages over a test involving birds from only one loft. If the birds depart appropriately in the two homeward directions when they are released alternately and one at a time, this fact goes far toward establishing that homing orientation has occurred. When the birds are all from a single loft, even though they depart toward home it is never possible to be quite sure whether the direction of departure represented a reaction to the distant home situation or to some purely local factor, such as wind or a topographical feature. In our work on this problem at Duke University we have therefore sought to have available pigeons living in places 100 miles or more apart for use in joint releases. The experiment to be presented made use of birds from Durham, North Carolina, and Richmond, Virginia, which are about 135 miles apart.

Simultaneous releases were made from two points, each involving birds from both cities. The experiment was set up on a "rectangle" design. One of the two release points was 101 miles north of Durham and 75 miles west of Richmond, and the other was 81 miles east of Durham and 94 miles south of Richmond. Dr. Ursula v. St. Paul was co-experimenter in this research, and we were ably assisted by Dr. Gordon Mangan and Miss Rhea White of the Parapsychology Laboratory staff.

The Richmond birds had never been displaced from the loft before this experiment. Some of the Durham birds had made short homing flights of as far as 20 miles from different directions, and they were assigned to the release groups in this experiment to give them a home direction different from their preceding release.

The birds from the two cities were transported during the night to a centrally located meeting place. There the birds from each city were divided into two groups and reassigned to transport vehicles for the remainder of the indirect journeys to the two release points. The birds were carefully shielded against any view of the landscape or sky along the way.

Releases at the two places were made during the forenoon, with an irregular alternation between Durham and Richmond birds. The details regarding the vanishing points, the number of birds homing to each city from each release point, and the approximate speed of return may be seen from Figure 1.

The Richmond birds gave very good homing returns for first flights at this distance, 19 out of 25 birds completing the journey. In spite of the fact that about half of the Durham birds had homed previously from distances of 5 to 20 miles, only 9 out of 28 returned in the first experiment.

I am getting a bit ahead of the story in mentioning homing success here, but this helps to explain how we came to be able to make a second rectangle release. The Richmond owners* of the birds had not expected to get them back and

* Mr. R. R. Grundy and Mr. David Beard, to whom we are greatly indebted for their participation, which made the experiment possible.

they had no need for the ones that returned. Accordingly, we used them again in a second experiment in which the release

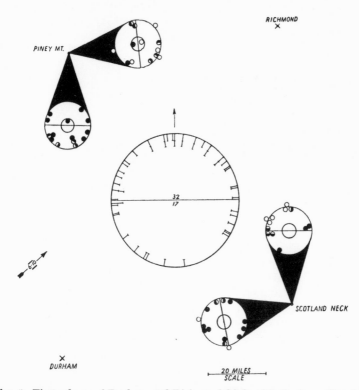

FIG. 1. First release of Durham and Richmond birds with the home lines in a "rectangle" design. EXPLANATION :—Projections of release points show bearings of vanishing points and homing performances of birds from the two cities as observed in single flights. Outside outer circle : birds homing faster than 15 mph. Inside outer circle : white birds = home on release day but slower than 15 mph. ; half shaded = homed after release day ; fully shaded = lost. Within inner circle ; vanishing points not observed. The large circle in the centre summarizes the departure bearings of all birds, with the vertical representing the home direction. The arrow shows the average direction and force, in m.p.h., of the wind over the test area on the release day (Oct. 1, 1954).

points were reversed. Eight of the nine Durham returnees were also taken for the second experiment, and other Durham birds were added to increase the number. The results of the second experiment are shown in Figure 2.

The flight pattern of the first experiment showed only a vague choice of the home direction at the release point.

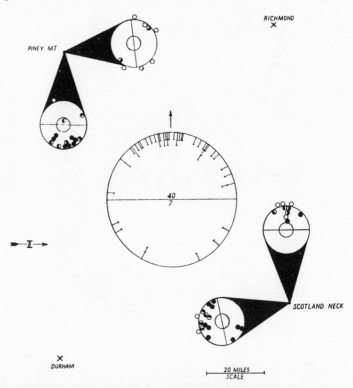

FIG. 2. Second release of Durham and Richmond birds with the home lines in a "rectangle" design. EXPLANATION: See Fig. 1. The arrow shows the average direction and force, in m.p.h., of the wind over the test area on the release day (Oct. 17, 1954).

However, out of 49 birds observed long enough to record a vanishing point, 32 were lost from sight in the home half of the circle ($\chi^2 = 4\cdot59$, 1 df., $P = 0\cdot032$). In the second experiment the flight patterns at both release points show more accurate choice of the home direction. Forty out of 47 vanishing points recorded were in the home half of the circle ($\chi^2 = 23 \cdot 17$, 1 df., $P = 0 \cdot 000002$). In both releases combined, 72 vanishing points were in the home half of the circle and 24 were away from home, a highly significant difference ($\chi^2 = 24 \cdot 0$, 1 df., $P = 0 \cdot 000001$).

There was some difference in the weather of the two days but none that could account for the difference in departures. The first day was more cloudy, with approximately an 8/10 cover of thin cirrus clouds through which the sun was visible. The wind was approximately 6 to 10 m.p.h. from the southwest. On the second day there were widely scattered small cumulus clouds against a clear blue sky. The wind was approximately 8 m.p.h. from the west. Temperature on the first day was warm (approximately 85° F) and on the second day moderate (approximately 65° F). Yet there was a striking difference in departures, as shown in the comparison of homeward and away-from-home vanishing points on the two occasions.

	First release	Second release	Total
Vanished toward home	32	40	72
Vanished away from home	17	7	24
Total	49	47	96

$$\chi^2 = 5 \cdot 02, 1 \text{ df.}, P = 0 \cdot 025$$

We welcome such unexplained differences in the Duke work, as well as differences among the findings reported from the separate locations where investigations of pigeon homing are being conducted (chiefly Wilhelmshaven, Cambridge, Duke, and Middlebury College). We consider that valuable discoveries may be made by following up the clues given by the differences.

On the second release 16 out of 18 birds homed to Richmond, whereas only 14 out of 30 homed to Durham. In this release, as in the first one, the percentage of homing success of the Richmond birds was greater than that of the Durham birds. The difference in homing performance for both releases combined is shown in the following 2 × 2 table, which gives a highly significant value of chi square.

	Durham	Richmond	Total
Birds Homed	22	34	56
Birds Lost	36	9	45
Total	58	43	101

$$\chi^2 = 16 \cdot 9, \, 1 \text{ df.}, \, P = 0 \cdot 00004$$

It is not possible to say definitely why the Richmond birds homed better than the Durham birds, but the situations were different in at least the following four general respects:

1. The Richmond birds were given regular daily periods of enforced exercise flight, whereas the Durham birds were left free at the loft to come and go as they pleased. It is conceivable that the Durham birds may not have been in as good physical condition for a long flight.

2. There were differences in stock, as shown by an earlier experimental comparison (Pratt, 1955).

3. Dr. Kramer has suggested that the locations of the lofts may be the important difference. The effects of displacing pigeons west and south of Richmond may be greater in terms of the change of the physical factors in the bird experiences than the corresponding effect of displacing Durham birds to the north and east. We have found a direction preference factor in the North Carolina situation, with a general favouring of homing on a northward flight, and we may have some indication that it was working here.

4. The average distance was less for the Richmond birds than for the Durham ones, though the difference is not very great and this factor alone cannot account for the striking difference in their performance.

These two Durham-Richmond releases are the first homing tests conducted with an experimental design which made it necessary for birds to depart in the four main compass directions on the same day in order to register a preference for the home direction. The necessity of choosing the four different compass directions offered a measure of control against the possibility that the initial orientation was brought about by some local condition (e.g. wind direction at the release point) or some general effect that caused the birds to turn in a direction that just happened to coincide with the home direction.

The fact that all such flight-deviating factors were balanced in this "rectangle" experiment is the reason why it provides strong evidence, perhaps the strongest available from a single experiment, that pigeons show a basic homing orientation that is not to be explained by directional training, local experience, or random searching.

What is the basis of homing?

A physical basis for what the pigeons did in the Durham-Richmond experiment is conceivable in either of two forms. First, the birds may have experienced at their home locations some geophysical characteristic by which they identified that spot on the globe, and when they were displaced they experienced a change in the special home-identifying feature or features which enabled them to turn toward home at the release point. Or, secondly, the pigeons may have recorded the enforced outward journey in some way which enabled them to compute the home direction. Establishing either of these two modes of homing behaviour would strongly imply a sensory basis, even though further research might be required to identify the mechanism involved.

What, on the other hand, is implied by the question whether the birds were homing by ESP? This is to ask whether they were reacting at the release point to the familiar home-plus-environment as a psychological situation and responding to this distant goal directly, in the absence of any conceivable sensory mechanism registering some external or internal physical energy system for the direction.

The ordinary type of homing experiment, in which birds are forcibly displaced and released to return to the starting point, does not distinguish between the sensory and extra-sensory possibilities. Of course, if the study of homing under this general situation ever reveals an adequate sensory basis, there would no longer be any reason for raising the ESP question in this connection. So far, no adequate sensory basis has been found, and it is therefore relevant to consider how the situation might be modified to enable us to take the first major step toward testing for an ESP factor in homing.

In theory, the experiment that is needed is simple. Move the home situation as well as the pigeon and then observe whether orientation occurs in relation to the old latitude and longitude or to the home situation in its new location. In practice, however, the experimental procedure may be difficult to arrange or even to approximate sufficiently closely.

Please observe that I said that, in theory, we move the "home situation", and not simply the "home", or the building in which the pigeon lives. Dr. Kramer has suggested that one way in which this might be done is to establish a pigeon loft aboard a ship anchored out of sight of land. Assuming that the birds would learn to recognize the ship as their home environment, but not the specific expanse of water in which the ship was anchored, it would be possible in time to conduct homing tests by moving both the birds and the ship over a sufficient distance (say 75 miles) and thus see whether the birds returned to their original latitude and longitude or to the loft in its new location. Thus far, we have not sought the opportunity to do a shipboard experiment as we have felt we need a more thorough general knowledge of homing behaviour before starting upon such a major undertaking. But I have been devoting some of my efforts to looking for a suitable compromise procedure using a mobile loft on land.

The mobile loft explorations have shown that the pigeon's home-ties for the familiar environment are very strong, even stronger than those for the loft itself. At the moment, therefore, I cannot say whether we shall be successful in developing an ESP test of homing with a land-based loft. These, briefly, are the steps already tried toward this objective:

1. Pigeons housed in a mobile loft were shifted every few days between two locations 25 miles apart. I hoped that the uninterrupted familiarity with the loft would accentuate the pigeons' attachment to it, and that the two familiar environments would become of secondary importance, balanced one against the other, by virtue of the divided but equal exposure to the two. A fire-tower observation point was midway between the two locations, and the plan was to release the pigeons there in due time to see if they homed toward the location where the loft was or toward the other one. However, the birds soon showed that the two environments were not equalized by the procedure. Once the birds were in either location for more than a day or two, they preferred to be left there, as shown by the fact that after the loft was moved to the other place the birds would abandon it and fly back to where they had been during the immediately preceding days. Then they would drift back to the loft after two or three days of self-imposed food and shelter deprivation. A few tests made from the fire-tower showed that the birds always returned to the location where they had been most recently.

2. Starting with a new group of pigeons, I moved the loft every day. Still the birds developed perferences for the *locations*, as shown by the fact that after each move a few of them went back to where they had been the day before (average distance about one mile) and did not return to the loft. However, when the loft was brought once more to the previous locations, the birds readily entered it.

3. At the next stage, and again with new birds, I restricted the experience with the environment still further to see if the birds could be made to accept the loft regardless of where it was located. The birds were closed inside the loft during most

of the day to prevent them from forming an attachment to the environment. Late in the day they were let out for exercise flight in a location where they had not been before. But the birds were reluctant to accept the loft in a strange place, and on the third day they completely failed to do so, despite the fact that some pigeons were in an aviary on top of the loft as decoys.

4. A "walled-aviary" experiment was undertaken, with pigeons being raised inside a large enclosure which only gave them a view of the open sky. Homing had been obtained from as far as 200 miles on the first release of pigeons raised in an enclosure of comparable size but without opaque walls (Kramer and St. Paul, 1954). It seemed worth while to try a suggestion, first offered by Dr. Karlis Osis of the Parapsychology Laboratory, of walling in an aviary to see if homing to it could be obtained. If so, the way would then be open for moving the aviary after the birds were displaced to see what happened. Releases in the preliminary stage showed no evidence of orientation toward the walled aviary on its original spot, and the aviary was wrecked by Hurricane Hazel before further tests were made. I have been urged to try further work along these lines, but it seems advisable to wait to see if pigeons now being kept in a walled aviary in Wilhelmshaven show homing orientation.

These efforts show that the task of finding a suitable test for an ESP factor in pigeon homing is not an easy one. But the failures themselves help to define the conditions under which success may ultimately be achieved. As long as the problem is unsolved and the possibility remains that some homing may have an ESP basis, the question will continue to be worth our best efforts to find a crucial test. Sound logic requires that we continue to try out procedures that do not depart too widely from the normal homing behaviour from which the ESP question arises. At the same time, it is important to explore for methods of testing "homing ability" under laboratory conditions, provided always that the procedures do not inhibit the basic function they are designed to study.

REFERENCES

BECHTEREV, W. (1924). *Z. Psychother. med. Psychol.* Abstract translation in *J. Parapsychol.*, **13**, 166.

KRAMER, G. (1953). *J. Orn., Lpz.*, **94**, 201.

KRAMER, G. (1955). *J. Orn., Lpz.*, **96**, 173.

KRAMER, G., and ST. PAUL, U.v. (1954). *Orn. Beob.*, **51**, 3.

MATTHEWS, G. V. T. (1953). *J. exp. Biol.*, **30**, 243.

OSIS, K. (1952). *J. Parapsychol.*, **16**, 233.

OSIS, K., and FOSTER, E. B. (1953). *J. Parapsychol.*, **17**, 168.

PRATT, J. G. (1953). *J. Parapsychol.*, **17**, 34.

PRATT, J. G. (1955). *J. exp. Biol.*, **32**, 70.

PRATT, J. G., and THOULESS, R. H. (1955). *J. exp. Biol.*, **32**, 140.

RAWSON, K. S., and RAWSON, A. M. (1955). *J. Orn., Lpz.*, **96**, 168.

RHINE, J. B. (1951). *J. Parapsychol.*, **15**, 230.

RHINE, J. B., and RHINE, L. E. (1929). *J. abnorm. (soc.) Psychol.*, **23**, 449; **24**, 287.

DISCUSSION

Parkes: There is one point I would like to clear up immediately. Dr. Pratt, when you say ESP in connection with birds and mammals and so on, do you mean simply something which cannot at present be attributed to any obvious activity of the known senses?

Pratt: I mean that, but not simply in the sense of our ignorance of the known senses. I mean that we must apply criteria to this behaviour to see if it would conform to the predictions we would make if it occurs without dependence upon any specific sense organ.

Parkes: So when you use the term ESP in this connection you do not necessarily rule out the discovery of a new function of the known senses, or of a new sense?

Pratt: That is true in general.

Hardy: I have listened to these two papers with the accounts of their experiments with the greatest interest. My inclination is to agree with Dr. Matthews: I think it is difficult to see how ESP can fit into what one sees of the orientation of birds in relation to the sun. I was very interested in Dr. Pratt's suggestion of using ships at sea, and I think the weather ships might possibly help. Weather ships remain on one station for a time and may then go away to another position; they have been very co-operative with work in oceanography.

I would like just to make two points. I know I was asked to open this discussion because I have expressed my interest in the implication of telepathy for biological theory. In that respect I would say in the words of Dr. Matthews "that I still carry the pimples of the young biologist" and I have not outgrown them. I agree with Dr. Pratt in thinking that it is likely that what has been shown in true telepathy experiments may be of profound importance to biology, although I cannot imagine its immediate connection with the problem of homing. Instead of discussing actual homing, I will briefly say why I regard telepathy as so important for biology. At first I welcomed the experiments in card guessing that seemed to put telepathy on a quantitative basis. I have, however, never been really happy over the question of clairvoyance. I find telepathy and precognition not impossible concepts because mind and mind, or mind and time, are concerned; to say, however, that one mind can tell what is on the back of a card that has never been seen by any other mind, that to me is something like magic which I simply cannot swallow. Now because the same kind of statistical results are obtained in telepathy as in the clairvoyance tests, and may be obtained also, as Mr. Spencer Brown has shown, in matching series of so-called random numbers, I have become sceptical as to the meaning of this card guessing side of the work. I am greatly in sympathy with Mr. Spencer Brown's attitude, but I don't think he is destroying all the work done at Duke University and other places; he is showing it to be something different but equally interesting. Just as Priestley was mistaken about the nature of the oxygen he had discovered and it was Lavoisier who showed what it really was—so perhaps something different will come of all these experiments, and none of Dr. Rhine's work will be wasted. I do believe however that telepathy, apart from the card-guessing experiments, is a reality.

I should like very briefly to mention some of the early experiments in the *Proceedings of the Society for Psychical Research*, Vol. 2, and refer to some of the results which were obtained in the Liverpool work of Guthrie and Birchell. I will show a series of drawings (Fig. 1) transmitted in these experiments; in the line above are the drawings made on one side of a screen and below are the ones drawn by the percipient at the other side. This is a set of six consecutive results from one experiment, containing indeed all the results for that particular test. These experiments appear to have been made under the strictest supervision. I think you must agree that they are very remarkable—more remarkable, to my mind, than any of the card-guessing experiments. These results are not alone, there are the experiments of Smith at Leeds, also recorded in volume 2 of the *SPR Proceedings*; there were also the experiments done by Schmoll and Mabire in Paris, and various others. Considering it biologically, if it is true that there can be a transmission of form to this degree, I cannot believe that it is something appearing only in a few human beings—perhaps only a few human beings are conscious of it; if this kind of telepathy is really true, then it must have some very profound biological significance.

I am not convinced only on this evidence, although I think it is most striking, I am convinced on an entirely personal experience which, although it is anecdotal and not scientific evidence, I will mention because it illustrates so well this transmission of ideas of form. In the early days of the first war I was placed with my unit on the Lincolnshire coast, and there was a Mrs. Wedgwood living there who was the widow of Arthur Wedgwood, who with Hensleigh Wedgwood was a prominent figure in the spiritualist movement at the end of the last century. When I met her Sir Oliver Lodge's book *Raymond* had just come out; we were discussing it one day at a tea-party, when she told me that she herself had been an amateur medium. We later tried some table-tilting seances of the kind described in *Raymond* but without the slightest evidence of anything "spiritualistic". However, on one of these occasions something very remarkable occurred—she knew that my brother was a prisoner of war in Germany, and she knew that he was an engineer; she suddenly turned to me when we had our hands on the table and said: " I can see your brother now, he is in a small room in a prison camp with his camp bed, and he must be drawing one of his engineering drawings, he is making big squares and oblongs in red and blue on a sheet of paper." Now she was describing exactly what *I* had been doing that afternoon, and nobody else in the world knew I had been doing it. Our Colonel was giving some lectures on military history, and he was going to lecture on

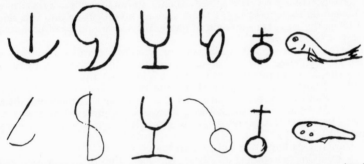

Fig. 1. (Hardy) A complete consecutive series of six drawings transmitted by telepathy from Mr. Guthrie to Miss E. without contact during the Liverpool experiments. The original drawings are shown above and the reproductions by Miss E. below. When No. 6 was being transmitted Miss E. said almost directly, " Are you thinking of the bottom of the sea, with shells and fishes ? " then drew as above. (From Hardy, A. C. (1953). *Proc. Soc. psych. Res.* 50, 99.

the Franco-Prussian war, and he asked me during the Sunday to prepare a map for him. So I took a big sheet of paper and drew in the rivers, mountains, etc.; now, it was my own idea, and not his, to represent the opposing forces by cards of red and blue, oblongs and squares for artillery and cavalry, etc.—so he could not have told anyone about it. That was exactly what Mrs. Wedgwood said she "saw" my brother doing.

I am very interested in colour, it makes a very strong impression on me; two years later I became a camouflage officer, and I was attending a course in London when I went out to dinner with Mrs. Wedgwood who had gone to live there. That afternoon we had been doing some experiments in dazzle with brilliant colours; cutting them up into shapes to give dazzle effects. I had painted a big sheet of cardboard a brilliant pink and spent some time looking at it, waiting for it to dry before cutting it up. The moment we sat down to dinner with Mrs. Wedgwood she said: "I don't know what you have been doing, but there is a large pink square on the table cloth in front of you". It was not as if she often did this sort of thing with me and that these were two lucky guesses out of many they were the only two cases of that kind. That experience, together with the early drawings I have mentioned and the telepathy experiments of Gilbert Murray, where he described many series of elaborate incidents, make me believe that there is some way in which ideas of design and pattern can be conveyed other than by the ordinary senses. And if they can be transmitted between human beings, occasionally consciously, I think it may have some considerable biological significance.

I am a Darwinian and I believe all the modern findings of genetics as far as they go, but there are certain problems in evolution which I believe have not yet been solved. If only we can find suitable sensitives who can do these drawings, I think such an investigation into this side of telepathy—the transmission of ideas of form—would be of profound interest to biologists.

L.-Davies: One point arising out of Professor Hardy's remarks—a definite challenge. On one occasion, very rapidly, I drew six pictures of a simple diagrammatic nature in one house, put them in my pocket and said nothing about them; that evening, I got A to sit in one room and look at each picture in turn, and E to sit in another room and draw them. And out of the six pictures, four, if not quite as close copies as those Professor Hardy showed, at any rate had elements which clearly showed telepathy.

Hardy: I do hope you will publish that.

Nicol: On the subject of these drawings, they are very old and apparently impressive, but in very recent years vastly greater amount of work has been done on the transmission of drawings, with assessment by quantitative methods. Those were done by Whately Carington and the whole collection is to be found in the SPR files, and Professor Hardy or anyone else has a gold mine there if he wants them. The results were significant, and incidentally it was those experiments which led on to Dr. Soal's great discovery of his two remarkable subjects. It is a mistake to suppose that the only drawings available go back 70 years, however interesting they are. Even more impressive work by quantitative methods is available in the literature to the extent of several hundred pages of reports.

Hardy: Yes, I am aware of the work of Whately Carington, but surely his results depended upon the statistical evaluation of an enormous number of views as to what was being transmitted? They are not the same as the drawings I have mentioned; they fall, I believe, into another category.

Wassermann: I have been longing for about two years now to reply to Prof. Hardy, and I hoped to publish some remarks on this, but unfortunately the Society for Psychical Research has not given me the opportunity. First, although there may be slight disagreements between Dr. Soal and myself, I wish to come out in full support of Dr. Soal and Dr. Rhine, because I feel that whatever Mr. Spencer Brown may have proved, he has certainly not invalidated an iota of Dr. Soal's or Dr. Rhine's major experiments. And as far as I am aware, Prof. Hardy has nowhere given any concrete arguments why the interpretations of the Shackleton experiments are wrong. In fact, I gather from conversation with Mr. Spencer Brown that his arguments have not invalidated any of the work of Soal and Goldney at all. Secondly, although the early experiments described by Prof. Hardy are very interesting, they were not statistically evaluated, and they were not based on a reliable method of scientific research. Whatever they proved, they were spontaneous cases and they did not permit any well-founded conclusions. It is Soal's and Rhine's work which has put the thing on a scientific basis.

To come to Dr. Matthews, with whom I am in great sympathy, I would like to state that I am of his own opinion that physical explanations should be invoked wherever possible, but where I would like to differ is this: ESP is just a name for certain faculties at present. It shows certain correlations happening in certain experiments, and I think it is far too early to say they cannot be due to physical causes. In fact, I have been putting forward yesterday and today a tentative theory which suggests that one can interpret these data entirely in terms of physical mechanisms. They are not necessarily mechanisms which are familiar from the elementary school book, but certainly they are physical mechanisms of the same type as modern physicists have described. The only question, therefore, is, are these physical mechanisms which I propose the right ones to interpret these data, or should we resort to others?

Now there is an immediate point I wish to raise, why I don't believe that Dr. Matthews' experiments point to a parapsychological origin. We know that parapsychological data are rather erratic, in other words, they do not crop up at a continuous level, they are not 100 per cent reliable. Getting 25 cards correct out of 25 is a very rare event indeed, and even in the majority of experiments the level of significance may be much lower, people may just guess 8 or 9 cards consistently (which is already a very important fact and highly significant). But what the pigeons seem to be doing is something much more reliable; although they fail also in a number of cases, their reliability seems to be much higher. It is for this reason that I am a little doubtful.

Gaddum: Dr. Matthews, is it possible to deceive your pigeons with an artificial sun? If the pigeon is in a cage, with an artificial sun rising vertically, would the pigeon think it was on the equator, and fly in the direction it thought was north? Has that sort of experiment been done?

Matthews: I hope to give you the answer in about a year's time. I have just finished constructing a mechanical sun which will do as you require, but I have not used it yet.

Wolstenholme: Have any experiments been done with permanently or temporarily blinded birds, or with any other animal which shows homing instincts? Is there any evidence that what is homing in birds is the same as has been shown in even, I believe, so low a form as a limpet?

Matthews: There have been some experiments, but mostly by rather dubious experimenters, I think. No large-scale work has been done. I doubt if there is necessarily a basic form of navigation throughout. Certainly this "homing" or whatever you like to call it, does seem to run right through the animal kingdom, as you say, but I am sure they use different methods.

Lewis: Have animals been studied who were not blinded but had had their cortex damaged or certain parts of the brain ablated?

Matthews: No, I am afraid our investigations are very crude experimentally and nothing like that has been done; only the outlines have been drawn so far.

Brown: Is it not true that a blinded bird cannot fly?

Matthews: Hooded birds have been tried and they could fly.

Brown: They didn't go into spiral dives?

Matthews: Some did, but not all; in fact some flew several miles, but it is not the sort of experiment one would wish to do in England.

Brown: I also wanted to ask if there was any evidence that birds, like bees, orientate themselves by polarized light?

Matthews: The evidence as far as it goes is no, they do not. It would only be able to give them a compass orientation; it would not be able to give them a complete navigation system.

McConnell: Dr. Pratt, how well established is the zone of no orientation of pigeons, mentioned by Dr. Matthews?

Pratt: I welcome that question, because on the basis of the work both in Wilhelmshaven and at Duke we find no zone of lack of orientation. At Duke we have used distances of from 1·7 miles for a first release, through 5, 6, 7, 10, 14, 15, 16, and so on, up to more than 100 miles, and we find orientation at every distance. We think this is a very significant fact. As I left to attend this symposium Dr. Kramer came in to say good-bye, and he began by making a bow and saying: "Let me announce very ceremoniously that I have written the first page of a manuscript by Kramer and Pratt on 'Short distance orientation in homing pigeons'." So we hope in due time that you will hear about it.

Matthews: I, too, have got short distance orientation up to 18 miles. It is interesting that when I recently went to Duke University, and Dr. Pratt was kind enough to let me watch some releases of his birds, we did precisely that experiment of which I was speaking, together, half the birds being released at 50 miles and the other half at 18. We got good orientation at 50 miles, and bad orientation at 18.

Pratt: We have had other instances in which we got anomalous results on a given day, but taking the picture as a whole, based now upon scores of releases, I think the general statement I made regarding homing orientation at all distances is the one which will emerge when we prepare our report.

Parkes: Dr. Matthews, may I clear up a point? You think that navigation along the route is by the sun?

Matthews: Yes, that position fixing is by the sun at the release point.

Parkes: That is what I wanted to clear up—I could not understand how the bird knows which way to go, although having decided which way to go, it had a means of doing it.

Matthews: To put it crudely, it does it much the same way as the human navigator does. It gets its longitude by its chronometer and time differences and its latitude from differences in noon sun height.

Parkes: That is what I cannot swallow, because the internal chronometers in mammals with which I am acquainted adjust themselves to environmental time very quickly.

Matthews: Yes, and after treatment with these artificial out of phase days I have had birds orientated in the wrong direction.

Parkes: But they don't have time to get disrupted in the normal orientation process?

Matthews: Most of these releases are within 24 hours—they are taken away and are released next day, and haven't seen the sun in the interval.

Wassermann: Could you upset the timing mechanism by drugs?

Matthews: One could try that.

Perry: Dr. Pratt suggested that the speed of orientation was too fast to be based on the sun. I don't think we should accept that suggestion because a reflex reaction of orientation to a visual stimulus of that kind would require only a very short time, a time measured in milliseconds.

Parkes: But with the shearwater, for instance, Dr. Matthews, are you suggesting that by the time it got to New York or wherever it was, it realized that its internal clock was 5 hours in front of local sun time, and from that knew which way to go back?

Matthews: It sounds a bit silly when you put it like that, but for instance how does a bat realize it is near a wall when it makes an echo? I am not trying to explain these fundamental mysteries of biology. An animal reacts to stimuli. All I am saying is that here are the stimuli to which it could react, and to which it does seem to react. I am not saying how it can react.

Parkes: It could correct the 5-hour difference by going back to the meridian of Greenwich, but it fixes its latitude in addition?

Matthews: We can put it in very simple terms. Let us allow that the bird could visualise the sun arch at the release point. If that arch is tilted down too low, this can be corrected by flying towards the arch. Similarly if the sun is not far enough round the arch, this can be corrected by flying against the sun's movement. Such a correction of stimuli is frequently found in animal behaviour.

Parkes: Yes, by some kind of sensory acuity which is quite beyond us, for instance.

Matthews: Well, I don't think it is, because I was perfectly aware when I went to America that my stomach was out of time.

Dingwall: It seems to me that if we are going to discuss the ESP factor in homing, we ought to hear something about the so-called trailing experiments, because these are something essentially different from homing. In homing the animal goes to its own home, but in trailing the animal follows to the new home where it has never been. Now the first thing is carefully to examine these anecdotes—I consider them anecdotal, in fact when I first read in the *Psychological Bulletin* the case of this famous Doolen Dog (wasn't it, Dr. Pratt?) it struck me as an anecdote which was certainly interesting, and I had never heard of any other examples before. Now I am told that a certain number have been collected at Duke. If such anecdotes can be collected and analysed, and found in nearly every case to depend on the kind of normal sources there are, with which all parapsychologists are familiar—pathological lying, for example—if they are all proved to be worthless, then we must turn to something else, but if we could get *one* really ironbound case of trailing, in which an animal travels, say, 400 miles and follows the family and turns up in its new home, that would—and I think Dr. Matthews would agree—bring in an element which would suggest very strongly that there was something which we could call ESP coming into the problem. I would like Dr. Matthews and Dr. Pratt to give us very roughly their opinion about these experiments, because I have not had the opportunity to examine any of them yet.

Pratt: I made the statement that there are a number of these cases in our files. I also said they are anecdotal, and as far as I can see they are going to remain anecdotal. But they at least did something to me, in that they started me working on this problem with the idea that there may be in pigeon homing something which is directly comparable to what these trailing cases suggest. So, rather than expound on the anecdotal cases, I am proposing experiments in which the same thing might be expected to happen. Only if trailing happens reliably in our experiments am I going to be ready to say: "Here is ESP in pigeon homing." That is not a stopping point; that is a beginning for further inquiry. Now suppose we do the ship experiment and we find that the birds go back to the old latitude and longitude and search that empty area as if to say: "Here it is, but it must have sunk or become invisible." Even though we might not know the physical basis, I would be ready to say that we should all be looking for the sensory mechanism by which this occurred. Then I would have to decide whether to try to become a biologist and hope to join the fraternity in order to continue working on pigeon homing, or whether I would go back to ESP experiments with human subjects.

PARAPSYCHOLOGY IN THE MODERN APPROACH TO PSYCHOSOMATIC MAN

ROBERT AMADOU

Paris

THE two preceding papers have been devoted to pigeons and other animals. My main purpose is to talk about man —or at least to emphasize the necessity of talking about man when we deal with that particular human behaviour called ESP.

I welcome Dr. Matthews' statement that it might be dangerously misleading to equate ESP as shown in man, for example in the context of quantitative tests, with apparently similar occurrences in animals. The analogy between the two orders of facts might very well be illusory.

I wonder whether we do not believe in statistical assessment and experimental tests intended to establish the existence of ESP more than in ESP itself.

If ESP exists, it must play some other part than merely hitting the right target-card in modern demonstrations. Perhaps, if we remember that, we shall learn more about ESP because we shall look at it wherever it is; and that is all I shall endeavour to say as briefly as possible.

The title of this paper, including the word "parapsychology", implies, in the author's view at least, that parapsychology exists as a science, or more precisely as a true scientific discipline. It therefore implies that parapsychology is not solely concerned with the exposure of frauds, the denunciation of fallacies, and the discovery of some hidden processes, the study of which would fall within the scope of another recognized science. We shall assume that parapsychology has its own original object, or rather that it has, like all other sciences, its own relatively and temporarily original object: ESP.

Let us consider that ESP has been established in the last twenty-five years by the admirable series of experiments conducted according to the experimental method by Dr. Rhine and the "Duke University school" and, in this country, by Dr. Soal and Mr. Bateman.

Let us first notice the importance of that affirmation. Parapsychology is in the very peculiar situation of being obliged to establish the very existence of the phenomena it intends to study. Of course, the real nature of the objects of actual science have been ignored in the past. But no discipline has ever been constituted in order to prove that meteorites come down from the sky or that so-called thunder-stones were made by the hand of prehistoric man. Furthermore, the existence of the object itself was obvious and no one cared to deny it. So, as soon as serious studies were made of the origin of meteorites or thunder-stones, a consensus was reached and the research could go on.

The peculiar obligation of parapsychology has been referred to very often. It is to be hoped that the profound reasons for that situation will be examined closely. The logical processes that lead to the deduction of the existence of ESP should be clarified, as well as the affective motives underlying the development and admission of that logical process. Some men certainly want to demonstrate the existence of ESP, and, as certainly, some men want to demonstrate that ESP does not exist. All of them are moved by reasons which have little to do with purely scientific spirit and intellectual curiosity and are indeed very far from reason itself.

Of course, what men believe—or do not believe—about paranormal phenomena is quite independent from the reality of these phenomena and cannot be used in favour of or against their possible reality. But it makes us understand how hard it is for parapsychology to gain universal scientific recognition. It makes us understand too, I feel, the courage and tenacity of parapsychologists. Above all, it reveals how men are "sensitive" about paranormal phenomena and gives us an idea of the deep roots of those phenomena in human beings.

Indeed, crisis appears to be the normal state of psychology and periodically affects any particular psychological discipline. Such seems to be the case with parapsychology at the present moment. Parapsychology has found something and seems very much embarrassed with that thing, and wonders what it is and how to handle it.

Dr. Thouless, I remember, wrote that parapsychology needs the achievement of two different enterprises: (1) experimental work and (2) philosophical reflection. But I think that conception of the successful evolution of our discipline must be examined most carefully.

Repetition of statistical tests, in the present state of our knowledge of psi phenomena, will only bring out results that will accidentally confirm the best results already recorded. If anyone is not convinced by the amount of evidence produced so far, it is very doubtful whether he will be convinced even by a dozen Shackletons. As we shall see later on, we do repeat our ESP tests; but until now, we have not been able to set up repetitive tests. Of course, the study by means of tests, of the correlations between personality factors, etc., and ESP correct guesses might be a confirmation of the existence of ESP that it establishes differentially. Such a study also teaches us something about the experiment upon which it is based. But let us take care at this point; the only teaching brought out by experiments such as have been devised by objective psychologists in the field of parapsychology is this and only this: which conditions are favourable and which unfavourable to *the manifestation of ESP in a Zener card-guessing session*.

On the other hand, and again referring to Dr. Thouless' scheme, philosophical reflection, in the proper sense of the word, is certainly premature, as long as we cannot offer any more data to the comprehensive speculation of the philosopher; and it is quite clear that philosophical reflection does not provide us with the necessary scientific hypothesis that would stop the infernal merry-go-round of card calling.

I suggest that experimental work, the gathering of facts in

parapsychology, should be understood in a much broader sense and that theoretical work should be exercised first in the direction of scientific hypothesis.

The latter statement may seem of the utmost banality, and quite probably it is so. Or rather, it would be so, if parapsychology and the object of parapsychology were not, for very definite, strong reasons, exceedingly overrated, if parapsychologists were not tempted to ignore the treatment commonly imposed upon all objects of scientific research.

The crisis of parapsychology is none other than the chronic crisis of psychology; and the only solution of it lies in the realization of a synthesis by which the set of hypotheses called psychology would be completed and by which, at the same time, parapsychological hypotheses could be related to and therefore strengthened by more general psychological hypotheses.

If all sciences are longing for unity and if the hope of all scientists is to unify all sciences into one, the first task is to achieve unification first inside every science. That task has been performed or is being performed in some sciences: physics provides an instance. Psychology is undoubtedly very late in that respect. But opposition to unity, within the psychological field, should not come from parapsychology.

Experimental, quantitative parapsychology has proved the existence of ESP. It has proved it in the most abnormal (if not paranormal) conditions. Modern parapsychologists are inclined to consider ESP exclusively, or almost exclusively, as what is left of ESP under laboratory conditions—and to consider that what is left of ESP under those conditions is ESP itself.

When we talk about experimental parapsychology, we mean experimental in the same way that we talk of astronomy being an experimental science. But we do not produce psi phenomena; our tests are merely tracks in which we try to catch some parts of occurrences escaping our power, in their fundamental determinism.

Since, in an ESP test, we only find a tiny manifestation of

a behaviour we do not apprehend in its complexity, we are
tempted to give substance to that manifestation and to give
ESP a very arbitrary individuality and autonomy.

One of the dangers along the road of parapsychology is, I
believe, the seduction of a new theory of faculties—at least
the idea of ESP as a faculty.

ESP had to be isolated in order to be recognized, recorded,
registered, admitted as something more than a ghost. Have
we any right to preserve that artificial isolation?

If we ask the question, "What is ESP?" all serious parapsychologists will be unanimous: no answer can be given. No
definition, and especially no operational definition, of ESP
can be given. Even the definition to be found in the inside
cover of the *Journal of Parapsychology* implies that certain
mechanisms are involved and that implication is gratuitous.
Indeed, all that has been pointed out by parapsychology is
a certain behaviour of man and it is even too much to assert
that ESP is a communication (or a mode of communication)
between one man's mind and/or body and another man's
mind and/or body (so-called telepathy)—or that ESP is a
communication between one man's mind and/or body and a
material event (so-called clairvoyance). We speak of communication; but we do not even know the terms of the
relationship, nor the way a communication is established
between them. Shall we rather speak of a transfer of information as being the best description of ESP behaviour? Indeed
we may. The ESP behaviour is the expression of an information, but the stimulus or the source of information is
absolutely unknown. All we know is this: the information
expressed by ESP has been, or is or will be, acquired normally
(and not paranormally) by someone and/or the subject
of the ESP experience himself. If we are not entitled to use
the word "communication" or the word "transfer", *stricto
sensu*, how could we accept the word "perception", either
sensory or "extrasensory"? The failure of all essays of explanation in terms of a physical theory (waves, radiations of
a new kind, fluid, etc.) and the metaphysical character of

Rhine's idealistic theory, that the scientific data are far from making unavoidable, should be recalled here. They confirm our embarrassment when facing a communication or a transfer to which nothing can be applied that applies to communications and transfers.

We also could recall C. G. Jung's theory of synchronicity. Jung considers there are two orders in the world, two principles governing the universe. The first order is that of causality, and the second one is that of synchronicity, which leads to significant coincidences. Coincidence means here that no causality relation can be found nor even thought of between two synchronized events. Jung's theory is of interest to us in as much as it shows the non-compulsory character of a "communication" or a "transfer" definition of ESP.

If we do not consider ESP as a faculty but instead try to understand the whole situation in which a so-called ESP behaviour or more generally a so-called paranormal phenomenon occurs, we shall escape from formulating wrong and pseudo-problems. For instance, we cannot say that someone has got or has not got ESP. ESP cannot be considered as a genetic character. Dr. Booth says: "A subject has not got ESP as he has blue eyes". Also, we shall not forget that, when we talk about a gifted subject, we talk about a subject gifted for quantitative tests, which is completely different.

But if ESP exists at all, how could it be considered as showing itself only in the presence of Zener cards? The hints given by spontaneous cases should be taken. Perhaps I may say a few words about that matter, which has not been raised at all in the course of this Symposium. Indeed, in a symposium devoted to ESP, and especially to the value of the evidence for ESP, only statistical procedures have been dealt with.

It is extremely difficult to establish the authentic paranormal character of a spontaneous case. Recently, some parapsychologists have emphasized that difficulty with great intelligence (Dr. West, Dr. Soal) and it has not been overlooked in the past. But it seems that one of the greatest difficulties in admitting any such case as paranormal was the fact that spontaneous occurrences were not convincing by themselves. It was legitimate to consider ESP, the existence of which was under discussion, as the most improbable hypothesis. Now, since ESP, as we assumed at the beginning, has been demonstrated, the ESP hypothesis becomes quite often more probable in the qualification of spontaneous cases than other hypotheses we had to accept before. To postulate that ESP is at work in a statistical test, so contrary in its very principle to the natural, living situation of man, and that it is not at work in everyday life, seems just absurd. Of course, the criterion of statistics can hardly be used in the appraisal of spontaneous cases (in spite of the interesting propositions of Carington) and the investigation of them is extremely painstaking; yet it is more, much more promising, and it can be carried out as long as those cases oblige us to look at ESP in its context and not as an arbitrarily though necessarily isolated function or faculty.

ESP, if it exists at all, plays a part in every psychical activity, just as do the "faculties" of memory, will, intelligence, etc. If we are to believe seriously in ESP, let us find out what part it plays in normal perception, for instance, or in the learning of a language.

Modern psychology has shown that any psychical act is a complex and that finally there is no psychical act as such, but only the psychical act of an individual, and perhaps we should say of a person, at a certain time of his life and of the life of the world, at least of the world that surrounded his life since his birth. It is certainly important to analyse that personal act and to describe some of its physiological, physical, and chemical foundations. Every psychological act might be supposed to have a physiological, external aspect. Alexander himself admits that we practise psychosomatic medicine instead of corticovisceral medicine, for the only reason that we have, at present, more powerful means of psychological than of physiological action. Some day, the advantage might pass on to the physiologist. But to answer that question in advance supposes that we take a metaphysical standpoint, which is not our purpose here. Let us not underestimate the value of objective psychology (including parapsychology). But let us not either overestimate it and take the shadow for the prey. C. G. Jung, whom all psycho-analysts would follow on that point, writes: "Any experiment is conceived in order to answer a definite question. Therefore, it eliminates as much as possible every useless, irrelevant element. It dictates its conditions, it imposes its conditions upon nature itself and thus allows nature to answer the question asked by the experimenter. . . . When we proceed in such a way, we deliberately, carefully exclude the free play of nature in the plenitude of its potentialities. He who wishes to understand that game with infinite possibilities, should ask a question implying very few conditions or no condition at all."

It is at least as important not to isolate permanently in our view all aspects of human behaviour as to analyse that behaviour in its constituents. Provided, of course, that a synthesis (and, much more so, a single act) is not equal to the sum of its constituents.

One of the most striking facts about ESP is that it is always closely connected with and related to another person; very often it is concerned with the subject himself of the ESP experience.

I fear we cannot rely upon mechanical devices and logical arguments to solve the almost "classical" problem of telepathy versus clairvoyance. So far, the defenders of telepathy and the advocates of clairvoyance have been able to translate all experiments intended to verify the other theory into the terms of their own theory, whether they talk about precognitive telepathy or material traces of telepathic messages. Two of the most prominent parapsychologists hold two opposite attitudes in that respect, Dr. Rhine, in the U.S.A., being in favour of pure clairvoyance, and Dr. Soal, in this country, being strongly convinced of the existence of pure telepathy.

But, leaving aside an imperfect terminology, we shall realize that ESP always appears in a personal context, that it is meaningless to talk about some sensory process being excited by an entirely external, dead object. Such a description would hardly apply to normal perception. It certainly does not fit with the manifestation of ESP, as we might observe it in the natural frame of an *existential* situation, that is to say, in less pedantic terms, a living situation, or the situation of a living man. The importance of personal relationships in the ESP occurrences has been discovered and statistically evaluated in the test-situation. But, as we well might expect, it is much clearer when we examine spontaneous cases.

In talking about psychological context, about the psychological unity of a complex in which we try to isolate an ESP element or an ESP tracer-effect, we also mean social context. Existential situation (or living situation) requires, to be fully described and understood, a sociological analysis as well as a purely psychological one. That distinction again is very arbitrary in the study we are advocating.

Martino, the Italian ethnologist, whose name was mentioned in the report on "ESP in archaic societies", insists upon the importance of social factors, and probably over-emphasizes that importance. But it might be worth stating his theory. Martino denies to parapsychology not only the right but the very possibility of exploring paranormal phenomena in archaic societies. He adopts a strictly idealistic point of view and maintains that the structure of the archaic society contributes in creating the so-called reality; an experimenter, or let us say the mere introduction of a pack of Zener cards, would change the whole picture. Martino thinks it meaningless to ask the question whether paranormal phenomena reported in archaic societies are "real", since our concept of reality does not cover the world in which they live and which they make.

Not going so far in that idealistic direction, it seems worth remembering that it would be nonsense to talk about psychological context without thinking at the same time of the cultural and social context.

I wonder whether you would now follow me one step further. The crisis of parapsychology at the present time is the crisis of objective parapsychology. And the very expression of "subjective parapsychology" includes a contradiction in terms, since it isolates what it is supposed to enlarge and replace in the whole picture. But psychology must include parapsychology and such should be the task of all modern psychological disciplines where subjectivity and objectivity are made to co-operate and to be dialectically linked.

We have noticed before that the words "communication" and "transfer of information" (if the latter word is taken in a more or less spatial sense) applied to ESP behaviour were not springing out of the facts themselves.

Let us consider precognition for instance. Precognition is the most extraordinary, the most abnormal, the most revolutionary—so it seems at first sight—of all reported parapsychological phenomena. But its very complexity is, I believe, an advantage for our study. It might be the cross-roads where all particular psychological disciplines meet, as all psychical tendencies and functions have met in order to produce the phenomena.

In the best authenticated cases, precognition is concerned with the personal future of the subject himself or of another person. The idea of future events standing in front of us and waiting for us to meet them first in precognition and then in the course of life must be admitted only if we are forced to do so. The same would apply to the theory of a dimensional time. If we are bound by facts to admit it, of course, we will admit it. But is there not another possible way of explaining precognition? That way has been hinted at in my book on parapsychology. Indeed, modern psychology—and I mean here depth-psychology, and not only psycho-analysis considered as a therapeutic method—has very clearly shown what can be understood by personal fate or personal destiny, and how those notions of fate and destiny, though unacceptable if one refers to them as some entities independent from man, some mysterious, almighty deities, cover the mechanisms by which man directs his life, meets some people or does some things. The part of chance, of external chance, and the part of freewill are both much smaller than we could—or than we would like to—imagine they are. Some examples are so astonishing that it is hard to know where to stop and when an event in the life of an individual has not been willed—though unconsciously—by himself. Now, how that event is introduced into the life of the individual according to the profound images (or rather *"imagines"*) and tendencies of the individual himself, I cannot say, and I very much doubt that anyone could say it. Here again, we could refer to Jung's theory and explain away the difficulty by refusing to consider any causal relation between the *imago*, for instance, and its realization in the material world. But let us remain in a more classical perspective: we shall have to admit that the relationship between man and the external world is not so simple as classical psychology or even experimental modern psychology might assert. There is a reciprocal creation that cannot be described in terms of communication or action modelled on the traditional ideas of communication and action. That is particularly clear in the case of precognition. It also could be found in all occurrences generally referred to by the non-committal term "ESP". Of course, I am sure those ideas are implied in the idea of ESP, as parapsychologists use it, but they fail to appear clearly in the context of statistical tests and it is fortunate that other approaches might help to restore their full value.

My main point is to emphasize the need for co-operation between all psychological disciplines. I wonder whether paranormal phenomena, through their being more complex, richer than others, are not a very favourable place of meeting.

In any case, I believe this is a direction in which parapsychology might progress considerably—until it dies. It has been repeatedly pointed out that any satisfactory definition of parapsychology is suicidal, implying that parapsychology is condemned to die more or less in the long run. But we should be ashamed of, or even troubled by, that suicidal character of any definition of parapsychology. Indeed, the constitution of psychology will only be realized by the death of every particular psychological discipline as such. But the suicide of parapsychology is not to occur every time parapsychology studies an alleged paranormal phenomenon. It is to occur when those phenomena, that are at present unexplainable by the recognized sciences, will have to be integrated into hypotheses also covering facts already belonging to psychology.

Now, the same could be said about psychology and physics, as it has been by Dr. Wassermann. Of course, I believe the unification of psychology is only a step towards the unification of knowledge—the unification of all sciences. But I am not sure that unification means reduction, nor that a synthesis of all sciences means a particular reduction of psychology to physics and chemistry. Is this the right time to purport a reduction of psychology to physics when physicists themselves seem to put some hope in psychology, or at least to consider that psychology has something to say about the picture of the universe they are discovering and the way they are discovering it, therefore about the validity and fidelity of the picture? Whereas scientists insist upon the unavoidable part of the observer, who is always an experimenter modifying the conditions of the observation whether he wants it or not, I understand they do not consider man, his behaviour and his mind, as just another physical element. At any rate, it would be a privileged physical element and, in a true sense, the centre of the system—that is, of course, the system as we might know it—and it would be a purely metaphysical question to ask what the system is itself, or even whether the system is in itself. The physicist, I think, would be the last one to pretend to be able to answer that question, which is perhaps meaningless.

Now, I am not a physicist, and I would be quite unable to explain or even to understand the scientific significance of Heisenberg's equations, for instance. But I cannot avoid hearing or reading what physicists say, and what they say does not appear to be a simple rejection of psychology for the benefit of physics. I therefore wonder whether this is the right time to attempt or even to foresee a reduction of psychology to physics. Dr. Eisenbud and Dr. Ehrenvald have seen the necessity of unifying all our particular sciences—but they have understood the necessity first of unifying psychology.

The main task before us is the synthesis of parapsychology and psychology—in other words, the building up of psychology. Here again, I shall not speak of reduction of one to the other. Of course, reduction, in the simplest acceptance of the term, is one of the commonest tasks in parapsychology. Parapsychologists make reduction of alleged paranormal phenomena every time they discover a fraud, either voluntary or unconscious. But what is needed now is a general hypothesis, or a set of general hypotheses in psychology. New discoveries in parapsychology occupy a front-row seat, and point to a certain, still vague notion of man, of his relations to other men and to the universe. It is necessary to compare, to bring together those facts, to formulate scientific hypotheses. We used the synthesis of data from psychoanalysis, psychosomatic medicine, ethnology, sociology; and experimental psychology, and particularly experimental parapsychology, should not be forgotten. Let us hope for the coming of an experimental genius, who will design new types of experiments and take experimental parapsychology out of the vicious circle in which it revolves. But the experiments of that supposed, expected genius will be useful only if they are inserted and analysed within the framework of a general hypothesis of parapsychology, or rather of parapsychological facts considered as psychological facts.

When psychology exists as a true, unique science, parapsychology will exist no longer; but it will have been most useful in bringing out a magnificent result: learning from science all that science can teach us about man.

DISCUSSION

Gillespie: First I would like to express my personal sympathy with the point of view that Dr. Amadou has been putting before us, in as much as he is inclined to bring us back to parapsychology as being related to psychology, as well as to statistics. We are dealing with a phenomenon concerned with man, and therefore with the other disciplines concerned with man. Having said that, however, I must add that although I am happy to be asked to open this discussion, I am really in no position to do so. I have no claims whatever to be regarded as a philosopher, and I think this is really the philosophical part of this symposium. All I can do is to approach the matter from the rather naive point of view of the psychiatrist and the psycho-analyst—naive, that is to say, philosophically speaking.

I think that many psychiatrists had, probably naively, felt fairly happy about this body-mind problem, before the facts of parapsychology began to impinge upon them, in the sense that one had learned to deal with it as being essentially a pseudo-problem. That is to say, one had absorbed the doctrine of psychosomatic unity, one felt convinced that body and mind were artificially separated entities, and that they were really the same thing looked at from different points of view, just as a dome looks entirely different from inside and from outside. That orthodox psychiatric position has been shaken by the findings of parapsychology. If these facts of parapsychology are indeed facts, and particularly if precognition is a fact, this point of view is shaken to its foundations, and it looks as though we must start thinking about it all over again. This seems to me to be the most shattering impact of parapsychology on science, and yet at the same time the most stimulating one.

I fully agree with what Dr. Amadou has said about the need to integrate the facts (if we admit them as facts) of parapsychology, with those other facts which we already know about man, and so make parapsychology an integrated part of psychology. I think he hinted, and I would agree with him here, that this is probably a task for psychiatry, psycho-analysis and related subjects, rather than academic psychology, because I think if psi exists at all, then it is part of the psychological underworld, rather than the psychological superstructure or surface which is the field of academic psychology, in other words part of the world explored by Freud rather than the world of the academic psychologists. It is not a question of the physiological psychology of the special senses.

I would like to remind you that there are some remarkable resemblances between the modes of functioning of psi as they have been described by parapsychologists and those that Freud called the primary process of the mind, that is to say the mode of functioning of unconscious mental processes, processes which are untrammelled by considerations of logic, of the real possibility of wishes, of the limitations of time and space, and which freely assume the validity of magic. The difference is that it has been assumed that this primary process, this unconscious mode of mental functioning, does not work, that it is a tale told by an idiot, and that it has to be replaced in the course of individual and racial development by the conscious, secondary process. Nevertheless, there is a sentence from *The Interpretation of Dreams* by Freud that I would like to read out: "Some other observations lend support to the view that these processes, which are described as irrational (that is the primary processes), are not in fact falsifications of normal processes, intellectual errors, but are modes of activity of the psychical apparatus that have been freed from an inhibition." That was written in 1900. Perhaps we are sometimes too apt to assume that evolutionary change is pure advance, pure profit, and to forget that it usually involves losses as well as gains, even if natural selection favours gains on balance. Thus, for instance, our assumption of the erect position has presumably led to some atrophy of our sense of smell, and this in turn, as Freud has suggested, may have had adverse effects upon human sexual function. Is it not possible then that man's development of his sensory functions, and especially of the distance receptors of vision and hearing, and of all the immensely elaborate cerebral discriminatory apparatus that goes with them, may have led to an atrophy, or more accurately a suppression of more archaic modes of making contact with the surroundings? May it not be that these supposed primary mental processes, whilst lacking the manifest advantages of the secondary mental processes, the advantages of certainty and discrimination, possess other qualities which the secondary processes by their very nature cannot have—qualities such as independence of time and space?

Assuming such a hierarchy of primary and secondary mental processes, is it likely to be easy for us, working in terms of the secondary system, to form an unbiased opinion about the potentialities of the primary system? We all know how difficult it has been to accept the concept of the primary system in Freud's sense, that is unconscious mental functioning. I think it is easy to understand that resistance may be very much stronger against the idea of an unconscious system that works, than against the idea of one that is purely delusive—like the difference between talking of witchcraft as something that happens, and discussing it as a mediaeval delusion.

That leads me to what I think is an important point. From the point of view of psycho-analysis (and Eisenbud has particularly expressed this), we are playing with fire. In parapsychology we are not playing parlour games. We are dealing with things which produce tremendous amounts of anxiety, and I think this has a good deal to do with unconscious resistances of parapsychologists themselves, which lead to a tendency to discredit the work of others and to clutch at straws which may give the hope of some other explanation. We have seen some of that in this symposium. I think, also, these same unconscious and irrational forces may be connected with a tendency to regard ESP as a freakish property of a few exceptional individuals, which seems to me to be like the servant-girl's excuse that her illegitimate baby is only a little one.

Wassermann: In reply to Dr. Amadou, let me say this. The body-mind problem which he raises is a problem of subjective philosophy, not of objective psychology, and the sort of problems I am dealing with belong to objective psychology. Now, Carnap in the *International Encyclopaedia of Unified Science* has stated at great length what the modern idea of physicalism stands for, and my view is that of a physicalistic theory. Now, of course, one can never say when the time is ripe to build up a theory, the only thing is to build one up and see whether it agrees with the facts. Facts by themselves mean very little until you correlate them in terms of a theory. The type of things which I have been trying to interpret in terms of physics are the experiments of Thorndike, Hull, classical conditioning, trial and error learning, instrumental conditioning, Gestalt perception, and various other problems which I have not discussed here, but which can all be interpreted, I believe, in terms of physical processes. I am not denying the existence of mental processes, but the point is they can be eliminated from the discourse of science, as far as it goes. You can put forward an epiphenominalis theory, but Carnap and others have shown that there is absolutely no necessity for this. Now as regards the Freudian view which Dr. Gillespie mentioned, I have great sympathy but I think Freud's work can equally be interpreted in terms of physicalism, and so do others.

Brown: I don't think anyone denies that we can have a physicalistic theory such as Carnap's, but equally I think we can interpret all physics in terms of psychology; it is a matter of what we are willing to do for the sake of convenience. If we want to talk about a chemical reaction in only physical terms, we can do so, but we take very much longer about it than the chemist.

I should like to pass on to a question which Dr. Amadou raised about communication, and his reference to Jung's hypothesis of non-causal synchronicity, which is in fact the hypothesis I was stating in somewhat different terms, when I said that these phenomena might be chance after all. A chance coincidence is in fact a non-causal synchronicity. I agree with him that we cannot use the term communication in this case, and I think also the use of the concept of information which he used is ambiguous. I should like to say that there is in so-called telepathy no information transfer. But of course information theory adopts two meanings for the word "information"; for example, if we put a monkey on a typewriter to strike the keys at random, we say that if it goes on long enough it will write all the Shakespeare sonnets; and if it did that, we should say here was a definite information pattern. But in one sense the monkey has in fact no information, although the pattern is later defined in terms of information. The monkey has not in fact received information.

A discovery, such as the discovery of Newton's laws of motion can be likened to the case of the monkey on the typewriter; the information originated in Newton as the sonnets originate in the monkey. What is odd is that Newton's guess later turns out to correlate significantly with subsequent observations on the planets and other satellites. Precognition, perhaps? But in that case this is no declining faculty, of whose vestiges psychical research obtains the last glimpses before extinction: it is, on the contrary, the living power of inspiration necessary to all scientific advancement.

McConnell: I must just say in passing that I have been puzzled for several years as to what Spencer Brown was aiming at, and now I am delighted to be able to pigeon-hole him as supporting Jung's acausal synchronicity !

The question I want to ask Dr. Amadou is this: I don't understand acausal synchronicity, and I would like, if Dr. Amadou feels that he wishes to, to have him say just a word or two about what concept of causality is involved here, that makes this combination of words meaningful.

Amadou: Well, first of all, I may say that I am not advocating a theory by just mentioning a possible solution to the nature of what is ESP and what is an ESP manifestation. In Jung's view there are two principal orders of things, one is causality and the other synchronicity. I don't think Spencer Brown's theories are as close as he says to Jung's synchronicity; there is an element which is lacking in Spencer Brown's theory and which Jung emphasizes very clearly, that is the *meaningful* character of the coincidence. Jung says that in the order of synchronicity you have the coincidence, which is not a chance coincidence, which is not a causal relation, but which is a meaningful coincidence.

Brown: Yes, but what does he mean by "meaningful"? Is it a meaningful coincidence that my watch retains a certain non-causal synchronicity with the sun in the sky? There is a decline effect—my watch is not perfectly accurate—and after several months there is a negative correlation. But is it meaningful?

Amadou: Well, meaningful means two things. First, in Jung's view it means that it cannot be attributed to chance. At the same time, it means that it is correlated with the personal or psychological situation of the person who experiences the coincidence.

Brown: But when we say that it cannot be attributed to chance, all we are doing is noticing afterwards that there is this synchronicity, and saying this is not what we mean by chance.

Amadou: Jung follows the most classical notion of chance, and for instance he says that chance cannot explain ESP manifestations because of the results of ESP tests. That is why Jung says chance is not alone at work.

Brown: But we can just as well say that chance cannot explain the synchronicity between my watch and the sun, and yet there is no information transfer between my watch and the sun.

Amadou: There is a causal relation there; and Jung says that in the order of synchronicity there is no causal relationship.

Brown: But if I turn the hands of my watch round I don't flip the sun across the sky. Nor does the sun have any useful effect on my watch if I have forgotten to wind it up.

Parkes: I think this could well be sorted out over a glass of sherry. Mr. Amadou, would you like to wind up the discussion?

Amadou: I have nothing further to say except that I quite agree with Dr. Gillespie's remarks as an exponent of the psycho-analytical position, which so far provide us with the best point-of-view for relating so-called paranormal occurrences to the existential situation, and therefore for progressing towards the explanation and perhaps the understanding of those occurrences—which are not different from—but part of the explanation and understanding of man's attitudes and behaviours.

EXPERIENCES SUGGESTIVE OF PARANORMAL COGNITION IN THE PSYCHO-ANALYTIC SITUATION

W. H. GILLESPIE
London

Historical introduction

THE first psycho-analyst to publish material related to parapsychology was Sigmund Freud himself, and probably few people appreciated how much he wrote on the subject until the relevant passages were collected by Devereux in *Psychoanalysis and the Occult* in 1953. Although it is true that there is some repetition, nevertheless it turns out that Freud wrote on this subject on six occasions, from 1899 to 1933. The first two papers, published in 1899 and 1904, which deal largely with the same clinical material, are quite slight, and are concerned to show that rational explanations can readily be found for some apparently remarkable coincidences.

However, in the third paper, written in 1921, Freud says at the outset that "it no longer seems possible to brush aside the study of so-called occult facts". He discusses the difficulties of collaboration between psycho-analysts, with their traditional scientific background, and occultists, who are mostly believers who merely want new proofs, and who are apt to declare that their cause has triumphed the moment a first assent is forthcoming, holding that belief in one alleged fact constitutes belief in all others: there is a danger that such people may be welcomed as liberators from the painful obligation of thinking rationally. Freud proceeds to discuss two cases of fortune-telling which did not come true; but he is able to show that analysis of these two cases makes the prophecies understandable and meaningful, on the assumption that the fortune-teller was telepathically aware of the clients' repressed and unconscious wishes.

The first case described in Freud's next paper (1922) is an even more striking example of a very characteristic aspect of psycho-analytic contributions to parapsychology, namely, the coming to light of connections not otherwise obvious as a result of analysis of the material—connections of a kind which seem difficult or impossible to explain on ordinary assumptions. In this case a man dreamt that his wife had twins, at the very time that his far-away daughter unexpectedly and a month prematurely did in fact give birth to twins. The dream makes sense—but then also suggests telepathy—if we assume in the dreamer an unconscious incestuous attachment to his daughter. Although in this instance Freud preserves an attitude of complete impartiality regarding the possibility of telepathy (the instance is indeed by no means convincing), the principle involved is of vital importance, that is, that analysis may reveal telepathy where none was apparent without analysis.

Freud's next paper (1925) contains no new material, but in it for the first time he unequivocally expresses his belief in the possibility of transference of strongly emotionally coloured recollections, particularly at the moment at which an idea emerges from the unconscious state into consciousness. If this is granted, then such telepathic messages may reach someone during sleep and come to his knowledge during a dream; or they may reach him during the day and be dealt with only during a dream of the following night. Such telepathic material might then be modified and transformed in the dream like any other material. At the same time, however, Freud expressed his disbelief in prophetic dreams, on the grounds that their existence would contradict all scientific assumptions and would correspond to pure wishful thinking.

It is only in his last contribution, published in 1933, that Freud uses material directly derived from the analytic situation, instead of merely applying analysis to non-analytic data. The material here concerns a patient's apparently extrasensory cognition of the visit a quarter of an hour previously of Dr. Forsyth from London. Freud analyses this incident very elaborately, and although he finally concludes "We are left once more with a *non liquet*", he adds "I must confess that here too I feel that the balance is in favour of thought transference." Furthermore, he is able now to call in evidence publications by two other well-known analysts, Helene Deutsch and Dorothy Burlingham. Freud asks his readers to think more kindly of the objective possibility of telepathy, and revises his former fear that this might endanger our scientific outlook, a fear that, he says, displays no great trust in science.

Helene Deutsch's contribution to this subject (1926), which was cited by Freud, is remarkable as being the first example of an analyst recognizing that her patient's telepathic feat may have been called forth by the analyst's preoccupation with her own affairs and her consequent temporary failure to give the patient her full attention. A similar case has recently been published by Servadio (1955), but this case is more complex in that it appears to involve precognition.

Burlingham's paper (1935) deals with apparent telepathy between mother and child, both of whom were being analysed at the time.

In 1933 Hollós made the extraordinary claim that in the course of ten to twelve years of analytic work during which he had kept systematic notes he had observed over 500 instances of telepathic communication. Usually the analyst's thought is communicated to the patient in spite of the analyst's wish to conceal and even repress it, that is, expel it from his own conscious awareness. This happens, for example, when the analyst's own associations to the patient's material become too much self-centred and too remote from the patient's associations. Here he evidently agrees with Deutsch. This paper led to some controversial criticism from Paul Schilder (1934), based on the view that experiences of the kind reported by Hollós could be understood as being due to chance coincidence, having regard to the limited range and stereotyped character of human thought within a given cultural pattern.

In the next year (1935) Servadio published a paper strongly in favour of the telepathic hypothesis, and he has continued to publish papers on the subject up to the present time. Another psychiatrist (not actually a psycho-analyst in the strict sense) who has been writing on this theme since 1930 is Ehrenwald.

Much the most prolific recent psycho-analytic contributor is Jule Eisenbud, who since 1946 has been publishing long and detailed papers devoted to extrasensory factors in the psycho-analytic situation. His work deals largely with dreams, and it is distinguished by a minute attention to details of the dream content and a firm adherence to the principle of psychic determinism worthy of Freud himself—and also by a most courageous disregard of customary analytic discretion where the analyst's own intimate secrets are concerned. Eisenbud has pushed the study of parapsychological occurrences in analysis to a point far beyond what any other analyst has dared or attempted. An extraordinary feature of some of his reports is the way in which he discovers telepathy going on, not just between the individual patients and himself, but between one patient and another, who is completely unknown to the first; this sometimes takes the form of outspoken competition between patients in the telepathic field, in an endeavour to gratify the analyst and gain his love. Eisenbud seems to have developed in this way something quite new in psycho-analysis—a kind of group analysis *in absentia* so far as the actual presence of other members of the group is concerned. In this respect it stands in sharp contrast to the classical idea of the psycho-analytic situation as an absolutely private one, and all this must, of course, be anathema to the orthodox analyst. Furthermore, it is likely to be urged that Eisenbud's patients perform these extraordinary feats in order to please an analyst whom they know to be intensely interested in telepathy. Of course, this is true, but on orthodox scientific principles no amount of such desire to please should enable a patient to achieve extrasensory cognition; so that however deplorable Eisenbud's procedure may seem from the point of view of classical psychoanalysis, this is no way detracts from its value as a contribution to parapsychological research. As to this latter, I can only refer those who are interested to his very detailed papres, most of which are to be found in *Psychoanalysis and the Occult.*

Consideration of the published papers of psycho-analysts, as well as personal discussion with colleagues, shows that there is a tendency to take up one or more of the following attitudes.

1. A rejection of the possibility of extrasensory cognition, and an attempt to use analysis to explain the phenomena on orthodox lines—to analyse them away, as it were. I think even those who are most favourably inclined to the telepathic hypothesis would agree that this should be the first line of approach; that is, nothing should be attributed to psi—or, in other words, regarded as inexplicable—which can possibly be understood on ordinary scientific lines, provided this does not involve undue straining of the facts. However, in the case of some analysts one seems to detect a strong emotional bias leading to rejection at all costs.

2. In so far as the first attitude is logically justified and not merely a means of warding off anxiety related to occult possibilities, it is largely based on the knowledge gained from analytic work of the powerful unconscious forces at work in human beings impelling them to revert at times to primitive or infantile ways of thinking which involve a belief in magic, disregard scientific principles of causality, of the limitations imposed by time and space, and the impotence of mere wishes to achieve anything. Here is a crucial aspect of the problem from the analyst's angle: science in general and psycho-analysis in particular have tried so hard and for so long to disabuse the human mind of belief in phenomena whose real existence is now being asserted by parapsychology. But of course there is another most important side to the coin; for it is clear that we have one and all been forced in the course of

our development to discard these primitive, animistic and magical ideas, and to set up permanent mental defences against them. It follows that when we are faced with experiences that seem incompatible with the rational, scientific view of the world adopted by our adult selves, then these defences against magical thinking are threatened and tend to be reinforced in order to avoid the anxiety that always develops when the ego's defences are threatened. The effect may therefore be that our conscious rational selves deny the evidence in an irrational, emotionally determined way—paradoxically, indeed, in the service of rational thinking.

3. A different attitude has been shown by a few analysts, and among these Freud himself may be numbered. So far from using analytic understanding solely to demonstrate the irrational, wish-fulfilling and fallacious nature of any belief in the existence of paranormal phenomena, these analysts have tried to show that analysis may actually reveal such phenomena in material that did not appear to show them; or analysis may add a great deal of confirmatory evidence to data which were only suggestive of the paranormal. Thus, the analysis of a dream may produce many associated ideas which fit together, like a jig-saw puzzle, if one assumes that extrasensory cognition has taken place, but otherwise fail to fit satisfactorily into a meaningful pattern. For example, in two instances of my own experience, the patient had a dream of which some elements would have made sense had *I* had the dream, but which were apparently meaningless for the patient.

I shall now refer briefly to my personal experience of apparent paranormal cognition in the psycho-analytic situation. I may add that I have had no occult experiences in any other setting, and one of the features of my observations that seems to me remarkable is that they all occurred within the period of two years, 1946 to 1948. In all there were four experiences, two with one patient, one with a second, whilst the fourth seemed to involve two patients as well as myself, rather in the fashion described by Eisenbud. Considerations of time forbid me to enter into full details, for which I must refer you to my published paper in *Psychoanalysis and the Occult.*

The essence of one case was that on the last evening of my holiday I read Elizabeth Bowen's short story "The Inherited Clock". Next day a patient in the second month of his analysis began his session by relating a dream from that night which contained an essential part of the story—not only a similar clock but a similar sinister significance attached to it. He did not know Elizabeth Bowen's story. Relevant facts are that the story had made a strong, eerie and psycho-pathological impression on me, though *I* did not dream about it. In general, the patient's dream related to aggression, inquisitiveness, and exhibitionism.

In another case, the night after I had been to the theatre to see William Douglas Home's prison play *Now Barabbas* a patient brought a dream about being chased by a criminal, followed by another dream from the same night in which she saw a photograph of a little girl and said, "That's not Douglas Home, that's a little girl". In the dream she thought the photo looked like herself when little. She had no idea who Douglas Home was until I told her. Here again the play had made a profound impression on me (as to its theme rather than the treatment of the theme), but *I* did not dream about it. It is as if the patient is saying in the dream: "It is not Douglas Home you should be interested in, but me."

About a year later, the same patient brought a dream about the Horseferry Road, to which her first association was that the day before the dream, whilst in that road, the thought crossed her mind that there must have been a ferry for horses there once. Now on that same day, the day before her dream, I too had been in the Horseferry Road, a thing that rarely happens, had noticed the name-plate, and had had precisely the same thought about there having been a ferry for horses, though previously I had always taken the name for granted.

The patient's other associations had to do with sex, marriage, forbidden looking and curiosity. A further very relevant fact that emerged was that on the afternoon of the day before the dream the patient had suddenly remembered the Douglas Home incident of a year before. This recollection of the day before, which had come into her head for no apparent reason in a cinema, suddenly came back to her mind when I told her about my having had the same Horseferry thought as herself, and the total effect on her was dramatic and upsetting; it is my impression, however, that the incident had a favourable effect on subsequent treatment.

The last example was more complex and seemed to involve paranormal cognition on the part of a female patient (a) of my nocturnal sexual activities, (b) of a male patient's strong castration preoccupations, (c) of a dream of mine of the same night involving the same castration symbolism as her own and the same as the male patient's fantasy, namely amputation of both legs. Further cues were (a) the phrase in my own dream "phantom limb", (b) the female patient's introduction of her own dream with the description "extraordinary and supernatural", expressions she never used at any other time, (c) my own justified feeling, when she was coming to the amputation part of her dream, that I knew exactly what was coming, what was going to happen, that is, a *déjà vu* feeling. In this female patient's case, again, forbidden impulses to look and investigate played an important part.

After I presented these cases to the British Psycho-Analytical Society in 1948, someone asked me what conditions I thought were conducive to the production of such telepathic feats. I jokingly replied "gleichschwebende Unaufmerksamkeit", referring to Freud's famous advice to the analyst to preserve a mental state of "gleichschwebende Aufmerksamkeit", that is, of uniformly hovering attentiveness, to the patient's productions. In this I was echoing Deutsch and Hollós; but subsequent experience leads me to doubt the importance of analytic inattentiveness in forcing the patient to make contact telepathically. Although my analytic inattentiveness is, I am sure, at least up to average, I am equally sure that it has often been much worse in the subsequent years than it was between 1946 and 1948, yet I have had no further telepathic experiences worth mentioning, except perhaps one. Having recently returned from Sicily, where I had heard a good deal about Diodorus Siculus, I found myself, for no other apparent reason, whilst waiting for a patient to come along the corridor into my room, murmuring to myself the well-known rhyme "Diodorus Siculus made himself ridiculous by calling thimbles phallic symbols". On entering, the patient immediately mentioned a dream of stockings, and how her first thought was "Dr. Gillespie will probably say they are penis symbols", with the obvious implication that this was ridiculous. A colleague has suggested to me that there may be a connection between the fact of my communicating my experiences to the British Society in 1948 and the immediate cessation of any further experiences for the following seven years; I think this is a suggestion worth considering.

Paranormal phenomena occurring in the psycho-analytic situation are of the nature of spontaneous manifestations; but they occur in a relatively controlled and well understood setting. Whilst they are generally incapable of statistical treatment they have the unusual advantage of rather complete data regarding the psychological background of both parties and their immediate psychological situation. There is the further possibility, already mentioned, of otherwise unrecognized psi phenomena being capable of recognition in the psycho-analytic situation because of the ability of analysis to uncover hidden content and undo distortions of the material.

A difficult and important issue is that of the criteria of what is paranormal in a situation to which statistics are inapplicable. Ehrenwald has directed most attention to this problem, and I would refer you to his book *New Dimensions of Deep Analysis* (1954). The main points he stresses are the presence of elements having a certain uniqueness, e.g.

numbers—what he calls a tracer effect; and the factor of psychological significance—the meaningful fit of a jig-saw puzzle. In general, however, I think data derived from analysis can never convince the scientifically orthodox sceptic, among whom I may perhaps reckon myself. This can probably be done only by the prestige of statistics. What analytic data do hold out is the possibility, having once admitted the existence of psi, of coming to some understanding of its psychological function and meaning; for example, my own material suggests a close connection with forbidden desires to see and to know (scopophilic impulses).

Finally, one may ask, why have so few analysts published material on this subject? There are various cogent reasons, I think, apart from the obvious answer that they have nothing to report. I do not think this answer is true, for when I communicated my results to the British Society thirteen people took part in the discussion, and most of them seemed to have had highly suggestive experiences. It is important to recognize that the phenomena are two-edged and involve the analyst personally as much as the patient. The fact that the analyst's private life and personal problems are intimately mixed up with the phenomena makes publication difficult or impracticable. Eisenbud has been remarkably frank in this direction, especially in one or two unpublished papers. Were it not for these considerations, and others related to scientific orthodoxy, I am sure we should hear more reports on the subject from analysts. I have found, in fact, both in public and private discussion, that not a few analysts took it for granted that such things occur, so that I found myself somewhat in the position of the little boy who was the only one to mention what everyone else knew about the Emperor's clothes.

REFERENCES

BURLINGHAM, D. (1935). *Psychoanal. Quart.*, 5, 69.

DEUTSCH, H. (1926). *Imago, Lpz.*, 12, 418.

DEVEREUX, G. (1953). Editor, Psychoanalysis and the Occult. New York: Bruce Publishing Co.

*EHRENWALD, J. (1954). New Dimensions of Deep Analysis. London: Allen & Unwin.

EISENBUD, J. (1946). *Psychoanal. Quart.*, 15, 32.

EISENBUD, J. (1947). *Psychoanal. Quart.*, 16, 39.

EISENBUD, J. (1948). *Psychiat. Quart.*, 22, 103.

*EISENBUD, J. (1954). *Psychoanal. Quart.*, 23, 205.

FREUD, S. (1899). Collected Papers, 5, 70. London: Hogarth Press, 1950.

FREUD, S. (1904). The Psychopathology of Everyday Life. London: Macmillan, 1925.

FREUD, S. (1921). Gesammelte Werke, 17, 25. London: Imago Publishing Co. Ltd., 1941.

FREUD, S. (1922). Collected Papers, 4, 408. London: Hogarth Press, 1925.

FREUD, S. (1925). Collected Papers, 5, 158. London: Hogarth Press, 1950.

FREUD, S. (1933). New Introductory Lectures on Psycho-analysis. London: Hogarth Press.

GILLESPIE, W. (1953). *In* Psychoanalysis and the Occult, p. 373. New York: Bruce Publishing Co.

*HOLLÓS, S. (1933). *Imago, Lpz.*, 19, 529.

SCHILDER, P. (1934). *Imago, Lpz.*, 20, 219.

SERVADIO, E. (1935). *Imago, Lpz.*, 21, 489.

*SERVADIO, E. (1955). *Int. J. Psychoanal.*, 36, 27.

(All the references except those marked * can be found in Devereux, *Psychoanalysis and the Occult.*)

DISCUSSION

Lewis: I think one's estimate of the value of such data as Dr. Gillespie has put before us depends on one's estimate of the scientific status of psycho-analysis and of the situation in which psycho-analysis is conducted. Dr. Gillespie has given us a restrained and sober account of the matter. He has put the stress almost entirely on the evidence supplied during psycho-analytical treatment and has not allowed himself the licence of some other psycho-analysts, who endeavour to interpret the phenomena whose extrasensory or precognitive nature they take for granted. The evidence in Dr. Gillespie's data is of the anecdotal kind occurring spontaneously in a particular situation, and subject to all those opportunities of error with which we are familiar in material accumulated during the last century. In a collection like *Phantasms of the Living*, the Myers-Podmore-Gurney book, there are stories similar in essence to those that are told by psycho-analytical writers, and open to the same objections. The objection of fraud is not, of course, to be made against the reputable psycho-analysts who have written on this subject, but neither is it to be made against the people whose data have been accumulated in books like *Phantasms of the Living* or in the records at Duke University.

I think also that the analytical situation predisposes to uncertainty about the evidence accumulated. As psycho-analysts themselves, like Lawrence Kubie, have repeatedly pointed out, the psycho-analyst is not detached and cannot be regarded as an impersonal observer, because he is so deeply involved in the situation. Normally he makes no contemporaneous record, and therefore his memory is the fallible instrument by which the data are transmitted; there can be very few of the checks and safeguards employed in the more familiar kind of ESP inquiry. He uses intuitive methods in interpreting the data and knowing when and how to intervene, and finally of course he and his patient are aware of communications by gesture, by breathing, and other non-verbal signals, which must influence the evidence that comes forward. When one contrasts this situation with that which is found imperative, not only in card trials for ESP but in ordinary clinical trials of a particular remedy, one can see how unsatisfactory the controls must be in a psycho-analytic situation. In a therapeutic trial, one takes extraordinary precautions to ensure that none of those who are observing the possible effects shall know whether the patient observed has had the remedy or not: if those precautions are not taken, gross mistakes can be made by people whose integrity and scientific training are not in dispute.

So it seems to me that we are here dealing with evidence which is far less satisfactory, though of course far more complex, and far more personal, than that accumulated by Dr. Pratt and Dr. Soal and others in their rigorous experiments. Even if one were not disposed to be critical of the scientific status of psycho-analytic methods, one might still hesitate to accept as instances of extrasensory perception the occurrences that crop up during psycho-analysis, such as Dr. Gillespie has described to us. They often admit of a different interpretation. This applies also, I think, to the evidence of thought transference put forward by Freud in his well-known essay, e.g. the story of the fortune-teller in Paris who told a young woman that she would have two children before she was 32. Moreover, an analogy between spontaneous productions during psycho-analysis and, say, observations of an astronomical event is quite a false analogy to my mind. Many astronomical events can be described in such terms that any competent person can repeat the observation; but that is out of the question in dealing with the observations that psycho-analysts report. How then can they be regarded as on the same footing?

The evidence, then, seems to me incomplete and unsatisfactory, but I should not like to suggest therefore that the work of the psycho-analyst is irrelevant or unimportant in this connection. One doesn't quarrel with blank verse because it doesn't rhyme. The psycho-analytic observations provide the kind of material which is tentative but which assists in formulating hypotheses, hypotheses that may be of value here and also in other directions. Mr. Fraser Nicol said at the opening session that one of the difficulties about getting people interested in this field of study has been that it doesn't seem relevant to other branches of knowledge. To the psychiatrist, at any rate, it is extremely relevant, because he is constantly dealing with people who are convinced that they have this extrasensory power, and he rates it as a symptom of illness. He may sometimes be mistaken in that assumption, but depending on it as he does, he clearly has got to pay very close regard to anyone who, in a situation so closely related to psychiatry as the psycho-analytic one, obtains evidence that purports to show the reality of the phenomenon. The data which have so far been put forward by psycho-analysts, regarding the personality of those who are most prone to throw up spontaneous evidence of telepathy during psycho-analytic sessions, suggests ways of selecting percipient subjects for experiment. I agree wholeheartedly with what Sir Charles Harington said at dinner last night about the importance of discovering techniques whereby suitable subjects can be recognised. The findings of psycho-analysts might help to shorten that search, if further observations lent colour to the suggestion that schizoid persons on the verge of schizophrenia are particularly suitable, that certain hysterical subjects are suitable, and so forth. I believe that the psycho-analytic work has value, not as providing evidence in the way that card studies provide evidence, but providing suggestions whereby technical developments might occur.

Gillespie: What Prof. Lewis said to begin with seems to suggest a misconception of what I have been trying to say. I do want to stress that I am not suggesting that psycho-analytic experiences of the kind I was mentioning are evidential. I don't think they produce anything that a scientist would accept as evidence for parapsychology. It is much more, I think, a matter of application of the hypothesis, and seeing what happens then, seeing whether it is fruitful. As regards records, it is perfectly true that most analysts are not in the habit of taking notes while the patient is talking, because they think it interferes with the analytic session, and in fact I never do it myself. But I did make records immediately after the session in all of these cases that I have mentioned, and I made a record of my own dream at once when I woke up. So I am quite satisfied myself that there is no retrospective falsification.

Prof. Lewis also made the point that psycho-analytic observations are not such as can be repeated by any competent person, like astronomical ones. It is perfectly true that psycho-analytic observations can only be made by trained psycho-analysts, but I am not sure that isn't analogous to astronomical observations and trained astronomers.

However, something that Professor Lewis said later on made me feel that after all he was in agreement with me, or that I am in agreement with him, namely the rôle of psycho-analytic research in relation to parapsychology. It is not a method of establishing the existence or otherwise of ESP, but rather of co-ordinating it with our other knowledge of man. And in that of course I find myself in agreement with Dr. Amadou.

L.-Davies: It struck me that the value of Dr. Gillespie's remarks for an experimenter in parapsychology may be this: hitherto in defining experiments, our object has been almost entirely to learn from the statistician how to devise a technique which will obey his rigorous requirements; should we not also go, not only to the psycho-analyst, but to all the other psychological schools and request from them ideas as to how our experiments might usefully be varied and enriched? For example, Dr. Gillespie made the great point that in the psycho-analytic situation the paranormal phenomenon, if it does exist, involves two people. I have already pointed out in my own paper, and others have done so too, that we are still not quite certain how many guinea pigs there are in the card-guessing experiment. And it seems to me quite possible that if we ask the psychologists for some suggestion as to how we should deal with the problem from the psychological point of view, just as we ask the statistician how we should deal with it from the statistical point of view, we may get a great deal of help in finding the answer to the challenge which Sir Charles Harington put out at last night's dinner.

Wassermann: Dr. Gardner Murphy, in a paper to the Society for Psychical Research, has I think effectively dealt with the point that Mr. Langdon-Davies has raised, namely the interaction of a multiplicity of people. He takes up a position which I feel is not very strongly represented at this conference; he belongs to a school which has perhaps more adherents in America, and I personally think it is a very sound school. I am more in agreement with that school than with the one which is represented at this conference, in spite of the very great admiration I have for the views held here. Dr. Murphy maintains, in extreme opposition to what Sir Charles Harington said last night, that it is the totality of guinea pigs which matters. There is a vast amount of evidence which has not been discussed here, which supports this. There are numerous papers which suggest that it is not only the agent or percipient that matter, but that a multitude of people may interact simultaneously. There is, for instance, some evidence that when Dr. Soal went out of the room in some experiments, things changed. There is also evidence that in some experiments when he was present there was no success at all, and the same applies to some of Dr. West's experiments. On the other hand, Dr. Soal seemed to succeed only with a particular type of person, for he experimented with 158 people with whom he did not succeed. Again, Dr. Soal did not succeed with Mrs. Eileen Garrett, whilst Dr. Rhine did, which suggests very strongly that there is a difference between Dr. Rhine and Dr. Soal.

To demand, therefore, that repeatability must occur in such circumstances means that we must state *all* conditions under which such an experiment was performed. I suggest that fixed conditions in such an experiment mean that the agent as well as the percipient and all witnesses remain the same. To say otherwise that the experimental conditions are the same in two experiments would be very dangerous; even people passively present in a room can change the experimental situation. I think much the same thing seems to come out in the psycho-analytic situation as well.

West: I have been very much impressed with the fact that more or less the same thing has been said by several speakers on different days.

I remember Dr. Perry said that he wished we could get more interesting and fruitful statistical experiments, because the statistical approach could be applied to more than card guessing. Sir Charles Harington last night suggested that we should look for new techniques of investigation, and Prof. Lewis to-day has said that the psycho-analytic material might suggest new hypotheses for testing. I believe that there is no conflict between all these suggestions and the maintenance of a proper experimental approach. I think that one can test almost any hypothesis by a proper experiment.

I would just like to mention one example in which the suggestions of psycho-analysts have actually been put more or less to the test in an experiment very similar to the ordinary card-guessing technique. This was done recently by Mr. Fisk, an English experimenter. He found a subject who had a habit of calling particular symbols more often than others. In discussions with this subject Fisk found that the man had certain neurotic sexual conflicts, and that two of the symbols symbolized for him male and female attributes respectively, about which he was in a state of conflict. Thereafter, Fisk conducted an experiment in which he substituted for these two symbols male and female erotic targets. The subject produced quite high scores on those particular targets and not on the other symbols. This in a sense was confirmation of the suggestion often made that material of emotional significance, and particularly, as Freud suggested, partially repressed material, is likely to be more favourable towards the manifestation of telepathy. I do feel that there is no fundamental conflict between the application of properly controlled experimental techniques and the testing of almost any hypothesis, which might be suggested by study of the apparent manifestations of ESP in real life, in psycho-analytic situations and so forth.

Pobers: Problems very similar to those described by Dr. Gillespie can be and are being studied in other situations of clinical psychology. It has been suggested that telepathy can be a source of error in certain psychological tests. There is also an important problem of telepathic communication in general doctor-patient relationships; curious occurrences are sometimes observed. The peculiar way in which a patient feels and speaks may refer more to the doctor's problems than to his own case. A large number of situations have to be studied, but of course it is very difficult to imagine how statistical experimental methods can be applied to this type of situation.

Brown: I was rather interested in the Fisk experiment because I have done similar experiments myself, but perhaps I have not got the right sort of stimulus in the symbols. Have you managed to get the effect again?

West: The effect maintained itself so long as the subject was in contact with Mr. Fisk, and then the subject went away and has not been tested since.

Parkes: Dr. Gillespie, do you think there is any indication that the psycho-analytic situation is more likely to bring telepathic phenomena than other situations?

Gillespie: I don't know, but I suspect that it is—on general grounds I would think so. The patient usually becomes intensely interested in the analyst, and at the same time is kept as far as possible entirely in ignorance of the analyst's private life and so forth, and it seems possible that would stimulate any powers that might exist for non-sensory mode of information.

Parkes: So the psycho-analytic situation ought to be a regular gold-mine of telepathic phenomena?

Gillespie: Yes. I would like to hear discussion about my curious 2-year period and then complete cessation. It does seem to me to be rather analogous to what happens in the card-guessing experiments.

Soal: The trouble about this kind of thing is that the people who are apparently good at producing spontaneous mental phenomena, having hunches and that sort of thing, do not usually do well at card-guessing experiments. You would think that the best people at card guessing would be spiritualistic mediums, people who do produce something abnormal in the presence of their sitters, details about their past lives and so on. I have tried a good many of those people, and they simply cannot do anything with cards.

Gillespie: Yes, I would certainly say that one would think so, if this were a physical faculty, that some people have in a high degree and other people have not. But it may also be a fairly generally possessed faculty which is used in different ways by different people, according to their needs. Some people apparently have the need to guess cards correctly! On the other hand to be inquisitive about somebody that you are interested in is not at all such a rare circumstance.

Wassermann: It suggests altogether that in spontaneous cases it is usually an emotional situation which is involved. The need of the subject is most important, and Gardner Murphy has stressed this.

Lewis: Could I ask whether the Archives to which Dr. Pratt referred include psycho-analytical data of this type?

Pratt: You have read my mind, because I don't remember saying anything about these Archives, but I was thinking about them!

Perhaps I may take this opportunity of saying that I am impressed by the similarity, brought out in this discussion, between the psycho-analytic material as a source of suggestions as starting points for experiments and the work that Mrs. Rhine is doing in the Parapsychology Laboratory. Her programme is one on which she has been engaged for four or five years and in which she is collecting, at every opportunity that offers itself, reports from or about people who consider their experiences to be unexplainable in ordinary terms. Her collection at the beginning of this year contained something like 4,000 cases, and some of you who follow the *Journal of Parapsychology* know that she has been analysing these cases, classifying them and looking for general principles running through them which might bear on certain questions that are of interest. The point of view taken from the start, and one that has been repeatedly emphasized in her reports, is that nothing is claimed in the way of evidence or proof of ESP, but that the suggestions might be fruitful for experimenters. This year, owing to the fact that the *Reader's Digest* published an article inviting readers to submit their cases to Mrs. Rhine, her collection has doubled in a remarkably short time. She has three to four thousand unanswered letters with which she is dealing slowly. So if you know anyone who has sent her a case recently, would you tell them please to be patient.

Nicol: A small point that was raised at the Utrecht conference two years ago: Dr. Humphrey and I did an ESP card-calling test with a considerable number of subjects, and not only was ESP tested for in the usual way but there were also various psychological factors, one of which was emotional stability. It appeared with a considerable degree of significance that the more stable the subjects were the better their ESP scores. At that conference there were a fair number of psychiatrists experienced in psychical research. They pounced on this finding that emotional stability was favourable to psychical impressions, saying this was contrary to their experience. But of course the reply was made that they only see emotionally unstable people.

Gillespie: It is very dangerous to generalize on one small experience, but one of the patients I have reported was one of the most unstable young men I have ever known in analytic work, very near the borderline of psychosis. Of course one does have experience in analysis of people who are supposed to be very stable, namely students in training, and in my own experience I have never had an ESP experience with one of those. But my experience is far too small to generalize on.

Wolstenholme: Is it at all a usual thing for people to consult two psycho-analysts, or two psycho-analysts to work together on any case simultaneously?

Gillespie: No, most unusual.

Lewis: Dreikurs does that now, and Rioch tried it.

Gillespie: But it is not at all unusual for a patient to pass from one analyst to another, of course.

GENERAL DISCUSSION

Parkes: To open this general discussion I would like to give Dr. Butler an opportunity to tell us about the special mechanisms employed by bees in finding their way around and perceiving situations which are not obvious to the human being. Such use of faculties which to us seem astonishing, leads one to think that other remarkable faculties may occur in nature and await discovery.

Butler: I would say at the outset that apart from the considerable development of senses about which we already know a good deal, I cannot think of any sense, which we know the honey bee uses, that other animals do not possess. For example, a honey bee out looking for drinking water possesses the ability, as she flies within a foot of a hidden source of water, to appreciate the presence of the source, and it has been shown that she does so because sense organs on her antennae are stimulated by the water molecules in the atmosphere itself. She is able to fly up the humidity gradient until she alights on the spot nearest this particular source of water. All the behaviour patterns that I know of in the case of bees are explicable, I think (though they have not all been explained), on "super-development" of faculties which we already know something about. After all, aboriginal man is, apparently, able to appreciate the presence of water when he approaches a hidden source.

Several discoveries about bees have really excited people in the last few years. One of course is Prof. von Frisch's epoch-making discovery on communication in honey bees, the way honey bees communicate to one another not only the scent associated with a particular source of food and thus its floral source, but also the direction and distance of the source from the hive. The bee does this by means of a system of dances; the bee that has found the rich source of food, say a dish of sugar syrup placed at a known distance from the hive, does not dance on first returning to the hive. She only does so after she has visited the source of food on two or more occasions. Furthermore, the food source has to be very rich if she is going to react by dancing, very concentrated and in abundant supply. If the concentration is dropped or the supply fails, or if there are a great number of bees milling about on the dish trying to collect the syrup, then she does not dance when she gets home. A very important point is this: the dance is normally a figure-of-eight on the comb, and young bees who are going foraging for the first time in their lives, will not as a rule leave the hive until they have already learnt from the dances of experienced foragers the position of particular sources of food. Furthermore, they have to learn (as Dr. Lindauer has has recently shown) not to interpret the dance but rather to follow the dancer accurately in the darkness of the hive, so that they may obtain the necessary map to find the source. The dancing usually takes place in darkness inside the hive, where it has recently been shown that the force of gravity represents the sun. For example, if the source of food lies in the direction from which the sun is shining at the time, the bee then orientates her dance vertically upwards on the comb face; if the food lies in the opposite direction from which the sun is shining, then the dance is orientated vertically downwards; if at an angle to the sun then to the same angle to the perpendicular. But the young bee has to learn to follow the dancer accurately. At first when the dancing bee turns round to complete a loop of the figure-of-eight, the young bee who is following on behind tends to go straight on, and it very often takes her two or three days, and sometimes several hundred experiences of trying to follow a dancer, before she learns to follow round and complete the figure-of-eight. Once she has learnt to do this she soon appears at the feeding place. Bees can interpret the dances extraordinarily accurately, to within something like 50 yards in 2 or $2\frac{1}{2}$ miles.

Again, home finding is definitely something that has to be learnt. If one takes a young bee, who has never left her hive before, only a short distance away from her hive and liberates her, the chances of her finding her way home are virtually nil. If on the other hand one takes her after she has made one flight from the hive, she stands a slightly better chance of getting home, and after she has made ten or a dozen flights the chances that she will get home are very high, provided she is not taken more than $\frac{1}{2}$–$\frac{3}{4}$ of a mile from her home. Ultimately she learns to find her way over distances considerably greater than these. Despite these abilities of the honey bee, it would seem to me that everything that has so far been discovered can be explained without any recourse to the idea of extrasensory perception, or indeed to any sense about which we do not already know. There are, however, still quite a number of phenomena that cannot be explained.

Parkes: The bee is a prime example of the possession of abilities which seem quite incredible until you find the explanation, after which they seem entirely natural and biological.

Pratt: When four years ago I had an opportunity of meeting Dr. von Frisch I read all I could on this work, and I decided that there was nothing in this bee orientation problem that ought to distract or divert the parapsychologist. But in regard to what you say about homing, if I may talk about that, can you tell us whether the bees, when they are able to find their way back to the hive from distances of, say, up to half a mile, show evidence of direction in their initial flight from the release point, or is it all done on the basis of searching and familiarity within that area ?

Butler: The bee usually flies up in the air, and makes a circling flight, and then flies straight off home. But she must be released over ground over which she has already flown, or near to such ground, if she is to reach home successfully.

Pratt: I have heard, without being able to trace the story to its source, that honey bees have been used for homing purposes as message carriers, in the Orient particularly. Now that is the sort of story you do not lose much sleep over, just as you do not lose sleep over the story that homing pigeons are used on Chinese junks, with their home on the junk and the bird being released on the shore, so that messages can be sent wherever the junk has gone. Nevertheless, I am interested to know if you can tell us whether there is any truth in the story of bees as message carriers.

Butler: I have never heard of this. We have made use of "the language of bees", as von Frisch calls it, to find particular crops we have been interested in experimentally. For example, three to four years ago there were bees dancing unusually late in the year, in the middle of October to be exact, and carrying large loads of yellow pollen. Analysis of this pollen and of the dance showed us the exact field containing the flowers from which the bees were collecting this pollen, a field just three miles away.

Pratt: Well, we still cannot equate what the bees do with what the pigeons do.

Butler: I do not think so, no.

Dale: Dr. Butler, is there evidence that they have a special sensitivity to the plane of polarized light ?

Butler: Yes, but then so have a good many other animals, insects anyway.

Dale: Does that depend on the eyes? If they were eyeless, would they lose that?

Butler: It is believed to depend on the eyes, but I do not know that there is any very satisfactory evidence. You cannot experiment with eyeless bees as they will not behave normally at all. There is one interesting point, though, that we cannot explain. We know that the bee will orientate herself by any sensory landmarks she is able to appreciate, and we find that bees will sometimes fly out in dense fog in which the visual landmarks are virtually obliterated. In one case that I investigated, I could not find out even with a sensitive photoelectric cell in which direction the sun was, and yet the bees were flying about a mile to a mile and a half to a horse-trough full of water and performing perfectly orientated recruiting dances on returning home.

Wassermann: Do these bees have a delicacy of Gestalt recognition comparable to the the things which are described—in Tinbergen's book, for instance—such as the food begging habits of the herring gull, where a slight displacement of the spot near the beak can diminish the response quite appreciably? Is something similar to that known for bees?

Butler: Some experiments are being carried out at the moment, not on the homing but on the social organisation of the honey bee community. It has been found that its cohesion is dependent on the interchange of food between individuals, in particular, interchange of the substance which they obtain from licking the body of their queen. Consequently you find bees begging with extended tongues from other bees, and other bees offering food to their sisters between their open mandibles. Some work is being done on this, and it has been shown that if you start with the head of a dead bee on a pin with its tongue extended and thrust that into the faces of other bees, sooner or later one of them will offer food to it.

Brown: Can you actually tell the bees what to do? Can you put a dead bee or a toy bee on a pin, and describe a dance with it?

Butler: A certain amount of directing bees to crops has been attempted by feeding the bees just outside the hive with concentrated sugar syrup containing the scent of the flowers you wish them to visit. Great claims have been made for this method of directing bees to crops, but personally I am rather sceptical of them, as I don't think the data stand up very well to analysis. But we don't know yet: I have a magnetically controlled bee who does dance after a fashion, and so far we have found that other bees are extremely interested in her gyrations, but we have not yet tried to convey information.

Brown: My other question is, when you have a strong following wind to your source of food, does this mean that the bee coming back says to her colleagues: it is a very short distance away?

Butler: I do want to emphasize that I don't think the bee thinks a about it at all.

Brown: No, no. But they go out, and then there is a head wind coming back. Does this mean that some of them fall by the wayside?

Butler: No, because the successful forager will only dance if she has found a really rich source of food, so the recruits are able to refuel, so to speak, before setting out for home again.

Dingwall: Was your fog example one of the inexplicable phenomena you mentioned?

Butler: Yes. Von Frisch has also described one or two in which he has taken colonies of bees fairly high up on the Austrian Alps, moving them under conditions of low dense cloud, and has sometimes managed to get them to forage, and found that the dancing still continues normally. He cannot explain this. I think the real mystery is how the bees interpret the dance.

Dale: Can they follow without learning the interpretation?

Butler: They don't have to learn the interpretation apparently, but they do have to learn to follow the dance correctly.

Parkes: Thank you very much, Dr. Butler. Perhaps now we should come to the more general discussion. I shall ask you in turn to make your concluding remarks.

Nicol: I think one point to make is that people outside the field, and to a considerable extent inside it too, obtain their information from the books, yet we are always appealing to them to read the original reports, for otherwise they are not entitled to pass opinions. Just to illustrate that, I mention an incident concerning the late Whately Carington, whom I knew well. I once asked him how many people read his numerous reports on paranormal cognition. And he said "I should say about a dozen". I said "In the whole world?" "Yes". Years afterwards I mentioned this to a colleague in the United States, and he said "I don't believe half that number read mine!" Now although there may be exceptions—I know the Soal-Goldney report was long ago sold out—it is true generally, and it would be a boon to the subject if more attention were paid to the original reports and some analytical thinking brought to bear on them.

Secondly, the question of repeatability. Apart from the remarkable high scoring of some subjects of which we have heard, the group experiments which have been suggested can only stand up if they can be repeated. It is no use getting odds of thousands to one and claiming they are important, unless you and others can get the effects reproduced. One promising line was begun by Dr. Gertrude Schmeidler about 8 to 10 years ago, who asked her subjects at City College, New York, "Do you believe that ESP can be demonstrated?" I simplify Dr. Schmeidler's type of questions, but this will do for illustration. Those who said "yes" tended to get high scores, and those who said "no" tended to get low scores. There is also the personality work done at Duke University, which has been expanded. Since the subject is essentially a study in personality, clearly we should try to relate it to the whole man, in his psychological aspects and, as Prof. Gaddum said, also in his physiological aspects. I would like to see more of that work done, and possibly some critical work done on the use of drugs that would either raise or depress the phenomena.

McConnell: I wouldn't want to seem to be advocating the psi theory of pigeon homing—I think my position would be precisely that stated by Dr. Pratt—one of interest without any preconceptions—but I wonder whether Dr. Matthews has given us a quite adequate picture of the difficulties encountered in his sun navigation theory. He spoke of the arch of the sun, which the bird must perceive, and from this, in a manner analogous to the manner in which a sailor navigates, the bird would decide its location by means of his internal chronometer and sextant. Now, the bird has in some cases apparently ten seconds to do this, and I believe that the way it is assumed that he does it involves actually measuring the direction of the arch of the sun, since of course one doesn't see its entire path but only a ten-second segment of it. This introduces several kinds of interesting problems. Just how big is this motion in ten seconds? Is the resolution possible with the mechanisms—the eye, for example, —that the bird might have?

Then there are the interesting geometrical aspects, which I don't think are adequately conveyed by the expression "arch of the sun". I don't know the details, but I think that when you see the sun above the horizon the curve is not a circle by any means, it is something much more complex—there is reverse curvature in it, I believe —and so the problem which the bird has in sizing up from a small ten-second segment of the path of the sun by means of his precise internal chronometer, finding out where he is, is really quite a difficult one.

Matthews: I am grateful to Dr. McConnell for giving me something to talk about, because I have no particular advice to offer to the parapsychologists: none they would take, anyhow!

This ten-second orientation business is one I think I can answer here. The geometrical considerations of the sun's path would really take up too much of our time—after nearly two days at the bird orientation conference on this subject, the net result was that we all agreed to differ. The ten-second orientation which has been levelled against the sun-arch extrapolation theory has never been demonstrated by the pigeons or the shearwaters I have used, either in releases as a whole (that is the pattern of release up to ten seconds) or in the individual records of a large number of pigeons having several releases from different points. It fact, for the birds I have worked with, the orientation flight has been of the order of 1–1½ minutes. Pratt and Thouless have recently published a paper in which they claim there was a strong evidence of orientation after ten seconds. As Dr. Pratt knows I disagree with the interpretation, and, taken as a whole, their results show that after ten seconds there is a completely random distribution.

Finally, the pigeons I observed at Duke behaved just like the Cambridge birds; on those occasions when I was fortunate enough to watch them, they took a good time to get away, but with one difference, that they did show an early directional tendency, which from the points at which I observed them, at least, did not have any relevance to home; it was a northward tendency. Now that is a very interesting point, and Kramer's pigeons in Germany have also shown these tendencies in one direction, to the north. So if you have your releases to the south, you get this directional tendency coming in at once, and then the bird which is orientating itself while it is flying away recedes out of sight, apparently orientating from the beginning. But, if as in the case I observed, you are out to the west, the bird flies to the north, which is entirely the wrong direction, and then comes round to the east. I think the explanation for these ten-second orientations will lie in that sort of thing.

Pratt: I would hate to see the force of the recently published article by Thouless and myself lost through hasty judgment of the issue. We did not consider the question settled in that report, so we have gone right on working. We have now many times the amount of evidence presented in that article, and it is in the same direction and quite significant statistically.

Even after only ten seconds of observation of the sun the bird is able to choose the homeward direction. It is true that we have this directional factor, but we think it may be quite important. Why should birds show a preference for flying from south to north? But the homing orientation is not completely obscured by this directional factor; it shows up in spite of it. So we are studying the directional factor and homing orientation, both at short and long distances, in fact everything which may be relevant. Dr. Matthews has given me an advance copy of his book, and I promised him a "plug" in return so I say: by all means buy the book, but don't be too quick to buy the proposition.

I think we have reached a stage of the conference where no one's intention is to be provocative, except of thought. But there is a question raised by some remarks after the recording machine was cut off yesterday afternoon which I think might have left some wrong impressions, especially as I hear that the discussions were continued over the teacups. It happens that the question in this instance is one which can be quickly cleared up by reference to the scientific literature; and I thought it would be of interest to some of us to have our memories refreshed as well as to others to have them initiated, on the issues of the imperfections in the Duke laboratory ESP cards. The *Journal of Parapsychology* (1937, 1, 305) has this brief statement: "Imperfections in the commercial reproductions of the ESP cards preclude their unscreened use for experimental purposes. As reports of screened work have indicated that subjects do practically as well and in some cases better when they have no sensory contact at all with the cards, the screen should be so uniform a condition that card imperfections are not a matter for experimental concern. However, the publishers of the cards have been able to overcome the principal difficulties and future printings will therefore be much improved."

I turn now to Vol. 2, 1938, pages 308 and 309, and read from an article by the late Dr. Charles E. Stuart entitled "A Review of Recent Criticisms of ESP Research": "The most frequently raised criticism of method has been the observation that the commercial ESP cards printed by the Whitman Publishing Company are so warped by the inking process that symbols may be read, under certain lighting conditions, from the backs of the cards." And this footnote: "This 'discovery' has been attributed to a number of individuals. In fact the warping did not show up in the large proof sheets examined by a number of people (including the present writer)" (and the present speaker). "It was found immediately when the first shipment of cards reached the Parapsychology Laboratory, and reference was made to the conditions in the December, 1937, number of this Journal." And this further sentence from the text of the article: "The most obvious method for eliminating such cues is to screen the cards entirely from the sight of the subject."

Goldney: On that subject, whereas all experienced investigators would understand that screening must always be employed, there is a greater danger in faulty cards of the Zener type going out and being connected in inexperienced people's minds with either the SPR or Duke Laboratory. Dr. Dingwall and I found, in an investigation in Sweden with Dr. Pobers, that whereas instructions had been wrapped round faulty packs from Duke Laboratory stating that the cards must always be screened, these instructions were lost and the cards were used unscreened because people said "Naturally cards coming from Duke University would be perfect in every particular". It was not only Duke Laboratory that had been guilty of circulating faulty cards, because on returning to the SPR I found that certain of our Zener cards which had been isolated by one of our Research Officers knowing that they were faulty, had, after a change of personnel at the office, been put back into circulation by mistake. I of course removed them all at once. Faulty cards should not be circulated in any circumstances, even with instructions regarding screening.

I would like to take this opportunity to say that we are often asked at the SPR for news of what other workers are doing, and we can only give this information if workers keep us informed of what they are doing.

Brown: The loving cup has come and I hope I shall be forgiven if I return briefly to my clock and sun analogy, since I am surprised it should have caused so much resistance. After all, we set a clock to go with the sun and gradually it gains or loses. It is right, or nearly right, on significantly many occasions, but there is a slow "decline effect". A randomizing machine is rather like a very complicated clock: and a subject guessing is another simplified randomizing machine. The rest follows. This is not entirely my idea; Babington Smith first introduced it at a British Association meeting, in which he gave the analogy of two randomizing machines as two pendulums which get in and out of step. I think this might be a very fruitful line for future research.

Gaddum: I haven't anything new to say, but I would like to emphasize what has been said already, that the most important thing is to find new methods of testing. It seems to me that guessing cards must be extraordinarily dull, and that it would be much easier for people to go on doing experiments if they had something of more emotional significance, and it is quite likely that they would get more results. But the most important thing is to increase the performance, either by finding sensitives, analysing personality and finding out what kind of person is sensitive, or by improving the conditions for performance until we can get away from having to use statistical calculations. People have tended to say that they don't like statistics, as if it were an experimental technique. Any result that is not of statistical significance is likely to be untrue, but sometimes it is so obviously of statistical significance that there is no need to calculate the critical ratios, and I believe the most important thing is to increase the performance of people until it is not necessary to calculate critical ratios. I think Mr. Langdon-Davies is holding out some hope of being able to do that.

West: I would like to make one comment about the very dramatic drawings which Professor Hardy showed us which he had extracted from the *Proceedings of the Society for Psychical Research.* These drawings had apparently convinced Prof. Hardy of telepathy, whereas other more recent and perhaps more elaborate evidence had failed to convince him. I would like to say that the reason why many modern parapsychologists are less convinced by these early tests with drawings is not for any statistical considerations—for we can all see the obvious significance of the resemblances—but firstly because the conditions under which those early tests were carried out would not satisfy us to-day, and secondly, because we have not succeeded in obtaining comparable results in modern times. There is perhaps one exception, namely the Upton Sinclair experiments in about 1930.

I would also like to say a word about the question of the ESP hypothesis in general: from listening to much of the discussion here, it seems to me that there is a tendency to attribute to ESP things which are unexplained. One might say, for example, that because one cannot find an explanation of homing, therefore it must be due to ESP. But I don't think this is a very sound method of argument. It reminds me of the situation in medicine, where one has the difficulty of deciding whether a symptom is organic or psychogenic, and some physicians say because we cannot discover an organic cause for this symptom, therefore it must be psychogenic. That, too, is an unsound method of argument. If we could find some positive characteristic whereby ESP would be recognizable, I think we would be in a much better position. I have said before that it is very difficult to establish characteristics of ESP, but there is one suggestion from Dr. Soal's experiments, namely that ESP can function just as well precognitively. If that characteristic proved to be general, it might provide the criterion we need.

Gillespie: I can only suggest that, in the psycho-analytical line, if papers are published it may encourage other people to publish more material, and cumulatively we may get more information about the conditions in the psychological situation which are associated with these phenomena.

L.-Davies: Recent experiences have made me optimistic that when I penetrate into my neighbour's kitchen I shall find a considerable supply of paranormal guinea pigs, and I propose to examine them under the avuncular shade of Dr. Soal. At the same time, I shall be only too happy to get suggestions from anyone here or elsewhere as to any particular kind of information that they think might be got out of the guinea pigs, if they do materialize. I very much hope, therefore, that anybody who is interested in making suggestions along their own line, but lacks material, will write to me. I don't promise that I will give my "sensitives" half a pint of lysergic acid, but short of anything which will destroy morals or physical integrity, I am interested in any experimental suggestions.

Pobers: The first thing that seems to be important is a standardization of conditions in card-guessing experiments and in their statistical evaluation. I believe that Dr. Soal's book can play a very important rôle in bringing about standardized conditions and techniques. Some of the discussion we have had here about the validity of one experiment and the conditions of another should have been avoided.

Many speakers mentioned the need to find new methods, and techniques involving less fatigue, eliminating the danger of boredom, restoring to ESP some of its emotional and human content.

It is equally important to find new methods of observation and analysis of spontaneous cases. Psychical research started with spontaneous cases; later they have been discarded, and all attention has been devoted to the measurable, to scientifically sound statistical work. It is high time to devise new experiments and research methods for spontaneous cases. As far as paranormal phenomena among primitive peoples are concerned, they are still observable in a few regions, and it is important to devise some kind of co-ordinated research project involving parapsychologists, ethnologists, psychologists and sociologists. These phenomena have to be studied while they can be observed.

It is very important to promote observation and research on the lines described by Dr. Gillespie, not only in psycho-analytical situations, but more generally in psychiatry, in psychomatic medicine and in clinical psychology. The co-operation of parapsychologists with researchers of a more orthodox type would be most valuable.

Butler: I would like to ask one question. It was said yesterday afternoon that the particular value, as I understood it, of going to primitive peoples was that it was believed that extrasensory perception tended to die out rather than not. Now it seems to me, thinking along normal evolutionary lines, that that is most improbable, if it is such a valuable possession as one is led to suppose. It is surely likely to increase.

Wassermann: There are two papers, one by Dr. Thouless and one by Dr. Gardner Murphy in which this point has been discussed.

Dingwall: I have very pronounced views on the direction and scope of future research. First of all the paramount necessity is to find gifted subjects. This is illustrated by this symposium, because I doubt whether it would ever have been held if it had not been for Dr. Soal's work, the discovery of gifted subjects and their investigation in a way in which other scientific men can join and see that the work is done properly according to scientific mood. Unless we can do this we shall continue to travel the anecdotal road.

Secondly, I think more work should be done in the insertion as Mr. Fisk has started, of erotic material in telepathic experiments. I remember when I was working with Miss Jephson in the very early days, about 1934. We were thinking of submitting a series of illustrated postcards for telepathic material, and I said to her "Can't we smuggle into this set an obscene photograph and see the result? If at the same time we could link up our percipient with a psychogalvanic reflex, wouldn't it be remarkable if we got a sudden jump at that moment, and were able to present our material and have it registered and photographed?" She agreed, but said that the time had not yet come. Well, apparently the time has come; Mr. Fisk and others are doing it.

Thirdly, I think Prof. Gaddum will agree that we must have more work on the effect of drugs. We know a good deal about the effect of drugs in certain South American tribes, where drugs are thought to influence their supposed ESP faculty. That should be done in Western peoples, but of course it is extremely difficult without the co-operation of pharmacologists and others.

Fourthly, I agree with Dr. Pobers about the investigation of primitive peoples. I think the time has almost gone by. I remember in the early days I said to Dr. W. H. R. Rivers "Here you go out to the Torres Straits, as Psychological Adviser, here is the opportunity now of investigating these strange phenomena in primitive peoples". And he said "Dingwall, you are impossible. If they are not true, I don't want to have anything to do with them; if they are true, I will have nothing to do with them". The investigation is still a possibility, but as Dr. Pobers says it requires a Commission.

The other day one of our leading spiritualists came to me and said wasn't it about time the parapsychologists investigated the sex life of mediums and sensitives? You know as well as I do that the whole subject teems with sex, yet nothing is done. That is a line that I think ought to be begun by parapsychologists. There are not more than about three books on it, of which Freimark's is the best; there is a great deal in it, and it should be investigated.

Finally, I want to say a word to the younger workers. I would ask them to become acquainted with the older literature. First of all they would get the historical background, and secondly I think they would save a great deal of their time. Reports are sent to me constantly by younger workers, in which it is quite clear that they have not made themselves acquainted with the early work, and have had to learn all the old sources of error afresh. That is where I think parapsychologists can help other scientific men who begin investigations. Is it not possible to persuade other scientific men, and psychoanalysts, to learn something about the sources of error before they begin experiments, and prevent them from publishing work when, had they known about these sources of error, they would have avoided falling into so many pitfalls?

Soal: I agree fully with Dr. Dingwall that the most urgent requirement at present is the discovery of these subjects who have the gift so well marked that they can produce highly significant results over a period. If you can experiment with such a subject, you can change the conditions and you may be able to discover something about his gift. But if you just get a subject who produces an odd result that is above chance, and then you try another and another subject, you get nowhere. I think you must have a subject that you can observe over a period of months or even years, that is, if you can find such a one, and I believe Mr. Langdon-Davies's discovery does augur perhaps a new feature for psychical research; for if he has found three such subjects, I think there must be many more in the same community.

As you know, I am all for rigorous methods in physical research; I do not believe in studying ESP in slack conditions and working up to better conditions. I think you should make conditions as good as possible from the beginning. But I know that certain workers don't agree with that, and I am sympathetic to the other point of view, though it is not my own method.

Another thing which I have observed with Mr. Langdon-Davies's subject was the enormous rapidity and automatic nature of the response, and I think if we could get some method of registering ESP that was automatic and subconscious, we should take a great step forward. I know that the use of the psycho-galvanic reflex has been tried in America by Woodruff of the American Society for Psychical Research, but as far as I know it has never been tried on a good subject, and I think we should use this method on good subjects and see if we can get much more consistent results than by conscious guessing of cards. What is done, I think, is the subject is conditioned when attached to the machine to make a response to a certain symbol, say a triangle, and then this symbol is mixed with other symbols and when it appears and somebody looks at it from behind a screen, if telepathy is operating then the subject should make the response automatically and it would be registered. If this succeeded with a good subject you would have a very valuable means of registering ESP.

I know Mr. Fisk has invented a new kind of ESP card which wants thorough investigation, namely the clock card. Hitherto we have been using cards with five symbols, and the subject guessing the card is either right or wrong. On Mr. Fisk's cards there is a clock face with a pointer, pointing at one of the twelve hours; when the cards are randomized, the chances of getting the right answer are 1 in 12. The method, which has been worked out statistically, allows for near-misses: if the card registers 12, and the guesser says 1, he is not so far out; he has the right orientation. Mr. Fisk claims these cards are more successful than the ordinary ESP cards, and I want to try them out.

Another thing I think should be done is an investigation of the guessing habits of people. Does the general pattern of guessing of these sensitives differ from the guessing of ordinary people? Dr. Pratt and I did some work on Mrs. Stewart's guessing, and we saw that in some cases her guessing patterns were influenced by the occurrence of a double target, say, where you had a cross followed by a cross. I think this should be studied much more fully. We should use some kind of factorial analysis to investigate the difference between a subject's guessing habits when there was no question of ESP, and then compare them with what she was doing in an ESP experiment. And, of course, we should compare the guessing habits of different people.

One other thing. When I said yesterday that in some of the earlier experiments at Duke University the cards were laid on the table and guessed in that way, I do not want to give the impression that anything like that happens now, or has happened for many years. I am perfectly certain it does not. When I visited Duke in 1951 I saw nothing to complain of in any way about the technical methods used. I also fully agree with Dr. Pratt that when these faulty cards were discovered by Dr. Rhine, he immediately put an announcement in the *Journal of Parapsychology* that the cards were not to be used without a screen. But at the same time, it was true that in 1938 I did get a pack of cards from Dr. Rhine in which the symbols showed through when you held them up to the light at a certain angle. Of course I didn't use them in experiments.

Lewis: I don't feel entitled to offer advice to those already working in this field. What Dr. Soal has just said, however, prompts me to say that I think that to use a conditioned response of this kind would introduce some very awkward further problems into the experiment. In any case, the prerequisite, I would agree with other speakers is to find gifted individuals who thereafter could be used as their own controls and subjected to various kinds of interference such as drugs, or stress situations, or influences that would change their emotional state, and thereby collect the kind of evidence it is customary to collect in such experiments.

Parkes: Obviously, it is impossible for me to summarise in any detail the discussions that have taken place at this symposium. All I can do is to tell you how the information that has emerged appeals to a biologist.

Several times in the last three days I have been reminded of T. H. Huxley's aphorism, "It is the fate of new knowledge to start as heresy and end as superstition", and I have wondered at what stage of that cycle parapsychology has now arrived. Perhaps it is just emerging from the stage of heresy. To the biologist, as Dr. Perry said yesterday, it is convenient to discard all "borderline material", results which are just significant on elaborate statistical analysis, and so forth. But there is little doubt in my mind that when you have done so you still have a substantial residue of results which have to be accepted. We have referred many times to Dr. Soal's two subjects; there are undoubtedly some others equally impressive. I am more familiar with Dr. Soal's work, and I am fascinated especially with the experiment in which telepathic and clairvoyant situations were alternated, and the subject scored far above chance in the former, and only according to chance in the latter. To the ordinary practising scientist (I hope Prof. Gaddum will agree with me) that is a most convincing experiment, and the result would be accepted without hesitation if it related to any ordinary biological problem. The fact that such a perceptive subject is found very rarely does not invalidate the results, though it does, of course, increase the difficulty of explaining the phenomenon.

We have had various explanations offered, and a good deal has been said about repeatability. On any particular subject results are repeatable at least for a time; what is not reproducible is the same result on somebody else. Considering the scarcity of sensitive subjects merely as a matter of biological variation, in the sense that all properties are better developed in some people than in others, the occurrence of a lot of people who show little or nothing, and of a few who have the faculty comparatively well developed, is I think, biologically, curious. To my mind such a distribution suggests that this faculty, if it exists, is vestigial rather than rudimentary. In other words, it is going down in the evolutionary scale and not coming up. If there is anything in this idea, the faculty ought to be better developed in primitive peoples than in more sophisticated ones, and it ought perhaps to be more active in some animals than in primitive man. In this connection, though not susceptible of laboratory proof, the extraordinary stories of occurrences among primitive man which we have heard from Dr. Pobers are highly intriguing.

In conclusion, I should like to say again that, in my opinion, the expression 'extrasensory perception' is a singularly unfortunate one, in that it begs the question as to the nature of the phenomenon under discussion, and has a slightly supernatural or mystical connotation. I like Dr. Perry's suggestion that in our present state of knowledge a better expression would be 'extraordinary sensory perception', with its implication that whatever phenomena have to be accepted and explained depend on the exceptional development of some known sense or on the existence of an as yet unknown one. In making this essentially biological approach I may recall that we have heard something during the meeting about the astonishing faculties possessed by lower animals, faculties which might well be thought supernatural if they were not commonplace, but which one after another are being explained in terms of physics, chemistry and biology.

AUTHOR INDEX TO PAPERS

SUBJECT INDEX